PAUL NEWMAN

By the same author

GENERATION X
(with Jane Deverson)
WHO KILLED MARILYN MONROE?
(in US as THE HOLLYWOOD CAGE)
THE CRAZY KILL
(on location with John Huston)
THE LAUGHING ACADEMY
(play)
A LETTER TO THE LIVING
(verse)

PAUL NEWMAN

by
CHARLES HAMBLETT

HENRY REGNERY COMPANY • CHICAGO

For Paula,
who also knows
the meaning
of
marriage

Contents

Acknowledgements

The author wishes to express his gratitude to John Huston and Ernie Anderson for helping to initiate vital preliminary interviews with Mr Newman; also to Warren J. Cowan, President of Rogers, Cowan & Brenner, Inc., of Beverly Hills, California, and Margaret Gardner, Managing Director, International Division, headquartered in London, for their help in bringing about these interviews in Mr Newman's home state of Connecticut. It should be stressed that Mr Newman did not participate directly in the preparation of this book, since neither he nor the author believe that the time is yet propitious for a 'definitive' biography—there's so much more to come! Any faults of omission, therefore, are entirely those of the author and the present work is offered by way of an interim report on a man of the cinema still extending his range as an actor, producer—and, most important, a director of high sensibility and promise.

My gratitude is further expressed to Fern Long, Deputy Director, Cleveland Public Library at 235 Superior Avenue, Cleveland, Ohio; to the pleasant and efficient staff of the New York Public Library at the Theater Arts division of the Lincoln Center, New York; and the staff of the Academy Awards Library in Hollywood, California.

Further acknowledgements are due to Professor Frank McMullan, School of Drama, Yale University, Connecticut, and to Mr William G. Caples, Kenyon College, Gambier, Ohio, for confirming certain data regarding Mr Newman's academic years.

Thanks are also due to Marilyn H. Bender of Times Mirror Magazines, Inc., for tracing for me the article 'How we turned Paul Newman into a "winning" driver', extracts from which are reprinted courtesy of *Popular Science Monthly*. Copyright 1969 Popular Science Publishing Co., Inc.; and to the Editor and staff of *Motor Trend* of 8490 Sunset Boulevard, Los Angeles,

California, for permission to use extracts from Dick Wells's somewhat technical interview with Mr Newman—gems of lucidity for the present writer who has achieved a ripe age without once ever driving a motor-car!

I am also grateful for the insights gained from reading assessments of Paul Newman by writers in the showbusiness field whom I have long admired, particularly Rex Reed and Bob Thomas, and from whom I have quoted, wherever possible with acknowledgement to the source.

Finally, during the writing of my text I referred to the following books: *The films of Paul Newman* by Lawrence J. Quirk, Citadel Press, New York, which is a well-documented chronological source-book; *The celluloid sacrifice* by Alexander Walker, Michael Joseph, London, particularly the chapter on American censorship which spells out the conditions under which Paul Newman came to professional maturity; *Rebels: The rebel hero in films*, by Joe Morella and Edward Z. Epstein, Citadel Press, New York, for a background history leading up to the era which produced the Newman style; *Brando* by Bob Thomas, W. H. Allen, London, for succinct documentation of 'the other Newman'; *The fifth estate* by Robin Moore (author of *The French connection*) W. H. Allen, London, for a remarkable creative insight into the darker forces at which Newman was pointing, allegorically, in the film *W.U.S.A.*; and to the regular news reports from Washington since the Watergate hearings and their aftermath, as a salutary reminder that Paul Newman wasn't kidding when he told me, 'I'm not against the Establishment, I'm against stupidity.' Had he added 'cupidity' he would have put the American moral dilemma into a nutshell. It is tragic that artistes of the quality of Paul and Joanne Newman should feel beholden to 'stand up and be counted'; but there are many of us, less important or articulate, who have reason to be thankful that they did not simply settle for the cosy image of being the Doug and Mary of the jet age. We are additionally fortunate that they carry their honourable concern with such magnificent, throwaway panache.

My last, but by no means least, thanks go to Paula Hamblett, for the uncomplaining way in which she manages to keep the home fires burning when I am on my travels, and to Emma Elizabeth Hamblett for her enthusiastic help and advice during my labours at the typewriter. Looking back with hindsight at the track record of this remarkably gifted man I can only conclude—to paraphrase the title of his breakthrough motion picture vehicle—that *Somebody up there well and truly loves him,* and this is the central theme of the ensuing thesis.

Hollywood–New York–London
August '73–January '74

Introduction

'If you can make it in Bridgeport, you can make it anywhere.'

Old Bridgeport saying.
P. T. Barnum made his home here.

The orchestra was playing to an empty ballroom. Oblivious of the dreamy violins and the best of Burt Bacharach and the Beatles, the guests at the junior prom stood elbow to elbow in the smartest hotel in Bridgeport, Connecticut, trying to catch a glimpse of Paul Newman. News had leaked out that the star was having a quick early evening meal in the dining-room before leaving for another part of town to work on night location in a film with the jaw-breaking title of *The effect of gamma rays on man-in-the-moon marigolds*. This time he was working behind the camera, directing his wife, Joanne Woodward, in the lead part.

The crowd in the foyer was a cross-section of mainstream America, the 'silent majority' that makes money instead of headlines. Earlier in the day Paul had been shooting in the ghetto and had attracted the same kind of excitement, so there is no social significance in the reaction of the present crowd. It just happened to be where Newman was passing through. Expensively confected matrons with Man-of-Distinction husbands. Lovely young girls, fresh as face cream ads, in fabulous formals and trailing artificial bouquets from gloved fingertips. Surprisingly, their escorts, dashing in multi-patterned jackets and frilled shirts, seemed as much charged with suppressed excitement as the girls, their aunts and mothers.

Seated at a far from prominent table in the dining-room, Paul Newman, the man whose charisma makes a mockery of the generation gap, was reminiscing and telling me for the umpteenth time, 'I'm really terribly square. Lucky, yes . . . I've been incredibly lucky. But—' He broke off and sketched an invisible square with a stubby forefinger.

xiii

A table-hopping member of the film unit came over and, in passing, said, 'There's a bunch of kids waiting in the foyer, Paul. I thought I'd warn you.'

'That so?' the star drawled. 'Guess we'll have to get moving, anyway.'

But he lingered over the remnants of his meal. 'Kids,' he said thoughtfully. 'They're so sharp these days, so—mature— you'd think they'd lose interest in movie people.' He made the last two words sound like the victims of leprosy. 'Kids are terrific. They've got to face a whole set of problems, options, challenges . . . the job of pushing the human race into the next century is enough to drive anyone *nuts*.'

Memory opened up another thought-tangent. 'You know, compared with the intelligent kid of today, my generation was plain dumb. To tell you the truth, I wasn't much good at anything when I was a kid. My brother and I, we both went in for every single sport you could think of. And *I* was terrible at all of them. Really—notoriously ungifted.'

He thumped the table with the flat of his hand. 'Okay, we gotta go.'

The welcoming murmurs, the excited jostling, triggered by the actor's appearance in the foyer clearly disproved his self-disparaging comments. With his piercingly blue, hypnotic eyes, firm jawline and crisp hair faintly frosted with grey, he moved easily through the crowd with a hand-clasp here, a warm smile there, generating a human current, which animated the gathering like forked lightning. If this was being square, then hooray for squares.

When Paul Newman shakes your hand he clasps it firmly and looks you directly in the eyes, as if trying to imprint you on his mind for ever. Here in this crowded foyer he spread an aura of goodwill while moving steadily towards the exit, beyond which his car was parked, ready for a quick getaway.

Good-naturedly, his wife kept a few paces behind, chatting with friends in the unit, acknowledging the good wishes of fans, while determinedly staying in the backwash of her husband's royal progress. Joanne Woodward, great actress in her own right, willingly plays second fiddle to her husband's popularity.

Suddenly Newman was gone. He has a strange facility for disappearing at just the right moment. The crowd slowly came out of its collective trance and began to trickle back into the ballroom. 'Isn't he gorgeous?' 'Wish he could have stayed for one dance—with *me*.' 'What a dreamy smile.' And a husky youth with the build of a college football star, said: 'Gee, I'll just have to phone home and tell the folks that I've met Paul Newman.'

Rain turned the location, that night, into a complete washout. Literally, it fell for hours. But not once did Paul lose his cool.

The downpour had started while Paul was still dining. By the time we reached the location site in a remote suburb it was knifing down in torrents. Freak weather, beyond the computations of the experts.

A huge camera crane, towering above the rooftops, had been set up in front of the house where the scene was to be shot.

With rain streaming down his face, Paul, hatless, clambered into the tiny bucket seat beside the camera. The crane, like a frightening fairground contraption, tugged the bucket upwards, and five million dollars' worth of superstar soared into the darkness beyond the floodlighting. Cops nursing nightsticks tried to keep a crowd of rain-bedraggled fans at bay. But as Paul zoomed back to the sidewalk the crowd surged forward in time to hear his disgusted remark to the camera ace, 'It's like trying to shoot a picture in a monsoon.'

'Never mind, Paul,' a teeny-bopper yelled cheekily. 'You can always join us down at the neighbourhood disco.'

'Now that sounds like a great idea, baby,' Paul said with a grin that cut another swathe through the generation gap.

I sat with Paul in his caravan while we waited for a break in the clouds. 'London weather,' he said.

'No, worse,' I replied. 'Manchester weather.'

Several days later he told me, 'You know the rain, the other night, cost us forty thousand dollars.'

That is what it costs to set up a few hours of night shooting in an urban street, a far cry from the days when Mark Hellinger shot *The naked city* on a shoestring budget that today would scarcely cover the making of a TV pilot. Paul's own money had gone into this movie, but he never once during the weeks of intensive production betrayed his concern, always keeping a steady temper.

'He always concentrates on one thing at a time,' Joanne told me. 'I've never seen him panic at anything.'

Rain did not bother the fans, that night, as they continued to scratch and knock and whimper at the sides of the caravan. Whenever Paul dashed out to confer with his crew, the familiar roar would be heard: '*Paul*, PAUL . . . Look over here, just say hello . . . to me, *me*, ME! . . . Hi, Paul, HI.'

Sitting in the warm caravan with the rain drumming on the roof I felt a twinge of unease as I sensed the hunger, the desperation of some of the deprived and underprivileged existences scrabbling about in the rain, their night voices suggesting the subliminal cries and whispers of the Bergman movie. Strangers in the night . . . prowlers who could strike sharply in the darkness if they suspected rejection. The dangerous obverse of love.

A few nights later this was brought home to me for real as the garish floodlights cut through the midnight blackness of another night location in Bridgeport, the fotofloods laying bare every detail of the untidy backyard where Paul and Joanne stood huddled in close professional conversation while setting up a shot.

The occupational tensions of film production were heightened by the knowledge that a self-proclaimed would-be assassin might be lurking in this rundown section of town where there had been several shoot-outs in the past few days. Half an hour earlier I had been yarning with Ed Nerkowski, city sheriff of Bridgeport, in our night location quarters in the nearby Homeport Restaurant, in the welcome brightness of Boston Avenue, when a message came through from police headquarters.

The sheriff's face became grim as he listened. 'There's a guy just phoned in to say he'll shoot Joanne Woodward,' he said tersely. 'Nobody takes potshots at that little lady on my territory. Come on, I'll drive you back to the location.'

The cold New England air struck deep into the marrow bones as we stood around in the yard while the camera dollied back and forth to trap on film the kind of sensitive performance that wins Joanne awards and nominations, and only the discreet infiltration of extra police around the set indicated that something unusual was going on. Romantically, I weighed the prospect of hurling myself dramatically in front of Mrs Newman to intercept an assassin's bullet.

Shortly before dawn, over hot coffee, I asked Sheriff Nerkowski why the Newmans seemed to mean so much to him personally.

'I'll give it to you straight,' the sheriff said, flinty-eyed. 'They're decent people. I don't expect they see eye to eye with me on many things. They're for liberalisation and change—*I'm* just a law-and-order guy. But you want to know the secret? Paul and that nice wife of his—they're on our side. And there's one thing I feel about Paul Newman—he hasn't gone Hollywood. He'll come down to the poolroom, drink a few beers and shoot the breeze with the boys. He's a regular guy.'

A regular guy. One of the crowd, yet one who by reason of talent, looks, wealth, and sheer responsibility for others, must constantly move remotely above the crowd. Not for the first time I wondered what drives and inner compulsions had lifted this seemingly amiable, seemingly ordinary man above the crowd. How had this self-confessed 'square' who initially hated the idea of being an actor, ever become Paul Newman, superstar?

Hopefully, some of the answers are contained in this book. They are my primary reasons for writing it.

1

An Urban Huck Finn

'. . . how I ever survived that early period I really don't know. I was filled with irresponsibility and recklessness.'

There were no special signs or portents in the sky on that sub-zero day of 26 January 1925, when Paul Newman was born in Cleveland, Ohio. Or if there were, they failed to emblazon the night with the good news that a star was born. The cards were definitely stacked against his ever achieving the Hollywood pantheon then occupied by the likes of Douglas Fairbanks, Rudolph Valentino and Richard Barthelmess. To the staid uppercrust business community into which he was born, Hollywood itself was a shadowy lotus land much given to the worship of sun, sin and sex.

The chunky, incredibly blue-eyed eight-pounder greedily imbibing his first drops of glucose and warm water did not. trigger any premonitions in the family circle that he would become an actor of infinite grace, of brooding and charismatic power. Everything was cut and dried for him, his course through life planned and charted by parental predestination.

He would grow up with 'every advantage', enjoy a liberal education, marry a decent neighbourhood girl, and eventually, with his elder brother, Arthur, inherit the family business and prosper. Meanwhile, a nursery cot awaited him at his parents' home at 2100 Renrock Road, Cleveland Heights. However, they were getting set to move to a spacious home at 2983 Brighton Road, in the more prestigious Shaker Heights, and this is where he spent his childhood and youth and where his mother lives to the present day. All was set fair for a happy, uneventful childhood.

'Shaker Heights,' Paul told me many years later, 'was very provincial.'

It is difficult to quote this master of histrionic understatement without conveying the soft, ironic inflections of his speaking voice. More than most actors, he uses language the way many good writers do, sparingly, hesitatingly, with the caution of a man who knows the value of verbal coinage. There is something about the mature Newman which suggests the controlled flamboyance of the later Norman Mailer; their voices husk harmoniously on certain vowel inflections, and both have a way of shrugging off personal comment with a disparaging lip-smile which leaves the rest of the face static and unamused. It is a way of repelling obtrusive questions, wrapping an invisible cloak against the trepidations of strangers.

So whenever Paul Newman speaks of Shaker Heights, it's as if in apology for never having been obliged to peddle newspapers in some Hell's Kitchen. It is a trick to disarm the interviewer, setting limitations on discussion beyond which even old acquaintances step at their peril. Democratically friendly, even earthy and Rabelaisian, his star status is encircled by a round-the-clock ring of confidence.

'My father was of German-Jewish origin, a gentle man . . . bookish. My mother was a Catholic who became converted to Christian Science. So there I was, with a Jewish father, a Catholic mother, and being brought up from the age of five as a Christian Scientist.' Paul's laser-probing eyes challenged mine. 'So don't ever tangle with me on the subject of religion— I've been through the lot.'

Despite the influence of the Talmud, the Catechism, or the improper Bostonian inspirations of Mary Baker G. Eddy, Newman seems to have remained consistently earthbound. 'When my mother was converted to Christian Science,' he recalls, not without relish, 'though it is a faith based on divine healing, without formal medical aid, my brother and I still had regular medical checkups.'

Paul always speaks of his father with respect and affection. 'He was not a religious man in the sense of going to synagogue, or thrusting religion down our throats. But he was still suffering from the old Judaeo-Christian guilts, and the feeling that for anything to be meritorious it would have to be painful.' A rueful chuckle. 'I certainly have lived up to that.'

2

Newman, senior, also taught his sons a sense of values. 'Although my father owned a flourishing sporting goods store,' Paul says with approval, 'I didn't get my first baseball mitt until I was ten. This was intended as a lesson. Just because your father's shop was crammed with sporting gear, it didn't mean that baseball mitts grew on trees. They were gifts, tokens of affection . . . to be offered without anybody's arm being twisted.'

Thanks to his father's admirable prudence, Paul is mercifully free of the habits of reckless extravagance which afflict so many Hollywood characters once they hit cinematic fool's gold. As an actor he's become a shrewd assessor of the small print in a contract, as a director he is a careful custodian of a production budget, and as steward of a large household he has had moments when he feared his children's ice-cream bills were about to bankrupt him.

Paul, like Bernard Shaw, is convinced that the Internal Revenue authorities are out to shake him down to his last cent; and in the light of recent disclosures accusing the Nixon Administration of harassing its critics—particularly those on the infamous White House 'Enemies list' (on which Newman received an honourable mention)—by means of searching tax investigations and phone tappings, it's surprising he's kept his cool, his sense of humour, and his sanity. One man's paranoia is another man's strong, right arm.

Unfortunately for any investigator into the psychodynamic evolution of Paul Newman from provincial square and campus hero to the massively structured histrionic powerhouse and the household name we all know today, he has a genuine memory block about his early life. This reduces his conversation to an inchoate mumble, punctuated by the most pregnant pauses since early Pinter, whenever he tries to piece together the fragments of what to him seems a very ordinary childhood.

I put it straight on the line by asking him, point blank, 'Were you really all that square as a kid, or is this some kind of protective colouring you've cultivated over the years to check any possibly indiscreet disclosures?'

'Was I *square*?' Gargantuan laughter. 'You better believe it. I was *hopeless* . . . at *everything*. Even football created special

3

problems. When I was fifteen, I had to get a waiver to play in my class team. I was almost ready to graduate from school, but without a 2-lb. waiver I would have been forced to play with the lightweight team. Can you picture the agony while I waited for more than an hour outside the headmaster's room for a decision on this, to me, extremely weighty decision?'

It's the kind of traumatic experience that can make anyone weight-conscious for life, and this may explain his constant checking on the bathroom scales and pride in the fact that for years his weight has remained steady at 166 lb., give or take a pound either way. Considering the amount of beer he still manages to put away, though he now seldom touches the hard stuff, this is something of a biochemical triumph. It helps, of course, to have your own sauna, but it's not unreasonable to speculate that the hour-long wait outside the head's study has helped Paul Newman to avoid becoming another Oliver Hardy.

'I just scraped into the team and saved my pride,' Paul says. 'In fact, I only started putting on weight after I went into the Navy. When I first got into my Navy uniform at Yale University, where I went on a preliminary training course, a guy walked up to me and said: "Aren't you a little old to be in the Sea Scouts?"'

During our talks together I tried hard to prod Paul into remembering a single achievement—sporting or scholastic—of which he had reason to be proud. 'Nope,' he would say after long thought. 'There was absolutely nothing.' Once, though, he said, rather ruefully: 'I was always one of those students of whom it was said, "He is very promising".'

He added: 'If you follow certain film critics, you will find that this situation seems to have persisted to this very day. "Mr Newman is promising but miscast." "He is a promising light comedy actor but will never be a Cary Grant." I shouldn't be surprised, if I manage to achieve my three-score years and ten I might even become a promising Lear.'

'Or promising Walter Brennan?'

'Right!'

We drew a similar blank when I was trying to get him to remember some teacher who might have influenced his early

4

thinking. Or local preacher, or cracker-barrel philosopher. Anyone, anyone at all.

'*No-o-o*,' he replied after long consideration. 'I cannot recall such a teacher or influence. Perhaps I simply wasn't in the market for profound thinking at the time.'

He found it considerably easier to remember the landscape of his childhood. The sight of Lake Erie, black and mysterious as the sea, stretching to the frozen wastes of Canada, haunted his mind with intimations of an earlier, pioneer America. The works of James Fenimore Cooper further stimulated his imagination, particularly *The deerslayer*, *The pathfinder* and, of course, *The last of the Mohicans*. These stories helped him to establish his American identity, gave added awareness of the fact that modern cities such as Cleveland are recent eruptions on the face of the American wilderness, and that 'white' immigrants from Europe are new arrivals by comparison with Cooper's Mohican chief Chingachgook and his son Uncas.

'On fishing trips with my brother we would explore lakes and forests straight out of the pioneer past. You could almost see the early Indian hunting parties still stalking deer and buffalo at the edge of the trail, and fishing from primitive canoes.

'This was before television, you must remember, when kids still read books. I did a great deal of reading, went through the usual children's classics. Washington Irving, Edgar Allan Poe, Melville . . . and some of the poets.

'I was lucky in having a newspaperman-poet in the family, my father's brother Joe Newman, a great character. My brother Arthur and I always enjoyed his visits, he had an informal way of talking about the great writers that brought them alive to us boys. He gave me insights into literature that I didn't get from any of the teachers at school. There were times when I dickered with the idea of becoming a newspaperman— but nothing came of it. He encouraged me to read anything I could lay my hands on (chuckle) until I got interested in girls—when I stopped reading altogether!'

'*No-o-o*, there wasn't any particular girl-next-door romance. I rather played the field in those days.

'Shortly before the war started, I became attached to a girl

5

whose name I have forgotten. We remained great buddies till about midway through the war, when she sent me One of Those Letters.'

Paul put a wealth of meaning into the last word. 'You know, nearly every single fellow on active service in the war got one. There I was, in the middle of the Pacific, and I opened this . . . *letter* that went something like, "Dear Paul, I don't know how to break this to you, but I have met someone who loves me very much and wishes to marry me." I went and had a few drinks and when I woke up the next morning I was feeling no pain at all. It was over, just like that.'

It's quite a thought—somewhere in America there is a middle-aged matron, probably with grown children, who actually turned down Paul Newman in preference to another man! Such is the stuff of dreams.

In early childhood Paul preferred to run wild with other schoolboys, getting into the usual scrapes and generally living the life of an urban Huck Finn. Girls were either mysterious or silly, or both, and there was more kudos attached to capturing pond frogs and going on fishing trips than wasting time on their prattlings.

'Shaker Heights was a cloister,' he swears. 'It was originally a Quaker Colony, very respectable. It has one of the best public education systems in the world and it was taken for granted that I would go on to college.'

His life revolved around his home, the big family residence at Brighton Road in a socially impeccable section of Shaker Heights. His father Arthur S. Newman for thirty-five years secretary-treasurer of the flourishing Newman-Stern Company retailing sports equipment, was born in Cleveland and graduated from Central High School to become a pillar of the business community.

For a while he tried his hand as an advertisement solicitor and then as a reporter on a local newspaper, *The Press*, but then his brother, Joseph S., established Newman-Stern in 1915 and Paul's father joined him. A year or so later he enlisted in the US Army and served with great distinction throughout the rest of World War I.

6

On returning to Cleveland he really got into his business stride and was active in the Retail Merchants' Board, belonged to the Oakwood Country Club and the Temple. The Newmans became a highly respected, well-liked Cleveland family. Theirs was not the highly charged world which John O'Hara so vividly describes in such novels as *The Ewings*, with its painful snobberies implanted from the Eastern Seaboard, its amoral tycoons and highfalutin matriarchs, its secret drinkers and shadowy financial deals. If the older Newmans did not choose to travel around in gleaming Pierce-Arrows and custom-built Stutz Blackhawks, and the Newman boys did not dine regularly in tuxedos with badges of the Psi Upsilon fraternity on their waistcoats or the keys of Kappa Beta Phi on their watch-chains, they nevertheless lived lives of unruffled ease and comfortable affluence.

Paul's mother, Theresa, came from a distinguished Ohio Catholic family. Refined and sensitive, she doubtless contributed much, genetically, to the actor's underlying brooding sensitivity and deep moral concern. Yet the influence of his father was stronger and is, perhaps responsible for Paul's passionate humanism. Later, one suspects, Paul would have many a struggle to contain the conflicting parental influences: the Freudian 'Moses' father-figure versus the 'Mary' figure of a dedicatedly Christian mother. Theresa Newman's strong religious convictions must at times have been a source of painful ambivalence to Paul, particularly when that time arrived when he was confronted with the choice of playing it safe or burning his boats and becoming an actor.

To his great credit he managed to become his own man less messily than most artistes. In Paul's case the struggle to kick clear of the nest was intensified by the need to think his way through the emotional tug of a 'saintly mother' as well as turning his back on the security offered by the business empire his father had built up. It's easier, after all, to take the plunge into acting if you're motivated strictly from hunger.

A clumsy young bull when it came to anything connected with sports, he found himself curiously at ease whenever he was pitched into school dramatics. At ten, he acted with the Curtain

7

Pullers at the Cleveland Play House as St George in *St George and the dragon*. In retrospect he recommends exposure to school plays. 'Getting up and performing in front of people has a certain value to a child.'

As an upper middle class child he spent comparatively little time at the local cinema. There were always so many alternative activities, 'not to mention homework'. His film heroes were conventional. Paul grew up during those prewar years when there were still clearly defined goodies and baddies, with clean-cut heroes as played by Spencer Tracy, Clark Gable, Gary Cooper, or baddies portrayed by the likes of James Cagney, Edward G. Robinson and George Raft.

The rebel as hero had yet to emerge, the anti-hero was unborn, and the young Paul Newman had no esoteric notions about film as an art form or movie actors as anything else than fabulously wealthy entertainers. He does not recall having ever fantasized about going to Hollywood or becoming a star. As we shall see, his drift into acting and, later, working in Hollywood was a largely unconscious process until he was well into his twenties. He freely admits he was a slow starter.

No matter how much he's prodded, Paul's recollections of his early life are frankly corny. 'One of the great memories of my childhood is snow in winter,' he once told me with an air of discovery. 'It would start falling around Hallowe'en and continue until well into March. From about the first week in December we would go tobogganing. It was sensational. There was also skating on ponds near our house.

'On Hallowe'en night gangs of us kids would prowl around, holding lighted pumpkin masks up to bedroom windows to try and scare the neighbourhood girls. We behaved rather badly, inexcusably so. Winter or summer we used to travel in packs. The older boys would get their father's cars and we'd hightail it out to the countryside and whoop it up. One time we put a guy's father's heap halfway up a tree in his own front garden. There was quite a ruckus over that but we didn't get into real trouble—nobody called in the law.

'But how I ever survived that early period I really don't know. I was filled with irresponsibility and recklessness.'

8

He was clumsy with knives, always cutting himself. 'But the worst cutting job I ever did on myself was with a packet of razor blades. I'd just started shaving and one morning I decided to save time and shave under the shower. Big deal. After trying out the razor I found the blade wasn't very sharp. So I stepped out from under the shower and grabbed a packet of blades from a shelf and stepped back under the water.

'The shower is drumming away and I shake out a blade and fix it into the razor. I'm now holding the packet in my left hand and the razor, and disused blade, in my right hand, you follow me? I think, "Ah-*ha*," if I leave the packet in the shower it will get soggy and the blades will get rusty. I'll throw them into the basin. Seems a bright enough idea, but as I turn to chuck the blades into the hand basin I lose my balance and—*whoosh!*—the blades scatter all over the bath. I trip and fall headlong into the lot! Blood all over the bath. One blade just missed a tendon—my Achilles heel—and blood is just everywhere.

'Boy, was I accident-prone. If there was a tree with a creaky limb you could be sure that was the one I'd pick to climb and snap—more bandages and plasters.'

His mother used to tell him, 'When you grow up you will have to marry a hospital nurse. There's no other type of woman who could cope with your constant falling down and collecting injuries. She'll have to be a fully qualified nurse with the patience of Job—what's to become of you I dread to think.'

Yet if Paul can only speak disparagingly of his early life, there are others from Cleveland and thereabouts who remember him as a strikingly attractive youth. Mrs Jane Connolly, now living in Akron, Ohio, furnished me with this vivid recollection.

'There was something dangerous about him, you felt he was not really tamed, that just beneath the surface there was a streak of violence. He was very popular, there were a lot of girls who wanted to date him. But he wasn't a chaser, he always seemed to be going someplace else.

'He was in his last year in high school when I first came to Cleveland with my family from Witchita. I was two years younger so this put me out of the running so far as getting to

9

know him was concerned. Yet he sensed my interest and always gave me a special smile when we passed in the corridor or met in the street. His eyes already had that intense, direct look and were bright blue just as they come across on the screen. He was always very sure of himself, you got the impression that here was a guy who really knew where he was going.

'Well, one Saturday morning I was out walking my dog, an itsy-bitsy Chihuahua, in Woodland Hills Park, when he was scared by a bigger dog and rushed to hide behind a tree. Well, the poor little thing got stuck in a crack. Next thing I knew, Paul was looming over us. He just talked the big dog away, didn't shout or run after it . . . just told it to scram. And it did. He then took hold of my dog and gently manipulated his neck back from this wedge, like he was a gynaecologist. Gentle, but firm. I'll never forget the patient way he handled my dog, soothing him down, easing him free. When he got the dog out he handed him straight to me, saying, "Here, you better hold him, he knows you better than he knows me." Thoughtful, you know? I'm sure he hasn't changed one bit, whenever I see him in a movie I remember him as he was that Saturday morning. He's one heckuvva man, even when he was just seventeen he was already a man, a real man. That's what people see in him, I guess, now he's a big star. Gentle, yet with that dangerous streak. Heaven help anyone that'd try to cross him, he'd walk all over them.'

Paul left Shaker Heights High School in January 1943, according to the registrar's office. Getting him to talk about why he should leave school at such an unpropitious time of the academic year is like trying to extract teeth from a carving on Mount Rushmore. Contemporaries say he was good at debate; he had learned the art of speaking in countless syllogistic dialogues with his father, his Uncle Joe, and his brother Arthur. The latter is a steady, easy-going character who fitted comfortably into the role of big brother without ever becoming overbearing. The two have always got along, and in later years Arthur Newman has become an important figure in his brother's production organization.

Already people noticed in Paul a certain fatalistic streak, the kismet-complex one finds in so many creatures of destiny. Paul seemed to enjoy testing his will . . . forging ahead in all activities which caught his interest, despite his shambling clumsiness and tendency to be accident prone. Though apparently unaffected by his mother's piety he seemed to leave much to providence. Ah well . . . Inshallah! If it is God's will, that was just jake with him. That was the Moslem way, as for himself, without stopping to figure things out too deeply he seemed to have persuaded himself that he had the *baraka*, the divine protection that gives a man immunity in a haphazard world. More prosaically, he had what he still calls 'Newman's luck'.

Even today when Paul is talking to you, he has a habit of rapping his knuckles on wood when he speaks of luck. He has a 'thing' about it. 'All my life I have been extremely lucky,' he told me. 'Being in the right place at the right time . . . it's happened so often I can't begin to tell you the whole of it.'

For a while Paul just drifted. Most people in Cleveland who knew him well agree that he was a born actor. He once created a minor sensation by playing an Italian organ grinder in a school play. He bounced all over the stage in acrobatic mimicry.

At Shaker Heights High School, he was coached by William Walton and Bob Fryer, now a stage and film producer. 'Paul's outstanding quality was the seriousness with which he worked,' recalls Walton, who became assistant professor of speech and drama at Allegheny College, Meadville, Pennsylvania. 'He was extremely intelligent and, unusual for a high school boy, was interested in serious drama. But he loved his fun. During rehearsal breaks he used to head for the piano and pound out a boogie-woogie. A flock always gathered round.'

'The important thing is to keep acting,' he has said. Friends and family insist that he has never stopped!

His mother recalls that even as a child at Malvern Elementary School his histrionics made their mark. 'Paul was the neighbourhood clown,' she says. 'He yodelled and sang and acted in all sorts of little stunts. Always into some mischief.'

She sighed and added: 'He was such a beautiful little boy. In a way it was a shame to waste such beauty on a boy.'

As he grew older he became more restless. During summer vacations he worked, for a while, as a sandwich boy at Danny Budin's corned beef palace in Shaker Heights. 'Paul had a habit of acting out any jobs he did,' Budin recalls. 'He would bow deeply to the customers and smile constantly as though he knew he was always on display. He had a good appetite too. As a matter of fact, it was a toss-up whether he drew in as much pay as he ate.'

Sometimes he would disappear for hours, just walking his dog, Cleo, wandering through the leafy streets and parks of Cleveland. Later he sold encyclopedias from door to door 'to see whether I could sell myself to people'. This was long before he ever heard of Stanislavsky, but unconsciously he was already practising the Method. Apparently carefree and extrovert, there was an element of self-consciousness in everything he did.

He sold himself and the encyclopedias to the tune of a nifty 500 dollars profit, which he promptly invested in a theatrical show. The show flopped and he lost his 500 dollars. But he had proved his point: he could sell.

His father began to wonder where his wandering boy was heading. 'He was a good-natured man,' Paul recalls, 'but he was strict about ethical things—basic morality and discipline. When my brother and I worked at the store, we had to show up half-an-hour before the other employees, and we left half-an-hour later than the others. My father never showed any favouritism. In fact, we were paid less than anyone when we were first initiated into the business. We'd go there to please him, but my heart wasn't in it.'

It was his reluctant interest in his father's business that caused Paul to enroll in nearby Kenyon College to study economics and business training. 'I wasn't as good in college as I should have been,' he admits. 'I just couldn't see myself as a businessman.'

After only one semester at Kenyon the attack on Pearl Harbor temporarily resolved all his problems, his filial guilts,

12

his doubts about the future. For the next two years he sailed the Pacific working for Uncle Sam.

The Japanese bombs had barely hit their targets on the Hawaiian Islands, than Paul had enlisted in the Navy. He was selected for Naval Air Corps training and sent to Yale, where his first glimpse of that stately old campus started a love-affair with this great university which has lasted ever since.

2

Dropout

'Talk about the Newman luck . . . *wow!*'

Unlike many Hollywood male stars who started out as truck drivers or elevator operators, Paul, no matter how earthy his role in a film may be, in private bears the unmistakable stamp of the more conservative type of college man. He has, as they say in Barney's Beanery, class.

But he does not wear his distinction on his Brook Brothers sleeve, even on those rare occasions when he is to be found wearing a jacket at all. His affection for Yale University is, for example, pragmatic as well as sentimental. His first impressions of Yale were the outcome of the accident of global war rather than any academic effort on his part, yet the moment he set eyes on the Georgian buildings on the Old Campus, founded with a gift from one Honourable Elihu Yale, a retired East India merchant from London, Paul was entranced by this enclosed, yet intellectually adventurous, world on the other side of the venerable façade of Phelps Gateway.

Yale opened the young provincial's eyes to this larger world where the 'clash of mind on mind' endemic to all good universities presented a cultural challenge. Even the newer buildings across the High Street, dominated by that outrageous Gothic landmark Harkness Tower, conjured up all the nuances contained in the words 'Ivy League'.

It was a second homecoming. America was at war and he was only briefly there on a Naval training course. But he had glimpsed Xanadu—and would return.

Paul's first exposure to college had not been an altogether happy experience. 'Mind you, Kenyon College was remarkably good at the time,' he says. 'There were some excellent teachers and its standards were pretty high. I think I would have been happier if I had enrolled for a liberal arts course or

Eng. Lit. instead of business training and economics. It's a wonderful place, really, but my heart wasn't in it; I just couldn't see myself as a future businessman. The Japanese air attack on Pearl Harbour had the indirect effect of postponing my prospective business studies for the time being. It gave me a breathing spell—I was barely into my freshman year when America entered World War II.'

Kenyon College in the small town of Gambier, Ohio, no great distance from Cleveland, was not to see the last of Paul, however. If he entered the war with mixed feelings he knew that if he survived he would be able, under the terms of enlistment, to resume his studies there on being demobilized. But for the time being, at least, all thoughts of a 'career' were mercifully postponed 'for the duration of hostilities'.

'I left to enlist in the Navy,' he says. 'I volunteered to be a pilot in the Navy Air Corps and was assigned to the V-12 programme at Yale. Then they discovered I was colour-blind and threw me out of it.

'For the next two years I served as a radioman, third class, on naval torpedo planes in the Pacific. No, I did *not* have any traumatic experiences at boot camp or, later, at sea. I think I am a rather adjustable beast. Later in Hollywood, I remember the publicity departments in various studios tried to build up lurid stories of Ironjaw Newman at war, but I'm afraid I had to disappoint them. Life at sea is ninety-nine per cent boredom.

'I didn't see any combat. People tend to glamourize these things afterwards. We went out on submarine patrols, things like that, but for most of the time we cruised around in readiness for action that simply didn't happen.'

A thought struck him, and unconsciously he started to rap his knuckles against the table at which we were sitting.

'Now here's a curious circumstance,' he went on, 'a perfect example of Newman's luck. On torpedo planes a squadron consists of six crews with a total of eighteen men. Every month a squadron would have to do what they call simulated carrier landings. When it came to the turn of our squadron to replace the one on duty, my pilot developed a bad ear and for that month we couldn't qualify. We were grounded and only five crews were sent out instead of six.

'I forget the name of the ship they were sent to, but it caught a Japanese "kamikazi" right in the "ready room" in which all five crews were sitting. Since pilots and their crew have no defensive position aboard a ship when under attack they just have to sit tight in the "ready room" and wait till the emergency is over.

'Of course, if they've sufficient warning to get the planes in the air in time, they take off from the carrier and hit back at the attackers. In this case there was no warning at all, the Jap suicide plane just swooped down and crashed with its bombs smack into the "ready room"—killing all my buddies.'

Paul gave me a thoughtful look. 'When you miss something like that because your pilot happened to have an earache . . . *wow*!'

Paul was in the radio room of a carrier, seventy miles off the coast of Japan, when he heard the atom bomb had been dropped on Hiroshima and Japan had surrendered. When I asked him whether he'd had any profound thoughts on the subject of war and peace, and the future of mankind, he gave me one of those penetrating, you must be kidding looks he kept in reserve for whenever I tried to lure him out from under his deadpan mask and put him across as a deep thinker.

If he had any thoughts at the time they certainly touched on the revived problem of his future career. But when he got back to Cleveland he put up no protest against returning to Kenyon College and resuming his study of banking and economics. Early in life he seems to have acquired the habit of holding his cards close against his chest.

'Kenyon really was a quite marvellous place,' he told me in a burst of nostalgia. 'It wasn't their fault that I hated what I was doing there. Money as a basis for a full-time career has never interested me. Fortunately the authorities agreed and after a few months, I managed to switch to literature and drama. I just had no feeling for banking.

'It was quite by chance that I drifted into acting. I really wanted to play football, but this ambition ended in sheer disaster. I'll never know whether I would have become a star football player, because before I had a chance to prove myself I became involved in a tavern brawl between some members of the college team and some kids from the town.

'Six of us were thrown into the clink. When the case was heard two of our team were expelled from the college and the remaining four were put on probation and tossed out of the team. I was one of the four.

'I hate to think what my parents must have felt when they read the headlines: *Six Kenyon footballers in jail for brawling. Kenyon's traditionally 'non-training team in trouble again.'* Shaker Heights was, no doubt, shaken to its sedate foundations.

Shortly after this incident Paul heard that the Drama Department at college was reading for a play. 'I was damned if I was going to let my football disgrace interfere with my extra-curricular activities. So I went along to read for the lead part and got it. I played Hildy Johnson in *The front page*, a corker of a play which still has a lot of dramatic mileage in it, and we got a big reception. I took several bows and had my first, heady taste of acting . . . but I never saw myself as anything but a teacher of drama in a college. I didn't indulge in any wishful thinking.'

After his initial success, Paul showed up regularly for rehearsals for a series of college stage presentations, demonstrating all the enthusiasm he formerly kept for the football field. So his tavern brawl proved an important turning point in his drift towards acting, but he still had no idea that he would ever become a professional actor let alone a Hollywood idol. At the time, however, his 'disgrace' was by no means a laughing matter, to himself or his family, and the fact that it cut deep into his psyche is implicit in the ironic comment he made, years later, when after some spectacular achievement, he'd say: 'So the campus drunk has made it at last'.

Although he had turned his back on the study of banking, Paul was not against pulling a shrewd business stroke.

'With time on my hands after being barred from playing football, I decided to go in for a bit of private enterprise on the side. I found a little bin of a shop for rent in the high street,

17

and converted it into a laundry. As a special service I offered my customers—all college kids—free beer on the side. I figured this would make the laundry chores more pleasant all round as well as knock the opposition laundries out of business.

'Every Saturday at ten o'clock I would get a keg of beer for about twelve dollars and the guys would come down and bring their laundry and sit around and drink beer with me till their laundry was done. No other laundry in town offered such an attractive service and I soon became a monopoly. With low rental and profits after investing in the beer, I was taking at least sixty dollars a week for myself.

'In my last year of college I sold the goodwill to a friend. He opened up—and closed down—in his first week of business. This is how it happened. On the first Saturday morning the new owner duly got the keg of beer and opened the premises dead on ten o'clock. The customers piled in and started to drink real hearty. Unfortunately, one kid drank too heartily. He staggered out into the high street and started masturbating a horse. The horse bolted with the drunk hanging on to its dangling appendage. Well, the cops moved in and closed the laundry down and the poor guy was out of business—lost everything.

'Talk about the Newman luck—*wow*; it could have happened to me at any time while I was running the business; there was enough booze floating around every Saturday to scare a dozen horses.'

Despite his prowess as a beer drinker, his playing the field with the choicest girls, and the shadow of his football mis-adventure which he was never allowed to forget by certain elements at the college, Paul graduated with a degree. In reply to my own enquiries I received in the fall of 1973 the following communication from the office of the President of Kenyon College.

Dear Mr Hamblett,

I have your letter of September 17, regarding Mr Paul Newman, a graduate of the class of 1949, who received the Doctor of Humane Letters.

18

Mr Newman was a student here over 24 years ago, and members of the Faculty or the Staff of the College who could give personal reminiscences or personal stories are not here any more. I am afraid that, as with anyone who has acquired fame, apocrypha and the fact would be at such variance that I should be very doubtful as a researcher about any reliability in regard to it.

The records we maintain contain no information other than academic scores, and it is fair to say that Mr Newman's scholastic record is a commendable one. I do not believe you would find the other records of consequence.

Trusting the above may serve your purpose. I am

Yours sincerely

(signed) William G. Caples

And so we draw a curtain over the early college days at Gambier, Ohio, pausing only to note that a scrutiny of the mimeographed programmes of student plays during this period in which Paul Newman is listed either as a performer or backstage assistant embrace a wide range of subjects from satiric reviews to high tragedy, from playing a dude in *Charley's aunt* to a robot in Capek's *R.U.R.*, from American tragedies to Russian comedies.

This variety suggests that while Paul still had no conscious idea of making a living as an actor, he was gaining valuable experience of drama in general. The frustrated footballer was at least making out pretty well as a thespian, and considering some of the solidly physical roles he was later to tackle it is as well that he had some athletic experience under his belt.

To this day Paul's competitive drive in sports is sublimated in his passion for auto-racing, and he still plays a mean game of tennis if he's up against worthy opponents. The ill wind that blew over Gambier and into the night club on the outskirts of Mount Vernon where a bunch of students were caught in a midnight brawl, possibly did less harm to the subsequent career of one of these students than he could ever have dreamed when he woke in the local jail 'the morning after'.

Paul must by now be weary of the often repeated crack that he graduated *magna cum lager*! But most two-fisted drinking men who have learned to hold their liquor the hard way would agree that he, at least, has never let his taste for good beer detract him from becoming *e pluribus unum* in his drive, *per ardua, ad astra.*

But at the time of his graduation, Paul still had no clear idea of where he was heading.

'I didn't know what to do. So I drifted into a season of summer stock in a small theatre in Wisconsin. Then instead of going into the family business I joined the company of another theatre, in Woodstock, Illinois, where I appeared in sixteen plays.

'It was here that I met my first wife, Jackie Witte, a young actress. We fell in love, married, and our first child, Scott, was born the following year.'

It was a comparatively carefree time. At the Brecksville Little Theater, where Paul had his first real taste of non-collegiate acting, he is remembered as a friendly young man with a penchant for wearing Bermuda shorts and munching popcorn during rehearsals. He was looked upon as an enthusiastic actor and a talented director.

It was an informal little theatre. Once a local clergyman took the role of a playboy and uttered the flippant lines: 'I wonder what they're up to tonight?' in reference to a young couple. Harmless enough, but someone in the audience took exception and the young minister was asked by his superiors to withdraw from the role immediately and for a time his position was imperilled. The company rallied round the unfortunate divine and in the end he was cleared, but it was enough to raise the hackles of the humanistic Paul, who was becoming increasingly conscious of the double standards that 'respectable' society was imposing on the mores of the day.

Distinctly on the lighter side, was the dog who wandered on stage during *Our town* and made a butternut tree his own, the undisciplined pig that got loose on stage during *January thaw*, the cat that ate up the fried chicken before it could be carried on stage in *Meet Me in St Louis* and the two goats whose bleats drowned out the lines in *Mister Roberts*.

The male star of *Born yesterday* broke his leg shortly before

20

opening night and played all six performances in a cast and on crutches. Theatre members outdid themselves in donating empty beer cans for the fence in the comedy *Suds in your eyes*.

During the farce *See how they run* one of the actors was caught on the wrong side of the stage without his trousers. Amid a period of mad antics on stage the poised actor simply ran across it in his long underwear to retrieve the precious garment. Action in the comedy *Papa is all* involved the bullwhipping of a son by his stage father. After one 'severe lashing' a voice from the audience yelled, 'You can't do that, he's my brother!'

Members of the Brecksville Little Theater continue to present their shows on the stage of their historic Town Hall which is only thirty feet long. It was in such places as this that the young Newman, almost haphazardly, learned his trade, and although he wasn't present at all the incidents chronicled above, this is the stuff that acting ability is built upon.

Brecksville LT was started in 1941 by two dozen individuals operating on a shoestring. In 1950 Paul directed a play for the group titled *Here today*, but though it was here today and gone tomorrow for the future Hollywood star he thrives on the green room gossip of these brave little theatres and the reminiscences of the rank-and-file performers and sweated backstage operators who still command his time and affectionate interest whenever pressures of 'the industry' allow. He cut his eye teeth in the amateur theatre and summer stock, and it was under these circumstances that he met his Marjorie Morningstar.

Jackie Witte was an engaging, lively actress with a sense of humour that appealed strongly to Paul. Talented, versatile, she was also a refreshing alternative to the campus queens and country club belles, with their sharp eye for a young man's standing in the community and financial prospects. To these charmers Paul was an enigma, an unknown quantity, who belied his solid family background with an offputting disinterest in such 'important' matters as money-making, homebuilding and asserting his proper position in the pecking order of the local junior executive hierarachy. The solid-seeming provincial, they sensed, was seething, just beneath the surface, with a Shelleyan 'divine discontent' disconcertingly aligned to a tendency to loaf, and dream, and question the status quo. There was, indeed, something dangerous about him—he just wouldn't conform.

To Jackie Witte this was an a-plus. As an actress, she was able to sense the real drive and determination underlying the surface scepticism and irresolution that made him a matrimonial risk among his own set. She had heard of others who shared this premonition of future distinction for the rugged yet sensitive young man with a Hamlet complex: *to act or not to act.*

Men like his old director of dramatics at Kenyon, J. E. Mitchell, who now says: 'I pride myself on the fact that I called the turn on Paul. I told him if he learned discipline, he would go far. He was not a faddist but a good technician and a no-nonsense actor. He had great intelligence, physical stamina and the ability to work hard—three characteristics necessary to success on the stage.'

Stories had filtered through to Jackie of some of Paul's theatrical successes at college. Kenyonites still talked, for example, about one musical which Paul not only helped to write and produce but in which he also played the role of the then Dean Frank E. Bailey. 'He played me better than I could have played myself,' Bailey would chuckle for years afterwards, while the late Dr Gordon Keith Chalmers, president of Kenyon, was so enamoured of the show that he saw it on three successive evenings. To Jackie, whose intuitions were reinforced by working with Paul in the theatre, it seemed a crying shame that this natural talent should be lost to commerce.

But when Paul's father became ill in 1949, his mother persuaded him to come to work with Newman-Stern, still jointly run by his father and Uncle Joe, who also continued to churn out lively newspaper verse as a sideline.

'Paul worked hard but his heart just wasn't in the business,' says Joe Newman. 'He bought a house out in Bedford, but after his father died he disposed of it.'

The carefree period of little theatres and summer stock was over, possibly forever. But when in May 1950, his father died Paul felt that his last obligation to the business was dissolved.

'I was very successful at being something I was not,' he later

22

observed, 'and that's the worst thing that can happen to a person. If you try to be something you aren't and fail—then you have a strong motivation to change. You say, "Well, I didn't do so well at that, I'll try this." But when you succeed at being something you're not—it's a lot harder to break away.'

And he told me, 'Altogether I spent eighteen months working in the family business, and hated every minute of it. I was no more keen on being in business than I was on studying to be a banker. I wanted "out".'

He didn't really make the big, definitive break until he was twenty-six, when, in 1951, he left Shaker Heights with Jackie, his baby son and four thousand dollars to enroll in the Yale Drama School.

At last he was in an environment in which he could stretch himself to the limit. Not only was he hopelessly 'hooked' on the beguiling academic climate of Yale; this was also the start of his long-standing love affair with the surrounding New England landscape, in fact the entire state of Connecticut, where he later planted his roots and set up a permanent home. Paul has told me that lack of funds forced him to end his studies after only one year, but it is possible that he took the plunge and moved down to New York to try his luck in the theatre and television on less flimsy grounds than simple blind faith in an off-chance hope of finding work as an actor.

Paul, while insisting that he was 'just plain lucky', adds the rider: 'Of course you have to have talent as well; and there comes a time when you have to be able to deliver. Still, luck plays a big part in everything you do.'

He initially 'got lucky' the night on which he played a minor role in a play staged by the Drama Department at Yale and . . . well, the facts are best told by Frank McMullan, Associate Professor of Play Production at Yale in answer to an enquiry I made in October 1973.

'In reply to your letter to Dean Howard Stein regarding Paul Newman's attendance at the Yale School of Drama, I can only offer the following:

'He was at the School during the academic year 1951-2. He proved to be a very good student. Professor Alois Nagler, who teaches a course on the History of the Theatre and Dramatic Literature, remembers him as a "good student".

'He was in my first year directing class, and he was interested in acting as much as directing and indeed showed talent in both of these fields.

'I like to think that I gave him a chance to be seen when I cast him in the role of Beethoven's nephew, Karl, in my production of an original student play about the life of Beethoven. It was apparent to me that his was a magnetic presence on the stage.

'The theatre agents, Liebling and Wood (husband and wife) came to New Haven to see the original play but were more impressed by Paul Newman as a potential actor than in the stage-worthiness of the play. The production was presented in the spring and Paul landed his first job in the theatre in William Inge's very successful play *Picnic*. Of course, this meant that he left the Drama School.'

Once again, Jackie was solidly behind Paul's decision to move on. One evening he found himself discussing the future with Jackie with extra urgency. Even before the favourable reactions of the agents to his part in the Beethoven play, his drama teachers had been most encouraging, some even suggesting he might be wasting his time at Yale since he was more than ready to test his talent in New York, on Broadway if necessary.

Exciting things were happening in the New York theatre of Miller, Tennesee Williams and Inge, and television was crying out for new faces. Plays were being imported from Europe. Sartre, Camus, Christopher Fry, were contributing towards that Indian summer of formal Broadway theatre, with the wild men—Kopit, Albee, Jack Gelber—waiting in the wings to usher in the new anarchy which culminated in LeRoi Jones, John Guare, The Bread and Puppet Theater and André Gregory's Manhattan Project.

Paul, feeling the stirrings of the wind of change on Broadway, wanted 'in' even if, as it happened, some of the changes would not eventually prove to his liking. But New York was where the action was, and he wanted a part of that action.

Uprooting his family once again presented another problem. Paul, that evening, opened a bottle of cold beer and took a thoughtful sip. 'It's possible,' he cautiously told Jackie, 'that I might, just *might*, make a go of acting right away instead of hanging around here at Yale for another two years in the expectation eventually of finding a teaching job in some prairie college.'

'What's stopping you, then?' Jackie asked coolly. '*I* have every faith in your ability.'

It was all the young husband needed to hear. The next day he told the college authorities that he would not be returning after the summer vacation, and began making preparations to transport his wife, son, car and few worldly goods to New York. 'It was either make or break,' he says.

Whatever the outcome, Paul Newman, the man who had turned down a surefire business career to follow a hunch, had taken the first step towards becoming Paul Newman, world star.

3

A method in his madness

'The Actor's Studio was like another home for many of us.
I really learnt to act there. Until I went there I was
terrible.'

'New York was a wonderful place, in the early 'fifties, for a
young actor to learn his trade.' Paul invariably speaks warmly
of this period of his life. 'The Actor's Studio, *wow*, it became a
sort of Mecca for all serious actors . . . Marlon, Jimmy Dean,
Rod Steiger . . . I arrived on the scene shortly after the first
wave had passed through.

'But before I could consider enrolling there, or even being
considered, I had to find work . . . make me some bread, and
find us a place to live. Things were pretty rough for the first
three months.'

Inevitably, the Newman luck held good. After only a few
days in a cheap downtown hotel, Paul and Jackie found a
suitable apartment for themselves and their baby son, Scott,
in an inexpensive yet quiet backwater on Long Island, close to
the smell of the Atlantic.

It isn't difficult to picture the scene as Paul knocked at the
door of the letting office, briefly crossing his fingers . . . would
his luck hold? So far it had carried him unscathed through
school, war service, college, without serious mishaps . . . well,
not serious considering the chances he'd taken, parental hopes
he'd shattered, opportunities deliberately missed. At last he
seemed on the right track, belatedly doing his own thing.

Passers-by stared curiously at the young man with the
hypnotic blue eyes and Greek god profile as he waited outside
the apartment building. Paul ignored them. Though completely
unknown to the public he was growing accustomed to being
asked by perfect strangers: 'Say, haven't we seen you on TV?
Aren't you a movie actor?'

His eyes could have come straight from an identikit picture of Monty Clift, his mouth was a refinement of Vic Mature's Magyar leer, and the shade of John Garfield hovered around the thrust of his jaw. Then there was this new guy who wore T-shirts, played bongo drums, mumbled . . . that emergent, giant shadow who was to blight Paul's early screen portrayals. What was *his* name now?

Lady Luck didn't let Paul down. The deposit of one month's rent in advance secured him the tenancy of a small apartment cheap enough for his carefully worked out budget, far enough from the noise and fumes of Manhattan for the child's health, quiet enough for the isolation he needed to study scripts and plays, and for that inner reflection needed to reinforce his kind of original talent, the kind that must ultimately be played out in public.

At the back of all great acting lies hours of self-searching, years of careful assimilation of other people's quirks and gestures: the way a drunk reaches for a shot glass, the brisk efficiency with which a bank clerk shuffles stacks of money, the trepidation in a lover's touch on a creaky garden gate.

Finding a pad was an essential step towards the freedom of movement Paul needed in his search for work, yet it also had to be sufficiently close to the city to get him there quickly— by rail and subway if necessary—for meetings with other actors and making the essential rounds of agencies and production offices and studios. Somewhere, also, for Jackie and Scott to settle into some sort of domestic routine.

Wisely, Paul's young wife had elected not to create a conflict of interests by continuing as a full-time actress. One actor in the family was enough; besides, she wanted to have more children, and was again pregnant.

Having secured his base, Paul began to make sorties into New York's theatre district around Times Square. During idle moments he would take a stroll down West 44th Street and stand uncomfortably outside number 432 and stare at the seedy, mock-Palladian façade of—the Actor's Studio.

'After those first three lean months,' he told me, 'by which time our savings had dwindled almost to zero, I found myself landed with parts in half-a-dozen television shows in a row. I also got a regular part in a soap opera called *The Aldrich family*, and then other spots came my way. Once again it was a matter of being lucky—boy, was I lucky!'

With the welfare of his small family secured, at least for the time being, Paul plunged into the New York scene with relish. 'These days we no longer have even an apartment in New York,' he says. 'It just doesn't make sense any more. The theatre has lost a great deal of its vitality. The streets aren't safe for Joanne to go out shopping with the kids even in broad daylight . . . or go anywhere alone after dark without being stopped every few yards and with every chance of being mugged while people pass by looking the other way.

'But when I first went to New York it was a simple joy just to walk along Broadway and feel that, with luck, you might get into the theatrical scene with a really worthwhile part. Marvellous new plays were being performed "live" on television by writers like Rod Serling and Paddy Chayefsky. Arthur Miller and Tennessee Williams were still bringing fresh concepts into the drama. It was the kind of action I imagined to have taken place in Elizabethan London. I wanted a piece of that action, and getting into television was the first step . . . the right kind of break.'

It could never be more than a first step for someone as bursting with energy, controlled energy, as Paul. 'I spent nearly the first thirty years of my life looking for a way to explode,' he said later. 'For me, apparently, acting is that way.'

Television work in those days was not, in any case, highly paid, and the ambitious young actor had no intention of getting stuck forever in a small apartment on Long Island. And now there was another baby on the way, another mouth to feed.

It was essential that he should run a car, pay stiffish telephone bills, keep up some kind of an appearance in the ruthless talent melting-pot of New York, meet kindred spirits in the Russian Tea Rooms, enjoy a few beers in some Irish joint on Third Avenue, eat regularly in good if unpretentious side-street cafés. Paul has never been a café society type, but in

New York he soon learnt that if he wished to maintain a comfortable standard of living he would have to earn, earn, earn.

Soon after getting a foothold on the television circuit, he found that the Man Upstairs who seems to keep a special lookout on the fortunes of Paul Newman had favoured him with another lucky break.

'I was cast in a play that ran fourteen months on Broadway. Some actors I know who started out around the same time as I did had to wait for years before getting *their* breaks. They didn't get launched simply because they were cast in plays that failed to stay the course. That fine actor, Tow Ewell, had seventeen flops before he made the big time in the hit play, *The seven year itch*. The same thing happened to Walter Matthau; every play they gave him flopped. He used to walk into a play, get a good part, but the play would collapse under him. Now he's one of the busiest actors in the world. You just have to stick to it, never let up.'

The play that launched Paul was, of course, William Inge's *Picnic*, directed by Joshua Logan, in which he played the part of a rich but very square college boy who loses his girl to a more sexually experienced class mate, played by Ralph Meeker. Since even now Paul insists on being a square from way back when, this must have struck him as ideal casting at the time, even if he didn't quite go along with the notion of the other guy getting any girl he had a mind to keep to himself.

He took to the role of wealthy Alan Seymour with studied grace, and earned himself good notices from the then five butchers of Broadway, the major drama critics of the day.

(Now there remains only one 'butcher' who means anything in New York, and there are many theatrical types in and around Broadway who fervently wish that lively 'limey', Clive Barnes, would get back to London's Fleet Street from whence the *New York Times* had plucked him in a mood of, to some, a moment of wild midsummer madness.)

Barnes' predecessor, Brooks Atkinson, claimed that Paul 'helped to bring to life all the cross-currents of Mr Inge's sensitive writings'.

Richard Watts, Jr, in the *New York Post* acknowledged there was 'excellent work by Paul Newman as the young man who loses his girl'. The other three critics agreed that the part was 'well played', that Paul was 'excellent' and 'did well', and that as they left the Music Box Theater, the first-nighters had risen to cheer the superlative company and their applause was 'ear shattering, spontaneous and heartfelt'.

The Newmans felt really secure for the first time since their arrival in New York. 'On the day I signed for *Picnic*,' Paul told me 'I had less than 250 dollars in the bank and a wife about to give birth to our second child. If *Picnic* had not been a good play, if it had folded after only a week or two, I don't know where I would have gone.'

Coasting along in TV soap operas, no doubt, with the occasional straight video drama thrown in as a cultural bonus to help maintain his self respect. However, the assurance of a long run finally also enabled him to make a practical effort to get accepted as a student at the Actors' Studio.

'It was like another home for many of us,' he recalls. 'I really learnt to act there. Until I went there I was terrible.'

Once again, lucky stars guided his way.

'You got two auditions,' he explains. 'One before a large group and then, if you passed that one, you would go on to another with just Elia Kazan and Cheryl Crawford. Well, one day some girl asked me if I would work with her for the second test. She'd passed her first audition, but the actor she'd worked with was out of town. She asked me if I'd take the male role during her second audition. So I did.

'The bookkeeper or somebody must have got things mixed up, because about four days later, I got a card saying I'd been admitted. And I hadn't even had a first audition! See what I mean? Lucky!'

He still goes to the studio whenever he can during his visits to New York, and remains defensively loyal to its controversial ideals.

'Sometimes what you see is pretty bad,' he admits, 'but you aren't trying to do a professional job. You're trying to work out something—a problem, a new approach.'

He thinks outsiders take The Method, as promulgated by

30

founding father, Lee Strasberg, arising from the theory of Stanislavsky, more seriously than do most of the people who actually work at the studio. This was demonstrated during the filming of *Cat on a hot tin roof*, when Paul pulled what he considered a really funny gag.

'Remember Skipper, the dead friend who was supposed to have been a homosexual? Well, anyway, in this scene, I'm in my pyjamas and I'm supposed to slam out of a door and when I do, my wife's nightgown, hanging on the door, brushes against my face.

'So, anyway, during rehearsal, when we got to that point, I suddenly tore off my pyjama top and started trying to climb into my wife's nightgown, crying, "Skipper! Skipper!" There were twenty people on the set, and do you know, not one of them laughed? To them, this was The Method in action and they stood in respectful silence. *So-o-o*, having bombed out on *that* mission, I mumbled something about, well, no, I guessed I wouldn't do that, after all—and we went through the scene again. This time I played it straight.'

He made a number of lasting friendships at the Studio. 'Geraldine Page was there and Julie Harris, Eli Wallach and Rod Steiger. Shelley Winters always went back there, as so many of them did. It's been the greatest influence on my career. It's a great thing for an actor to have a place where he can keep up in his work. Even when you're in a show, you become stagnant in a part after the first six or seven months. The important thing is to keep acting. That's the only way you can grow. I used to go to the studio twice a week whenever I was in New York.'

By talking with other students and actors who had already acquired reputations he found he could understand himself a little better. Yet he was still given to brooding at length over the relative failure of his school days, his inability to come to terms with the Shaker Heights community, and then his wayward behaviour at Kenyon. It took some time before he was able to realise that his behaviour patterns had always been part of his ruthless subconscious drive towards fuller realization of himself and his will to become a public performer, an interpreter of men's dreams and emotions, a communicator in a society which often hopelessly snarls up any attempt at simple communication.

Eli Wallach had told him: 'Nobody cares if you want to be an actor. It's not like becoming a doctor or lawyer.'

Trying to figure out what his own parents' feelings must have been as they saw him gradually slipping away from the protective fold, he said: 'I think my parents were positive about me. If they didn't encourage me, at least they didn't discourage me.'

With the world becoming easier to understand and his career at last nicely off the launching pad, he still suffered from his old Shaker Heights hangups and felt remorse for not having stuck it out in the family store. There was something almost indecent, he sometimes believed, about the rapidity with which he had left home after his father died.

'A man of respect', that's what they'd called his father. Would Paul achieve the same solid respect in the make-believe world of the theatre? Would his performances on the stage impress his mother as it had the critics? He doubted it.

There were times when he wished he had remained at Yale, and earned his master's degree if only to help find work as a teacher. He would tell people, 'I think I would make a better producer . . . an administrator . . . an actor.'

It was something that would nag at him over the years, a conflict that was only resolved when he made a success of directing pictures himself. He didn't air his doubts often, yet he aired them often enough and with such obsessive repetition as to make his predicament relevant to long-term friends such as Eli Wallach, Lee Strasberg and for a while a fey, wistful, soft-spoken yet curiously self-assured young actress who had casually drifted into his world.

It happened shortly before he opened in *Picnic*. He was calling on the agent, John Foreman, later to become his business partner, when he met Joanne Woodward for the first time.

A serious actress, born some twenty years earlier in Thomasville, Georgia, Joanne spoke with a melting corn-pone accent and had, he learned much later an IQ of 135—higher than the majority of Southland college professors. The way Paul remembers it there was no instant bubbling of chemistry, no blinding flash on the Ponte Vecchio, no ringing of distant bells.

'I'd called at this agency to talk business. She happened to arrive on time for an appointment and I'd kept her waiting. So I was introduced by way of an apology. She was an actress, and my part of New York was full of actresses. She wrote me off as a snobby college boy. I was wearing a seersucker suit of a conservative cut. It was, in fact, my only suit and it had just been to the cleaners. We exchanged polite hellos and I went on my way, no sweat.'

This might arguably have been the briefest non-encounter in modern romantic history, had not Joanne, quite by coincidence, been subsequently cast as an understudy in *Picnic*. Backstage they reminded each other of their earlier meeting, and as the play's run stretched into weeks and months they struck up a casual friendship, no more or less than the usual shared theatrical camaraderie.

Over late-night coffees they would discuss common interests: the perfidy of producers, the scandal of minimum wage rates, the scarcity of meaningful scripts. Was Broadway a weary anachronism? Was live theatre dead? Was Hollywood any better? Then she would return to her bachelor digs and Paul drive home to Long Island. Rarely did a theatrical twosome so commendably deserve to be called just good friends.

Towards the end of the run of *Picnic*, Paul was offered a contract which, he felt, he simply couldn't turn down. 'Warner Brothers would pay me a thousand dollars a week,' he says. 'Little did I know what I was letting myself in for.'

He had already refused several Hollywood offers and chances of screen tests. The brashness of these approaches were distasteful to him, they lacked couth. But how long, he wondered, would the studios continue to show interest in him? Hundreds of other actors were knocking at the gates. Hollywood was, in any case, part of any actor's essential experience. In the electronic age you had to diversify.

33

Shortly after *Picnic* closed, Paul headed west. Prudent as always, he left Jackie and the two children at home on Long Island. His journey was, in any case, to prove a walk on the near-side of disaster.

4

Hooray for Hollywood

'I was stuck with this mess—there was no way out.'

In New York, those of his actor friends who had already worked there were given to speaking of Hollywood with contempt. Compared with the creative satisfaction of working in the theatre, they claimed, incarceration in the dream factories was worse than being condemned to slaving in the assembly plants of the Detroit auto industry.

Studio chiefs pushed actors around as if they were cattle bosses on the Chisholm Trail, they further claimed, and hack directors sought only Pavlovian responses from them in short takes in front of sullen camera crews.

Even the best of the breed, so went the talk among the survivors who had been there and come back to the safety and sanity of Manhattan, were despotic sadists, autocratic egomaniacs. Watch out for Wyler. Avoid Hitchcock like the plague. Bypass Preminger. Don't question the status quo or you'll be run out of town like Orson, frozen out like the 'unfriendly ten', or pressured unto the point of death like John Garfield.

Paul had heard all the arguments. Now he was out there on his own creaky limb, wondering like many before him what he had let himself in for. He didn't have to wait long before finding out—the hard way.

'I checked into a motel near the studio. I had no intention of letting this apparent piece of good fortune go to my head: besides, I still had to be careful with my money. Bringing up a family in New York while launching a film career in Hollywood can be expensive. I needed every penny I earned.

'The moment I walked into that studio I had a feeling of personal disaster. As it happened, my first picture, a piece of costume hokum called *The silver chalice*, had the distinction of being the worst film made in the entirety of the 1950s—the worst American film in the entire decade. If I live to be a thousand years I would never be able to handle lines like: "Oh, Helena, is it really you? What a joy!"

'When I did my screen test there were several solemn-looking executives hanging around. The scene wasn't playing too well, so, after a whispered conference, they took me to the studio hairdressing department and had my hair dyed.

'There was a lot of that going on out there at the time. If a scene wasn't working out somebody would say: "The kid can't handle that part. Maybe if he has his teeth capped he might improve." Someone else would say: "That scene didn't play at all too well; maybe if we put him in a different costume it would come alive." They were all groping around in circles—it's a wonder any creative spark ever showed on the screen.'

It was enough to dishearten the most shallow-minded starlet: for a man of Newman's good taste and sensitivity this exposure to Hollywood at its worst was sheer hell.

'I played the part of a Greek slave—called Basil, if you please!—with a flair for sculpting. He's ordered to fashion a cup that would be used at the Last Supper. I was stuck with this mess . . . there was no way out.'

When Paul speaks of this low period of his career his expression gets moody, and you wonder how this stubborn, perceptive man ever bothered to stay the course. It was a betwixt-and-between time in Hollywood, with the wartime boom petering out and television presenting fresh challenges which were mostly ignored by the old guard.

The present writer knows the period well, since it coincided with his own arrival in California from London. But where an actor would be hurled in at the deep end, foreign correspondents like myself could dip their toes into the shallow end and gauge the temperature. As privileged observers we could enjoy carefree private lives on the beaches, ride over mountain trails or raise hell in Las Vegas, and watch from a comfortable remove the ghastly charades taking place in the studios.

Correspondents like me who were not tied to a newsbeat,

who could pick and choose their feature interviews from a plethora of stars, were given a unique view of the movie colony at every level. If he was lucky the simpatico reporter would, from time to time, get star actresses to weep on his shoulder and let down their hair, literally and figuratively, if only to upstage a director or settle a score with a rival barracuda.

Top directors would break out the booze, publicists would promote floozies over long liquid lunches at Chasen's, and rugged actors would show off the trophies in their gun rooms and invite you to visit glamorous movie locations in the interests of promoting their current activities among magazine readers in Wigan or Wagga Wagga.

Shortly after arriving in Hollywood this writer was able to watch Paul at work on the Warner lot and I remember asking the unit publicist *not* to set up an interview: he looked so miserable, so totally isolated in this artistic disaster area, that it would have been an impertinence to intrude, a negative exercise. What the hell could one have said that wasn't damaging, if not outright libellous to the studio? One could feel sympathy for Paul's predicament, but there was absolutely nothing one could hopefully say, or write, on his behalf while he was lumbered with playing Basil in *The silver chalice*!

Paul had, in any case, arrived at a curious time in the always chequered history of Hollywood. The reek of Weimar hung in the air, or, writing with hindsight, the odour of Washington as the ship of state floundered on the rocks of the Watergate. Instead of an avuncular Sam Erwin or an ironic John Sirica presiding over the last rites, however, there was a blustering caucus of tycoons—Jack Warner, Zanuck, Selznick, Skouras, Cohn, Louis B. Mayer and De Mille. They raged away like Old Testament prophets commanding the waters to recede, swearing that there was nothing wrong with Hollywood that couldn't be put right by a return to the Harpo Marx and gingerbread days when the entire industry flinched when they cracked their whips.

But nobody could really put back the clock, no matter how much the old guard kidded itself; and without realizing it, Paul was caught up in the tide of anarchy and individual

37

opportunism that was about to rip Hollywood apart and leave it wide open to solo directors and stars to set up their own production companies.

Eventually, of course, this new freedom was itself replaced by the big corporative battalions who took over the bricks and mortar in the late 'sixties and brought the creative rebels to heel. But at the time of Paul's Hollywood debut power units were grouping and regrouping around the established directors and their stars. Gregory Peck, Clark Gable, Gary Cooper, Robert Taylor, suddenly found themselves tempted into the dangerous waters of independent production: even those who had always been docile studio time-servers—Taylor, for example—sniffed the winds of change and found the air bracing. As on Broadway, Paul found the established values of Hollywood in a state of rampant flux.

Inevitably, considering the way the studio had so quickly confirmed his worst fears about the 'system', Paul aligned himself with the young turks who were streaming in from New York and making a mockery of all that the old Hollywood guard considered sacred.

He had briefly met James Dean in New York and now found himself sharing the occasional beer with the moody young iconoclast who had been known to relieve his bladder on the studio floor while members of the public were being escorted round the Warner sound stages. To save money (and originally to get through the New York traffic more quickly) Paul had taken to riding a motor cycle, and sometimes he and Dean would roar down to the beach and drive along the coastal highway, stopping off for drinks at waterfront hangouts like Jimmy's favourite, The Point, and talk into the night as the waves crashed around them.

Not for nothing did they cast Dean in a picture named *Rebel without a cause*. Jimmy was the archetype rebel of his time, more so than Brando, whose protest lacked the neurotic intensity of the young loner and stemmed more from his own personality defects rather than a passionate feeling for revolution or a horror of social injustice. This came later, when Brando had had a chance to read, study, and bone up on the wrongs of society. Dean didn't intellectualize; like Lawrence, *he felt it there*, in honest gut-protest.

One night Dean had been talking up a storm at Googies, next to the original Schwab's drugstore and now defunct, and at closing time this moveable feast transferred itself with scarcely a break in the conversation to an Englishman's rented villa in the Garden of Allah, just across the road. Towards dawn, someone asked Jimmy what he really wanted from Hollywood.

'Screw Hollywood,' he said with infinite contempt. 'Screw Jack Warner. Fuck the system. Shit on the producers, the guys in the middle, the moneymen in the East. Shit on the stars, the cult of personality, the phoney glamour. The best thing that can happen out here is for a fucken great earthquake like the one they had in San Francisco to shake the whole lathe-and-plaster idiocy down to powdered rubble.

'Then maybe some of us who survived could go out in the streets with lightweight cameras and shoot the naked reality of existence. Imagine the rats and gophers and wild dogs running around the ruins feeding on the bodies of all the fat studio bums who died of fright after the first few tremors of the 'quake.

'That's what these bastards are doing all the time, eating each other, acting out ritual murders and tortures, and cursing their enemies and banishing the faces that don't fit into the wilderness. When these guys have some goon threaten you, saying you'll wake up in the desert outside Vegas buried up to the neck with an orange stuck in your mouth, they ain't kidding. They're killers, man, killers. We should put up with such shit? When Los Angeles returns to the desert and the Navajos take back their land, that will be the time to make the big Hollywood epic. *Gone with the wind* will look like a home movie beside my picture: *When the shit hit the fan.*'

Dean's pre-dawn, apocalyptic diatribe silenced his little circle of bit players, amateur satanists, failed poets and jail bait. For a long moment they stared back into his mocking eyes, riveted by the force of his words. Slowly they got up and went away, singly and in couples. Nobody bothered to say goodnight. He watched them go, then stiffly, as if in pain, he left the villa and stood at the edge of the floodlight pool. He squinted up at the streaks of red high in the greying sky over towards Griffith Park, and then began to shake with laughter.

'Who the hell was I trying to convince?' he spluttered, and his merriment seemed close to tears. 'Give any one of them a hundred bucks and they'd lick Jack Warner's ass.'

Slowly he walked away from the pool and headed out towards the Sunset Strip.

Anarchy was in the air, protest was blowing in the wind . . . but who was there to throw the first stone? Or was everyone out on that crazy coast caught up by some gigantic, unseen yet psychically real, juggernaut that was sweeping the old order away without anyone lifting a finger to stop the process of disintegration?

Shortly after Dean's death I asked Elizabeth Taylor, who had worked with him in *Giant*, how, in her view, he might have developed had he lived. 'He would have changed the face of Hollywood,' she said without hesitation. 'I think he was ready to go into production, maybe starting as a director, his head was full of ideas. He would have contributed greatly to the future of this business, turned things upside down and then come up with some work of sheer genius. What a loss . . . for all of us.'

Kirk Douglas, a much older man than Dean, served as another model with whom Paul could identify. Not so much with his personal background, which was rugged to the extreme by Shaker Heights standards, but as an actor who had achieved star status while managing to remain his own man.

Kirk, who had been brought to Hollywood on the enthusiastic recommendation of a former drama school chum, Lauren Bacall, solidly backed by her husband, Humphrey Bogart, gave Paul some sound advice—and an insight into the setup—when the two men met socially. Unlike Paul, who was stuck with a seven-year contract with Warner's, Kirk had insisted from the start on only signing for one picture at a time—a brave undertaking when it is remembered that he had to make half a dozen so-so pictures till be became a world star in

40

Champion, a picture nearly everyone but its producer Stanley Kramer advised him not to do.

Those were still the rough and tough days for actors when the studio bosses ruled like oriental despots. Yet as Kirk told it he was one of the first to really challenge the system.

'Hal Wallis wanted to put me into a picture I didn't like,' Kirk confided. 'I'd just done a picture with Burt Lancaster, *I walk alone*, and then Hal said to me: "Listen, you've only had two movies, and I want you on a long-term contract or I drop you." Those were the days when everybody was still dying to be on such a contract. "I'll drop you," he said again. So I said: "Okay, drop me." And he did. I've been free ever since, except for the time I had a deal with Warners, after *Champion*. Well, I got out of that, too. I wanted to do a picture about Bix Beiderbecke, and I didn't like what Warners had lined up for me as an alternative. No way. So I said I'd do the next picture for nothing if they'd let me off the hook.

'That's how I became a free agent and my own producer long before the rest of the stars got out from under the old studio system. No wonder they call me the Ultimate Loner.'

Kirk freely admitted that his independent stance earned him many powerful enemies. For example, the ruling queens of the gossip columns were Hedda Hopper and Louella Parsons— 'the one with the hat' as Brando contemptuously called the first, and the 'carpet wetter' as the second was nicknamed owing to her habit of bladder-incontinence at moments of high excitement at public functions. Talk to them if you have to but don't ever take them seriously, was Kirk's laconic advice.

If Paul felt he was wasting time in Hollywood, he was also picking up invaluable guidelines from amiable veterans like Kirk Douglas and other seasoned soldiers in the celluloid battlefields. It prompted him to rethink his own approach and to move with caution as through a minefield—and also to scrutinise all future offers and contracts with the greatest of care.

As his pal Kirk put it: 'Once you've decided to be an actor it becomes an obsession and the final result is nothing at all like onlookers would think. The outsiders don't see any of the torment that goes into the whole area of evolving a part, the torment of making decisions and fighting the inner strife.

'The outsider sees only the external perks, the swimming pool, big houses, the smiling faces and newspaper write-ups and the lovely ladies all around you. They see so little . . . Me, I see so much of the anguish and torment. When I think of actors and actresses, I think of the loneliness. Just think of how many actors and actresses destroy themselves, who drink out of all kinds of needs and frustrations. I've seen great unhappiness and loneliness in Hollywood. I've seen certain people who have been able to survive it. I've also seen feeble attempts to cover it up, people having made a big success and then suddenly being at the bottom again and trying to rise up. They hang around, cling on to the dream that is just a nightmare. You know, what I see around here is not a happy scene. The survivors are few. By that I mean the ability to survive as individuals. I am not talking about the financial success. But to survive you have to be really tough . . . when they say it's a rat race, they're right, it is.

'Someone once described being a star as like being on a San Francisco trolley car; there are so many seats for the stars and there is always someone else jumping on to the trolley and trying to find a seat. They keep squeezing and pushing and finally the struggle gets too much and they jump off.

'To survive you must develop a kind of awareness of what it's all about and, hopefully, you also develop compassion. That happens when you realize that nobody is a genius. They're just talented people, some with more talent than others, working in a medium where occasionally things come together and the rest is due to luck, pal. Only then can you take off . . .'

Paul determined that he would fight every inch of the way to get the parts that really meant something to him, to achieve the kind of creative satisfaction which would make the rest of the Hollywood fantasia bearable. But he would never play the sycophant's game as so many of the old stars had done; like Kirk he would be his own man.

Thanks to his previous stage experience his agents had thoughtfully insisted on a clause being written into his contract which, if strategically applied, might at least help to counteract the inevitable private and public ignominy which, Paul suspected, would be heaped upon him when *The silver chalice* was released and the world at large had the opportunity of seeing him as Basil the Slave.

'You must remember,' Paul told me, 'there was no way at that time of getting into pictures unless an actor signed a stock contract like the one I had signed with Warners. There were as yet very few independent producers with the power to produce anything in America outside the studio system. It was about to happen, but it needed just a bit more time.

'So this was *it*. At the end of each day's filming, I would go back to my motel feeling absolutely lousy. Yet what could I do? I would tell myself: "For months they came knocking at your door. You had reached that point where you were beginning to feel that empty space in your heart . . . wondering, how long will they keep knocking?" I *had* to go to Hollywood. I *had* to sign a contract with one of the big companies, or get lost in the shuffle. What I *hadn't* anticipated was the absolute disaster of being cast in a lousy film. "Okay," I thought, back in the motel. "So you've got yourself into a mess. So *do* something, *anything* to get yourself out of it."

'Once again I was lucky. My contract gave me the right to do two plays in New York. I heard of a part going, in *The desperate hours*, of a crazy psychopath who holds up a family at gunpoint in its own home. Meaty stuff, and I'd learned one of the basic lessons of acting—unless the part has some real meat in it you're a dead duck. This part looked good to me, and I signed to do it even before they'd finished shooting *The silver chalice*.'

Those last days on the set, as Basil the Slave made his leaden progress to the final fade, held some of the tension of an early Hitchcock thriller as Paul strutted his stuff for the camera while keeping his fingers crossed lest some studio minion pulled him aside and told him he'd been assigned to another picture. But his luck held, and he had scarcely time to remove his

43

makeup and toss his Roman togs into a prop basket and check out of the motel, before he was at Los Angeles International picking up his reservation for the next flight out to New York.

5

The other Brando

'Some day, damn it, they're going to say that Marlon Brando looks like *me!*'

When speaking of his escape from Hollywood to the Broadway production of *The desperate hours* Paul raps the back of his hand on wood.

'Once again I was lucky,' he told me. 'The critics loved the play and gave me good notices. I don't think my Hollywood bosses were all that pleased with me for agreeing to do the play without previously consulting them—and giving them a chance to push me out on loan into some other movie monstrosity. But getting back onto the stage after those miserable months in Hollywood gave me a much-needed shot in the arm and helped to restore my confidence.' He shook his head and said with carefully spaced precision: 'Man, those Hollywood people sure can knock big dents in a guy's ego, given half a chance.'

In the prevailing climate of back-stabbing paranoia the slightest show of personal independence was considered an act of gross disloyalty, and now the powers-that-were at Warners decided that in Paul they had had one more New York indoctrinated rebel on their books. Speaking of his performance in *The desperate hours*, Paul, with his usual habit of under-statement amounting to self-denigration, plays down the chilling impact his role of Glenn Griffin in Joseph Hayes' gripping play had on audiences of the time, let alone the critics.

The play 'pulled the firstnighters forward to the edge of their seats' according to Robert Coleman of the New York *Mirror*, who nominated it 'the most absorbing chiller-diller of its kind to hit Broadway since *Blind alley*. Under Robert Montgomery's vigorous direction it is played to the hilt . . . Paul Newman, with but one previous Main Stem appearance, is fascinating as the mastermind of the escapees who wilts under pressure.'

Brooks Atkinson in the *New York Times* called it 'a graphic crime play that makes sense. It shows more interest in the characters than most thrillers do . . . Paul Newman plays the boss thug with a wildness that one is inclined to respect. The play shatters the nerves.'

These views were echoed by other critics. 'A melodrama that frankly sets out to pulverise your nerves,' William Hawkins commented in the *World Telegraph & Sun*. 'The most flamboyant of the criminals is a complex role played by Paul Newman. This is a real mental case, taking his hatred of his own father out on the world. Newman has exciting passages despite the fact that he tips the character's derangement much too early.'

'Paul Newman's grinning gunman,' wrote Walter Kerr, 'with close-cropped skull and a firm assurance that there's something in it—may start off with the throttle too open, but it is finally an effective performance on a splashy level.' And John Chapman summed up: 'There could be no more stir-crazy and animal-crafty desperado than Newman, (his) is a splendid, tensely maniacal performance.' Finally, from John McClain: 'Paul Newman, the top gangster, registers strenuously as the swaggering neurotic who masterminds the festivities.' Broadway toasted a new theatrical star.

The play was inevitably compared to *The petrified forest* in which a relatively unknown Humphrey Bogart played a similar hostage-holder. In fact, the play had already been made into a movie with Bogart playing Paul's stage part. There was no danger of Paul being called the new Bogie, though. Rather, it was a case of having to shake off the 'new Marlon Brando tag' that lazy-minded people tended to pin on him. But as Frank Schuerger reported back to the Cleveland *Plain Dealer*:

'There *is* a resemblance between the two actors and both are individualists. Newman, for instance, also has an aversion to ties and so, like Bill Veeck, sometimes has trouble getting into the "better places". The other day when I met him for the first time, he was garbed in a prisoner's outfit. This was at a photography studio where publicity pictures were being shot.

'When he changed into his civvies, they turned out to be a pair of slacks, a sweater and a cap. We retired to a side-street café for a beer. While I had three, Paul had one—plus a cup of coffee—plus a cup of tea. Before imbibing the variety of liquid refreshments, he dashed out to make some phone calls. One of his aims was to try to get a ticket for *The pajama game* for his mother that evening. His mom had travelled from Cleveland to be in New York for the opening of *The desperate hours*. Upon leaving the restaurant, someone asked Paul whether they hadn't seen him on TV. Newman replied that I was on TV and that he was a newspaperman. Unlike many actors, he doesn't go around hunting autograph hunters.'

Most nights after the show he hurried home to Long Island where Jackie would always have some food ready for him and beer in the icebox. By this time Scott was four, Susan two, and soon they would be joined by a third child, Stephanie, born in 1955. Though seething with professional conflict—especially over his feelings towards Hollywood, what with his expanding family and his triumph in his new role, those were anything but desperate hours for Paul Newman, private citizen.

When the notices for *The silver chalice* appeared it came as no surprise to Paul that the consensus reactions were less than enthusiastic. Possibly the nicest was the report in *Variety*. 'The picture serves as an introduction for film newcomer Paul Newman. He's a personable young man who will probably make an impression on the femmes. He handles himself well before the cameras. Helping his pic debut is Pier Angeli, and it is their scenes together that add the warmth to what might otherwise have been a cold spectacle.'

Anything else that could possibly be said of this multi-million misadventure was encapsulated by A. H. Weiler in the *New York Times*. 'In providing a modicum of excitement and generous portions of extravaganza, they have turned out a cumbersome and sometimes creaking vehicle that takes too long to reach its goal. In spinning the saga of the cup from which Christ drank at the Last Supper, they have employed a largely tested cast that rarely distills emotion or appreciable conviction.

'Paul Newman, a recruit from Broadway and video, who is making his film debut in the role of Basil, bears a striking resemblance to Marlon Brando but his contribution is hardly outstanding. As a youth who has been cheated of his inheritance by a covetous uncle, sold to slavery and eventually chosen to create the holy relic, he is given mainly to thoughtful posing and automatic speechmaking. And despite the fact that he is desired by the extremely fetching Helena and the wistful Deborra, his wife, he is rarely better than wooden in his reaction to these fairly spectacular damsels.'

The final insult came from John McCarten writing in the *New Yorker*. 'As the Greek sculptor, Paul Newman, a lad who resembles Marlon Brando, delivers his lines with the emotional fervour of a Putnam Division conductor announcing local steps.'

Still, even with a Broadway run to contend with, there was always TV. Apart from his bread-and-butter stint with the soap opera, *The Aldrich family*, and appearances in *The web*, *The mask*, and *You are there*, he was, during these formative years, kept busy in the plethora of video drama programmes which kept so many other fine actors and actresses going in New York before TV in the USA gave up and became almost completely an advertisers' medium.

Philco, U.S. Steel, Playhouse 90 could stretch from a musical version of *Our town*, in which he co-starred with Eva Marie Saint and Frank Sinatra, to worthy ventures like the 'U.S. Steel Hour's' Theater Guild presentation of *Bang the drum slowly* in which he portrayed a baseball player and *Five fathers of Pepi* in which he played an Italian merchant.

Of his live one-hour bravura performance in the Kaiser Aluminum Hour's telecast of *The army game*, Harriet Van Horne noted: 'Acting and production were excellent with special honours going to Paul Newman.'

Most of his work was 'live', for videotape was not yet in general use, and the busy actor had his embarrassing moments. On one occasion he went before the cameras with his fly

48

undone and the tail of his shirt hanging out, another time he went on with an excess of makeup to cover a black eye collected in a bar brawl. But he revelled in the unpredictability of it all, regarding it as next best thing to appearing in a stage performance.

Talking about this period later, he said: 'TV was exciting because it *was* live. Men like Tad Mosel and Paddy Chayefsky and Max Shulman were writing for television and they made it an inventive era. Call it kitchen sink, inner search, what have you—it was great.' He went on: 'The trouble was, as it turned out, that what could have been good Broadway plays were burned out in a single night on "Robert Montgomery Presents", "Philco Playhouse", "Studio One" and the rest of them. That whole glorious period of television has disappeared.'

It was left to Neil Simon, in the mid-'sixties, to revive the popular light plays which for a while brought some of the carriage trade back to Broadway. But in the television-hungry 'fifties the drama was cannibalized by the playwrights lured to write for the box.

After the first heady dawn of native TV drama, however, the advertisers and their hatchet men began to realize that 'kitchen sink' and 'inner search' was strictly for the birds, so far as selling soapsuds and cornflakes was concerned—unless it was packaged in sanitized soapers and oaters and labelled *Peyton Place* or *Gun smoke*, or wrapped up in cops-and-robbers fantasies with lashings of urban violence, car chases and synthesized sex.

The theatre of O'Neill, Williams and Miller was practically frozen out, and significant drama went off-Broadway or became the prerogative of Pop, Op and the Underground. The Living Theater and the Velvet Underground, William Burroughs, Andy Warhol, Jules Feiffer and John Cage encroached on territory formerly reserved for the luminous talents of Helen Hayes, Osgood Perkins and the Lunts. But with two long runs to his credit Paul was happy enough with the way things were in the theatre of the mid-'fifties. Hollywood remained the bugbear.

Many months were to pass before Warners could find anything suitable for Paul, and as Lawrence J. Quirk puts it in his

49

germinal record of *The films of Paul Newman*, after *The silver chalice* he was in danger of being dismissed by the men in the motion picture industry who made the important casting decisions 'as a Brando look-alike, another also-ran Actors' Studio product from TV and the theatre.'

Laurence Quirk tells how when offered, on loanout to Metro-Goldwyn-Meyer, the role of Rocky Graziano in the film version of the autobiography the fighter had written with Rowland Barber *Somebody up there likes me*, Newman decided to accept, as he recognized the fine opportunity for a solid, in-depth characterization. The deal included a starring role in another MGM project, *The rack*, but the Graziano story comes first in importance.

'Before embarking on the film,' Quirk writes, 'Newman spent considerable time in New York with Graziano, absorbing his mannerisms, his walk, his vocal tones, speech patterns, boxing stance. The two men talked for long periods of time, and Newman went back to Hollywood with the rudiments of his forthcoming characterization fixed firmly in his mind. Then began the second phase of this painstaking preparation: he worked out constantly in the gym at the Hollywood YMCA, and brushed up on his boxing with top professionals.

In peak condition at thirty-one, Newman reported on the MGM lot in fine fettle, and rarin' to go. This was his first picture with perspicacious director Robert Wise, who understood how to bring out the best in individual performers according to their special gifts and creative insights, and he guided Newman through this, his second film, with masterly control and tactful understanding. The Actors' Studio training that Newman had not been able to successfully apply to the Greek slave role in *The silver chalice* lent itself more readily to the Graziano part, and he incorporated what techniques he thought would best serve.'

This time Paul had nothing to fear from the movie critics, and most of them did him proud. With the Rocky part to his credit he had now secured a footing both on Broadway and Hollywood. Only the Brando look-alike tag persisted, and still had the power to hurt the up-and-coming star.

Brog. in *Variety* summed the situation up in two sharp sentences. 'For Paul Newman *Somebody up there likes me* is a showcasing that should help remove the Brando look-alike handicap. His talent is large and flexible.' And John Beaufort in the *Christian Science Monitor* conceded: 'Although Paul Newman's shambling, impulsive performance as Rocky has inevitably recalled Marlon Brando's portrayals of Neanderthal types, Mr Newman nevertheless adds his own insights and vivid portraiture. The writing and acting are pungent, racy, and down-to-asphalt.'

With the script in the skilled hands of Ernest Lehman and abetted by director Wise, an actor could scarcely go wrong and Paul milked his part to the limit. It also helped having the support of Pier Angeli, Eileen Heckart, Harold J. Stone, Everett Sloane and the then brightly shining Sal Mineo, and his rigorous workouts with tough pros in the gym paid off in spades when it came to putting conviction into his big fight sequence with Tony Zale.

But even in this physical area Bosley Crowther could not resist inter-larding his *New York Times* notice with the snide observation: 'Let it be said of Mr Newman that he plays the role of Graziano well, making the pug and Marlon Brando almost indistinguishable. He is funny, though and pathetic in that slouching, rolling, smirking Brando style, but with a quite apparent simulation of the former middleweight champ.' Crowther concluded that 'the representation of the big fight of Graziano with Tony Zale is one of the whoppingest slugfests we've ever seen on the screen.'

Other commentators added: 'His marbles-in-the-mouth stammer and sneer are in the neorealistic tradition of Marlon Brando' and that 'his chest and biceps measure up to the brawniest of Hollywood's beefcake actors.' Though generally admitting that he was excellent as Rocky, 'with his hunched, half-crouch, rolling gait and Italo-New Yorkese accent' the critical consensus still insisted that the overall effect of Newman's performance was 'Brandoesque.'

It was a maddening situation. Brando was in the happy position of getting in first with an arresting new style for which his generation was receptively prepared. Yet even non-look-alikes such as James Dean and Sal Mineo, suffered under the giant spell that Brando cast over an entire decade. It is argu-ably possible that a great deal of Montgomery Clift's sub-sequent disintegration was due to the fact that Marlon had stolen his best effects, if not his thunder. (Though Clift 'got in' well before Brando, he was a lightweight by comparison and would never have made a Kowalski.)

Newman, unfortunately, came closest to actually looking somewhat like Brando, and was consequently the worst hit by the Brandoitis of the day, a precursor of Beatlemania.

'Some day, damn it, they're going to say that Marlon Brando looks like *me*!' Paul would say in exasperation.

Privately the two men got along extremely well, considering how they were in constant danger of treading on each other's egos. Of the two, Paul was the more mature, while Brando was totally unpredictable. He could be as infuriatingly churlish towards actors as he was towards his usual whipping boys on the production side of the movie industry. The only time he was at the receiving end of being bracketed with anybody was in connection with Montgomery Clift. Seeing Clift strolling along Madison Avenue, one afternoon, Marlon jumped off his motor-cycle and ran after the shy actor. Grabbing Clift by the coat collar he peered into his face, and said: 'You're supposed to look like me.' Slowly shaking his head, he released the startled Clift. 'But you don't at all,' he mumbled, and got back on his machine.

Poor James Dean suffered a painfully shy admiration of Brando which he could never fully articulate. On the rare occasions when he found himself in Brando's company he was rendered almost speechless. Marlon generally ignored the younger actor, making it even more difficult for Dean to break the shyness barrier. And he could be hurtful.

Look magazine, in its coverage of *East of Eden*, said: 'Because of a similarity in their acrobatic mannerisms, Dean inevitably will be compared to another Kazan actor, Marlon Brando. But nobody can deny Dean's personal achievement in making his difficult role understandable and fascinating.' Yet Brando, discussing the same film, was quoted as saying: 'Jim and I worked together at Actors' Studio in New York, and I have great respect for his talent. However, in that film, Mr Dean appears to be wearing my last year's wardrobe and using my last year's talent.'

Brando must surely have been only too well aware of the effect such a remark would have on a fellow-actor as sensitively vulnerable as Dean, and would have been only too willing to tap the claret of any critic, or columnist, or assistant producer, overheard to be saying something of the sort about himself, Brando. It can only be explained away by assuming that even so great a humanist as Brando can become the victim of the working actor's worst trait, dislike of other actors who present a challenge or a threat to their self-esteem. As Laurence Harvey shamelessly used to say: 'Don't tell me about them, ducky. You know I'm only interested in talking about myself.'

Brando was never bitchy towards Paul. In some ways he may have sensed in the pleasantly mannered, disciplined college man from Shaker Heights a quality which he himself lacked: control. The brat of Broadway, the original crazy, mixed-up kid, was tormented and traumatized often to the point of eccentricity if not insanity. In this, Marlon had more in common with Clift and Dean, which possibly helps to explain his cruelties towards them.

Newman, on the other hand, was too tough, too well orientated, ever to play the victim, or allow himself to be the butt of Marlon's often sadistic ironies and crude practical jokes. It was okay for the greatest American screen actor of his generation to play pranks on the likes of Wally Cox, or the butch stuntmen and anonymous female hash slingers who frequently formed the nucleus of his various entourages, but Newman could not be patronized.

Try to shake Paul's hand while you're holding a hen's egg in yours, and he'd soon make you feel like a provincial oaf whether you're Marlon Brando or the King of Redonda. With Newman such japes simply 'weren't on', and from the very beginning of their friendship, which survives to this day,

53

Marlon treated Paul as his peer, one of the few that commanded his total respect.

In the same year as the release of the Graziano picture, 1956, Paul also appeared in *The rack*, a court-martial melodrama with shock flashbacks to tortures in a North Korean military prison camp.

According to the script, Paul played a Captain Edward W. Hall, Jr, who succumbs to torture and brainwashing to turn traitor. This somewhat lugubrious movie, based on a TV play by Rod Serling, is very much of its time; but the complex scenes between Paul and Walter Pidgeon, playing his father, generated a powerful acting chemistry between the newcomer and the veteran actor. The integrity of Paul's performance pleased nearly all the critics.

Bosley Crowther raved: 'A brilliantly detailed performance by Paul Newman gives a much more disturbing emotional impact to the film than is compounded in the drama unfolded . . . For the job of showing the soldier's feelings and suggesting the strain and agony he went through in the unseen prelude, Mr Newman is finely qualified. He truly achieves in this picture a remarkable tour de force. In his facial expressions, his gestures, his pauses and his use of his voice, he makes apparent in one figure a singular personal tragedy—the whole film is done with smooth dispatch.'

Not a peep out of anyone about the Actors' Studio, not a single crack about the Method. But at least one critic could not resist a gibe about Paul's friendly but formidable rival when he described his playing of Captain Ed Hall as 'monotonous sub-Brando'.

Paul once gave me a curious example of how, mysteriously, his path has sometimes been crossed by Brando. The point came up when we were discussing the extraordinary breakthrough for Paul as a universally accepted actor after *Somebody up there likes me* reached the world's cinemas.

'Since I believe in studying my parts through observation, I spent some weeks with Graziano, watching the way he walked, the way he carried himself and the way he spoke. Gestures, mannerisms . . . I watched him like a hawk.'

54

Paul chuckled as a thought struck him. 'Now here's a curious thing. People were always comparing me with Marlon, and this would make me good and mad since we know better than anybody that we have always been two distinctively separate people. Well, some time after I'd played Rocky I was having a talk with Marlon and the conversation got round to our so-called similarity of appearance. Marlon burst out laughing when I told him the way they'd been bugging me about this.

' "I'll let you into a secret," he said. "When I was studying for the part of Kowalski in *Streetcar*, I studied Rocky Graziano and based my characterization on him. The way he walked, moved, talked. I studied photos and newsreels, and built up my Kowalski from these observations."

'Marlon and I had both worked from the same prototype to put across our stage and film characterizations! People have often said that in private life Marlon isn't anywhere near like Kowalski and I'm pretty sure I'm not in the least like Rocky when I'm at home with my feet up and having a beer and watching television. After that, I felt a lot better whenever I was accused of doing a Brando.'

If anyone is still interested in the Newman-Brando controversy, there's a handy yardstick by which they can be assessed. Not in a million years would Newman have consented to play that other Paul, the character Brando assembled with such self-investigatory agony in *Last tango in Paris*. The very idea is as grotesque as the thought of Bogart playing the Marquis de Sade. Some will see this as an implied limitation of the range and depth of Bogart or Newman's talents. On the other hand, it could also be regarded as a demarcation line showing precisely how so many otherwise highly intelligent observers went wrong in confusing, for so long a time, two highly original personalities, with distinctly separate cosmogonies, on the strength of a superficial resemblance.

Where Newman has always been passionately but unflamboyantly hopeful of resolving the glaring injustices and inconsistencies of our post-war society through the exercise of reason and tolerance harnessed to community action, Brando has frequently lapsed into a sloppy nihilistic romanticism which

55

has rarely achieved anything and invariably diminished his credibility as a rational force for liberalisation.

Where Newman is a pragmatist, Brando is a Utopian. While Brando prankishly 'moons' his bare bum from the windows of New York taxis, or before the camera on a Paris dance floor, Newman solidly and methodically goes about his business of acting or directing with a minimum of fuss or extra curricular dramatics. Life is, after all, a matter of choice. Each one of us is exercising our decision-making mechanism round the clock: what to have for breakfast, whether to catch a train or use the car, which phone call to make first, where to have lunch, what paperback to buy, movie to see, TV programme to watch, nightcap to drink. Actors who reach a certain eminence have many occupational decisions to make, notably in the choice of themes, stories and roles most suited to their talents.

It is interesting to note that Brando might at one time have made himself available to play Newman's role in *Butch Cassidy and the Sundance kid*, one of several occasions when the two actors could with equal facility have tackled an identical role. Fair enough; but again, can anyone imagine Paul Newman getting involved in the absurd narcissistic mock-sexual exercises demanded by Bertolucci for the full realization of the original premise of *Tango*?

These divergent patterns have been consistently apparent in both men since their careers 'went public' close on quarter of a century ago, but it was not until Newman consolidated his career with a series of powerful screen characterizations which unmistakably sprang from his own resources, that the look-alike hubbub died down and the critics began to assess each of his performances in their own right, and not as carbon copies of Brando's protean acting ability.

These days Newman's feet are firmly planted in Connecticut, while Brando's neurotic inability to live within society is implicit in his compulsive escapes to his island of Tahiti, his extra-marital complexities, and his often eccentric choice of film roles. He will, commendably, concern himself with the plight of the North American Indian, and recreate his own microcosmic world on his Pacific island under the delusion of being an ardent conservationist, but these are in reality childish acts of defiance against a larger world which he cannot emotionally comprehend on an adult level.

This is not intended as denigration of one actor in favour of the other, rather it is an attempt to set the record straight. That there was confusion in the first place is sad: yet it happened; and for more than a decade was a subject for exhaustive debate among solemn cineastes, to their lasting discredit.

There is one thing the two men have in common with which they are in total accord, and this is their refusal to live according to their star status with all the flashy trimmings. They have been consistently against: owning Hollywood mansions, flashy cars, yachts, private executive aircraft; membership of prestigious clubs and societies; charity balls; drifting along on the golf-and-country clubs circuit, owning race horses, etc.

It's tough to be a nice guy in Hollywood, as Kitty Hanson astutely remarked at the start of Paul's career. If you prefer the simple life, you're a non-conformist and if you prefer New York to Beverly Hills you're a rebel. If you keep your sense of humour, you're a screwball. If you're serious about your marriage, your career and the state of the world, they call you humourless.

In the film colony Paul's interests and ambitions and the things that concerned him deeply, his likes and dislikes and his way of life, soon earned him, along with Brando, a reputation for being a rebel, a non-conformist, difficult and something of an oddball. To the Hollywood hierarchy, he was an ingrate, biting the hand that (they claimed) fed him because, even though he was to be considered one of the hottest properties in filmdom, he continued to keep his distance from the social life at the top executive level and insisted on making his permanent home anywhere but in California.

To Paul it was simple. 'Why be so defensive about it? Hell, when they come to New York to work, I don't tell them they have to make their home there, do I? All I'm doing is claiming the right to say what I think, dress as I please, and go wherever I choose rather than where other people want me to be. Is that too much to ask?'

For some people, apparently, as Paul was soon to learn, it was.

6

Putting his head together

'What measure of serenity I have in my life today is the direct result of analysis. It brought me every possible benefit. My acting improved and I achieved a greater control over myself.'

Control is the essence of all art, yet how many actors have mastered it? In Hollywood only a few major stars have achieved maturity in that prevailing climate of eccentricity which has made Los Angeles the laughing academy of the world. Gregory Peck, Charlton Heston, Kirk Douglas, these spring easily to mind, but these are the exceptions.

The roll call of renowned screwballs and ding-a-lings is much longer and easier to recite. Robert Mitchum, George C. Scott, Frank Sinatra, Lee Marvin, Dean Martin, Steve McQueen, Peter Fonda . . . these are the wild men, the characters, the hell-raisers who doggedly maintain the extrovert standards set in a more innocent age by Bogart, Flynn, Barrymore. In this arena of the ego dedicated to the pleasure principle and the personality cult, Paul Newman stands aloof, a tower of strength, a paragon of 'cool'; in a gallery of larger-than-life grotesques he offers few opportunities for the stock caricature of the flamboyant star. His liberal humanism, his genuine concern, his natural reserve, make him a figure of dignity in an élitist group predominantly populated by figures of fun.

Not that he is a prude, on the contrary he enjoys life in all its diversity. He appreciates decent food, good but not necessarily fashionable restaurants, private dinner parties with kindred spirits, and has the ability not only of making friends but keeping them. Chums like Robert Wagner and Natalie Wood, Peter Ustinov, Robert Redford—not to mention a small army of off-beat characters not known to the public—can always be expected to be warmly welcomed and informally entertained wherever they might reunite in their global wanderings.

The stabilizing factor in what otherwise might have become a time-consuming social chore is Paul's restraint and split-second timing; he knows exactly when to move on, is never tempted to overdo anything. I would nominate him as the most 'balanced' actor I have ever met in the course of a professional life largely devoted to observing actors at close quarters—a form of masochism which I would not in retrospect wish upon my bitterest enemy.

It was not always this way with him, though; even the Paul Newmans of this world must experience their darker moments. We have already noted how unhappily he reacted to his initial exposure to Hollywood, and how he fought against his home environment to make the breakthrough into acting. But these were reactions to external pressures with which most ambitious people must contend if they are not to remain permanently parent-fixated and chronically house-bound.

More devastatingly, at a time when he should have been enjoying his first film triumphs, with the world opening up before him, he was being subjected to certain internal stresses which threatened to sabotage his burgeoning career. Stardom was being handed to him on a plate, but would he take it?

The period immediately following the release of *Somebody up there likes me* was, in Paul's terse phrase, 'not a very good time'. He is reluctant to discuss the more painful aspects of this turbulent passage in his otherwise comparatively smooth journey to stardom, but he admits it was a time when the pressures of both public and private life began to mount alarmingly. For a while it seemed that the carefree college graduate, with the seemingly charmed life, was in grave danger of following his chum, Brando, into a temporary limbo of emotional and mental confusion.

What had happened was that Joanne Woodward, Paul's platonic pal and backstage confidante during the Broadway run of *Picnic*, had landed herself a contract with 20th Century-Fox studios in Hollywood and the couple were seeing more of each other than was healthy, certainly as far as the stability of

59

Paul's marriage was concerned. With every fresh meeting, they realized that their feelings had now become too involved to be written off as a casual mutual attraction.

Paul's upbringing, his entire code of conduct, was not programmed to accepting the idea of divorce as an easy way out. And he was deeply committed to his family life. By this time he and Jackie had three children. Scott, Susan and Stephanie had reached that stage when they had become distinct little individuals with clearly discernible separate needs, and a way of making their demands felt by their parents, and particularly by their doting dad—who, seeing less of them than Jackie due to his work, overcompensated by showering affection on them whenever he managed to get home to Long Island. In a dicy profession, *he* needed *them*.

Joanne, for her part, had no wish to be cast in the public role of home breaker. Having herself as a child been the victim of divorce, brought up by her mother and rarely seeing but desperately missing her father, whom she'd adored, she did not want to inflict a similar unhappiness on Paul's children. And yet, and yet . . . all who saw them together at this time felt that if ever a couple were 'made for each other' they were it. The real tragedy of this emotional impasse was that everyone involved was so damned nice.

With some misgiving Joanne and Paul agreed not to see each other again. On the surface this appeared a sensible decision, but subconsciously, it began to have a dire effect on Paul's behaviour. Always one to enjoy a few beers, he now began to sample more potent brews and this sometimes led to his getting into brawls in bars and at parties.

Hollywood is the easiest place on earth for anyone, with both the money and the inclination, to go to hell on wheels. There's always a crowd to be found that's prepared to whoop it up, and even for someone as fastidious as Paul it was not too difficult to find congenial alternatives to the quiet suppers and excursions to the beach, in Joanne's company, which were now forbidden.

Then on a trip back home to the east, shortly after the Graziano movie was prémièred in New York, his drinking met the inevitable consequences. On the night of 7 July, 1956, Paul was arrested on Long Island on charges of leaving the scene of an accident and passing a red light. He resisted arrest and was hauled in handcuffs into the police station at Mineola, and jailed. Trying to bluff his way out, the incensed Paul told the arresting officer, 'I'm acting for Rocky Graziano, beat it.' To which Patrolman Rocco Caggiano laconically replied: 'Yeah, and I'm Rocky, too, and you're under arrest, pal.' Paul spent the night in the clink, brooding perhaps that history was repeating itself from the low point of his Kenyon 'disgrace'.

Whenever Hollywood threatened to get the better of him, Paul sought refuge in the Actors' Studio, where he still considered himself a pupil. In an atmosphere of quiet dedication under the guidance and inspiration of Lee Strasberg, such questions as the relevance of his brush with the police on Long Island could be viewed objectively and placed in proper perspective. It was more important to persevere as a student of acting than worry unduly about what Hollywood time-servers thought of him, most of whom meant very little to him anyway. At the Studio, he found kindred spirits who shared his contempt for most of the Hollywood hierarchy . . . including, once again, James Dean.

'It was just after I'd completed the Graziano picture,' Paul recalls. 'I'd signed to do a TV play with Jimmy. In it Jimmy was to play a punch-drunk ex-boxer based on Hemingway's Nick Adams stories. I was to play the young Adams-Hemingway figure who meets up with this old pug, The Battler. I was looking forward to working with Jimmy in this when the news came through that he'd been killed in a car smash.

'Well, I opted out of the play. I wanted no part of it. I just backed out, I was so rocked by Jimmy's death. A few days later the director told me to forget about playing Nick Adams and asked me instead to play Jimmy's part. I said, "No, I don't want to have anything to do with the play in any shape or form". About four days went by before the director called me again. "You've got to save my skin," he said, "because we can't find anybody else. We go into rehearsal next Monday. I'm sure that if he were capable of knowing what's happening,

Jimmy would appreciate your stepping in and saving the play. You owe it to him if not to the rest of us.'

'So I did the show, playing the old punchy. Half an hour after leaving the TV studio I got into a bar-room brawl and walked straight into a left hook. One eye was completely blackened. The next day I had an important interview with a producer. I walked into his office wearing an eye shade underneath a pair of dark glasses. There were several important people in the office and my entrance caused a bit of a stir.

' "What's happened?" the producer asked. "Why are you wearing that shade and those glasses?" I said: "You know where I got hit in the show last night?" There was a lot of nodding of heads. They had all seen the telecast of the play. "Well, we put a bit too much realism into it—and this is the result."

' "Boy," said the producer, "that's sure some Method acting. You show real dedication, kid." '

Paul roared with laughter when he told me this, but his ability to joke about the Method does not in any way diminish his affection for either it or the Actors' Studio. His virtuoso performance as the ancient pug won him further respect as an actor in places where it really counted, and even the *New York Times* admitted that 'Paul Newman had to surmount grotesque makeup but was quite effective.' Did the shades of James Dean and Stanislavsky exchange congratulatory smiles as they watched from the celestial wings?

As Paul's acting ability increased he became thoroughly disenchanted with the type of film parts to which his studio had the contractual right to assign him, or worse, parts for which they hired him out to other studios—irrespective of whether or not he thought them suitable.

'They were still paying me a straight one thousand dollars a week while hiring me out for a few weeks' work at seventy-five thousand dollars a time. There was no possibility of my getting even a small percentage of the profits.'

Warners had only to hire Paul out twice a year to make well over two hundred per cent profit on their annual outlay. Yet from a little over fifty thousand dollars, Paul was obliged to pay

62

his agents' fees, business and legal expenses, and the massive overheads which went with the grind of commuting regularly between his work on the West Coast and his family residence on the Eastern seaboard. Paul had no intention of bringing up his children as just three more spoiled Hollywood brats, so he continued to spend as much time as possible on Long Island and with his theatre friends in New York.

The first picture he made after *Somebody up there likes me*, though again directed by Robert Wise, was a forgettable woman's weepie set in New Zealand and called *Until they sail*. On attending the press screening at the Metro studios I remember seriously wondering how much longer this potentially exciting actor could survive such insensitive casting. The film was largely concerned with the romantic adventures of four sisters (Joan Fontaine, Piper Laurie, Sandra Dee and Jean Simmons) with American troops in the antipodeans, and the male actors had little to do beyond registering the coy simulations of sexual arousal which passed for passion in the Hollywood of the mid-'fifties.

Jean Simmons and Paul managed to generate some genuine emotional warmth for which they received smatterings of lukewarm praise from the better critics, but it was again left to the *New York Times* to put Paul's dilemma into real perspective. 'The genuine tugs at the heart are few and far between in this bittersweet but basically restrained chronicle ... although Mr Newman's portrayal is sometimes glum and casual, it is, nevertheless, generally effective ... Unfortunately, there is a good deal of introspective soul-searching before this narrative arrives at its sad and happy endings. Although this is a disturbing chapter in their history, the women who have the affection of the visiting Yanks only "until they sail" generally react with cultivated emotions.'

You cannot admittedly win 'em all but Paul now needed something meatier if he was to keep the momentum of his career on an upward swing. Fortunately, Warners finally found something for him which at least gave him a chance to project some real sexuality into his part to the delight of his growing number of woman fans.

63

The Helen Morgan story, directed by Mike Curtiz, while never aiming beyond the requirements of the average paperback novel, enabled Paul to pull out the emotional stops with the kind of force that had galvanized his portrayal of the psychopath in *The desperate hours*. As the flashy prohibition-era gangster Larry Maddux, who seduces and then exploits the alcoholic singer Helen Morgan (played by Ann Blyth) he essayed a Cagneyesque role against a background of cheap tonks and speakeasys that brought him the biggest batch of fan mail he had hitherto received. Somewhere out there on the movie circuits a mass audience had reacted to that vital spark which confirmed his 'star quality' even within the restricted framework of a cheap gangster thriller.

Kirk Douglas had told him, 'It's the public that makes you. They see something in you that strikes a response inside themselves, and that's when you become a star.' Now his appeal was established beyond the confines of a degraded dramatic vehicle.

In Britain the title was changed to *Both ends of the candle*. The best the New York *Herald Tribune* could say was that the picture would 'not go down as a landmark of originality, but sentimentalists may have a good time and an occasional snuffle. Miss Blyth is appealing as the mournful heroine and Paul Newman is excellent as the selfish promoter, providing the hard crust on a soft meringue.' The fact remained that Paul's talent had salvaged a dog of a film. Even if some of the movies in which he was appearing were only so-so, Paul was at least beginning to build up a stockpile of good notices and a lot of favourable responses from the cash customers at the box office.

Meanwhile, Joanne was also building up a nice career for herself over at Fox. Her first efforts for her parent studio could scarcely be considered scintillating, but having no intention of being fast-shuffled into the role of a non-productive contract player trotted out by the bosses to entertain visiting distributors and promoters or posing for pin-ups, she preferred to take her chances before the cameras in undistinguished movies if only to gain practical experience of film making.

But not for long. After appearing in three formula pictures *Count three and pray, A kiss before dying* and *No down payment,* (the last, Fox production, was a fairly trenchant piece of social commentary relevant to its time) she began to accrue a reputation as the studio iconoclast.

Outspoken to the point of recklessness, Joanne tongue-lashed the studio brass, and their minions, with all the lethal eloquence of a Broadway actress let loose among the barbarians of the film factories. Nobody was spared the force of her logic, and in the end her war of nerves paid off.

Fox executives had for some time been casting around for an actress to play the triple role of a girl with a multiple-personality problem, based on a real case described in a best-selling book, *A Case of multiple personality.* Several big-name actresses were tested for the part, but it finally went to Joanne more or less as an act of desperation on the part of the studio hierarchy. Okay, they reasoned, let this loudmouthed blowhard who thinks she knows it all have a go at playing Eve. If she pulls it off, we have us a valuable motion picture property. If she falls short of absolute perfection, that'll fix her wagon once and for all time. She either earns herself an Oscar nomination, or she can get back to her beloved New York theatre and we'll personally see she don't ever work in Hollywood again.

Within a few days after the camera started rolling on *The three faces of Eve,* word got around the studio that Woodward was turning in a performance that was making people's hair curl. The hell with a nomination, this obscure southern belle might even grab herself the Oscar if she kept up the standards she had set herself with the early takes.

Big shots who had looked the other way when they'd seen— or, more likely *heard*—her coming now went out of their way to be nice to her and stopped addressing her as hey, you. It was *Miss* Woodward this, *Miss* Woodward that . . . and half the studio tried to get into the projection room to see the day's rushes of *Eve.* When the first rough cuts were shown, all Hollywood knew that another star had been proudly hatched, right there on the 20th-Century-Fox lot. Hooray for Hollywood, indeed; the old magic formula was still working and the nephews and sons-in-law could resume their card schools and other indoor games around the production offices.

Paul at this time was carefully putting his head together. The shrewd Clevelander had staked his life on becoming an actor, and he now swore he would not jeopardise his career through lack of emotional control, if that indeed was the source of his heavy drinking and general waywardness. It was all right for Brando to take a plane to New York to hole up with his psycho-analyst, it was part of his total genius. But it was not the way of Shaker Heights. If Brando wanted to go that route, fine . . . he was large, he contained multitudes. Paul, on the other hand, had enough trouble trying to live down that Brando look-alike tag without muscling in on his personal scene as well.

For a start, perhaps, he *would* consult an analyst but without making a big song-and-dance production of it. Since his involvement with Joanne, although he hoped he was handling *that* situation pretty well, he had declared a moratorium on interviews touching on his personal life and was cutting down on Press relations in general. From now on his public could find out all they needed to know about him from what he put into his screen performances.

The hell with the Press and public relations anyway. The gossipier sections had already begun trying to give him a hard time over that Joanne business. As of now he would preserve his private life from the snoopers, and as long as he didn't go in for any more 'Brandoesque' scenes like that sorry business with the cops on Long Island he saw no reason why he shouldn't be left in peace and privacy to get on with his career without amassing a stack of lurid press cuttings.

This was Paul's reasoning at the time; and it was to set the pattern of his attitude towards press interviews and personal publicity for many years, a pattern which exists in a modified form to the present day.

During interviews the conversational flow would dry up whenever the topic turned to Paul Newman, the private person, and for this reason some writers, columnists and press agents began to grumble about his inaccessibility and labelled him 'difficult'. When asked a direct personal question, he would either object vehemently or, more usually, simply not answer them.

'Anyway,' he told Kitty Hanson, 'they know better now than to ask me what kind of underwear I put on.'

His reticence about his personal life did not extend to his public life as an actor. In fact, he came to believe that being a successful movie star carries with it a responsibility to the public.

'Movie stars,' he claims, 'are a kind of royalty. They're the only royalty America has—and it's amazing how people look to royalty for answers to practically everything. If I am a member of that royalty, then it seems to me I have a responsibility to be honest with people and to talk about the things I consider really important.

'Some actors have had very colourful backgrounds—they were truck drivers or beachcombers or they worked on the waterfront. I don't have anything like that to talk about.'

He would tell interviewers that sixty per cent of his reading time was now devoted to scripts, in the hope of finding a new play or film. He'd give his eye teeth, he'd swear, to find a good 'stageworthy' script dealing with the problems of life in a thermonuclear age and once even offered to do a TV show of this kind free, if a suitable script could be found. 'Most of them are pretty bad,' he concluded. 'And let's face it, second-rate theatre—even with the noblest cause in the world—won't accomplish anything.'

At one time the actor embarked on a six-week crash programme to learn and read everything he could about atomic testing, fall-out, thermonuclear war, shelters, survival, retaliation and defence.

'I always go all out,' he grinned. 'When I drink, I drink and no nonsense about it. When I study, I study.'

No wonder he has a great deal in common with Peter Ustinov, who in his early twenties announced his intention of reading through the Encyclopaedia Britannica starting with page one of the first volume and ploughing on till he reached the index of the final volume. I'm not sure whether he succeeded, but the intention was there and very much in the spirit of Paul's approach to learning a little about everything if he possibly can manage it. In Paul's case, he read everything about the atomic threat he could get his hands on, talked to everyone who was any kind of an expert.

'The frightening thing, of course,' he concluded 'is that even the experts don't agree. How can you expect people to understand or care when there's no one who can tell them positively "this is what will happen" and "this is what you can do"?'

Newman's willingness to discuss his views in areas like this tended to alarm studio officials who feared he might offend some pressure groups and thus jeopardize some current movie with his name at the top of the billing. After all, these were the post Senator Joe McCarthy days of red scares and witch-hunts, with even Arthur Miller, before his marriage to Marilyn Monroe, being hounded by the authorities to testify against anyone he knew who might have been a Communist.

But as Paul's fame increased he still claimed the right of any other citizen to say what he thought, campaign for his preferred political candidates, and would always listen attentively to or talk earnestly with anyone who had anything interesting to say regardless of his background or status in or out of the Hollywood pecking order.

When years later I told him I found it difficult to imagine a time when his emotional problems drove him to seek help through psycho-analysis, he wasn't in the least put out.

'I found it a most enriching and rewarding experience,' he told me very calmly. 'What measure of serenity I have in my life today is the direct result of analysis. It brought me every possible benefit. My acting improved and I achieved a greater control over myself.

'People should not be afraid of it. Anything you can do to develop a realistic appraisal of yourself is immensely useful. The people who are against analysis usually haven't taken the trouble to find out what it really involves. It's more a problem of the ego with them. They must always be the great frontiersmen. They don't ask anybody for help. They are absolutely self-dependent.

'I find that attitude rather childish. People like that are also basically rather lonely. Analysis is always interesting . . . you never stop learning. It's never really finished.'

Back at the Fox studios the bosses were casting around for an actor to play the lead in their upcoming production of *The long hot summer* based on a collection of stories by William Faulkner in the smouldering style of the then fashionable Tennessee Williams melodramas.

A deal was eventually made with Warners for the services of their rising star, Paul Newman, to play the cocky young incendiarist, Ben Quick, the 'barn burner' of Faulkner's short story of that name. Whom better could the bosses choose to play opposite Paul, in the role of a shy, sexually unawakened southern gal, than Fox's own rising star their very own, three-faced Eve, Joanne Woodward?

Kismet. This was 'it', fate, call it what you will. Despite their good intentions Paul and Joanne *had* started seeing each other again. Now they would be thrown together before the cameras for the whole world to see what sparks these two were capable of striking from each other simply by looking into each other's eyes and saying absolutely nothing.

There were no poet's words to match the fires they lit without speaking, the electric charges they generated without moving, the love they expressed without kissing. This new screen partnership held all the power and promise of the creative marriage between Tracy and Hepburn, and even the Man Upstairs must have flickered a quick grin as he looked down and reckoned that there are times when you just can't buck your destiny, you can't fool fate.

As Paul and Joanne wended their separate ways to the location in Clinton, Mississippi, where they were to film their first co-starring movie, hardly a soul connected with the production of this sizzling saga of the Deep South did not feel that they were all in for a long, hot summer of the higher emotions.

And as things turned out, it became just that.

7

Summer lightning, winter dreams

'This was a happy time. It felt good, being married.'

In keeping with his Actors' Studio training, Paul spent some
time alone in Clinton, Missouri, long before the rest of the
company arrived for the location filming of *The long hot summer*.

For days he just hung around the bars and pool halls,
letting his beard grow and absorbing local colour and listening
to local speech patterns. When some local roughnecks confronted him one evening, asking him if he wasn't that actor
who'd played Rockie Graziano in a movie, Paul shook his
head and rubbed the back of his hand across his stubbled
chin. 'Nah,' he said slowly. 'You know something, I've bin
asked that before. What gives with this guy? Does he come
down to the pool room?'

Of course, his cover was blown when the rest of the company
turned up and he had to start working in front of the cameras.
But he had achieved his object of insinuating himself into the
enclosed, southland community and shaking off his Yankee
accent and college mannerisms.

As with Brando, who in private was never in the least like
Stanley Kowalski, Paul sometimes surprises strangers with his
off-stage bland personality which has nothing in common with
some of the overwrought Tennessee Williams characters and
pool sharks he has played.

Joanne, of course, had no such problems. The Georgia-born,
soft-spoken actress knew the southland from infancy. After her
mother divorced Wade Woodward—a born charmer with a
career in publishing which culminated in his becoming a vice-
president of Charles Scribner's Sons—they had moved on to
Greenville, South Carolina. She did not get to know the north
until she had spent two years at Louisiana State University
followed by some theatrical work back in Greenville, which

included playing in a little theatre production of *The glass menagerie*.

If ever a lady was born to highlight in her work the more attractive qualities of the south, it is Miss Woodward. It is not insignificant that one of Joanne's childhood heroines was Scarlett O'Hara (seeing Vivien Leigh in the flesh at the world première of *Gone with the wind* in Atlanta when she was ten was a traumatic experience) and were it not for the failsafe of her impressive IQ and exquisite sensibility she could have blended easily into the pillared Colonial life-style that still exists on the larger estates where rocking chairs creak on crumbling terraces and whippoorwills call from hidden swamps.

But with two years of New York's Neighborhood Playhouse and the Actors' Studio behind her, and with an Oscar nomination in the offing, Joanne was determined to put all of her accumulated skill and energy into her part of a browbeaten southern heiress dominated by her father, another variation of the Big Daddy figure so popular in the 'fifties, and this time played by Orson Welles.

Paul's preliminary research in the local bistros made him so popular with the tougher elements around town that when a Yankee snooper turned up from New York looking for a scoop on the romance between him and Joanne, they rounded on the unfortunate muckraker and steered him into the washroom at the back of the beer parlour and set about persuading him to get out of town, but quick. Paul was never told this, but the scene was worthy of some of his later characterizations, a combination of Chance Wayne in *Sweet bird of youth* and Eddie Felson in *The hustler*, the local boys making it clear that if the New Yorker hadn't left town by sundown they would be happy to take turns to castrate him and then chop off his fingers.

With Tony Franciosa, Lee Remick, Angela Lansbury, and a horde of character actors supporting them—and with that old rogue-elephant of an actor, Orson, to needle them into coming up from the floor to deliver their emotional punches— Paul and Joanne felt an exhilaration in their work which neither of them had previously known. If there were any

71

lingering doubts about their imperative need for each other they were finally resolved during those long, hot weeks in Missouri.

In Martin Ritt, Paul found a director after his own heart, and the two men formed a friendship based on mutual respect which was to develop into a solid artistic association. They later formed their own company, Jodell Productions, named after Joanne and Martin Ritt's wife, Adele. Their collaborations included the grossly underrated *Paris blues*, *Adventures of a young man*, *Hud*, *The outrage* and *Hombre*. Everything they worked on together was worthy, and if one or two of their ventures did not reach the heights they certainly never plummeted into the lower depths of Paul's least satisfactory vehicles—such as *Lady L*, *Exodus*, *The secret war of Harry Frigg*, and the ponderously farcical *A new kind of love*.

When *The long hot summer* was released *Time* observed that Newman's performance was 'as mean and keen as a crackle-edged scythe'. Hard consonants were coincidentally employed by most of the critics to acclaim the snap, crackle and pop of Paul's acting. *Variety* contended that 'Newman slips into a cracker slouch with professional ease, never allowing a corn-pone and molasses accent to completely disguise his latent energy and native intelligence'.

Bosley Crowther in the *New York Times* praised 'the tight, word-crackling script' of Irving Ravetch and Harriet Frank and voted Paul best of all 'as the roughneck who moves in with a thinly veiled sneer to knock down the younger generation and make himself the inheritor of the old man. He has within his ploughhand figure and behind his hard blue eyes the deep and ugly deceptions of a neo-Huey Long. He could, if the script would let him, develop a classic character.'

With the picture satisfactorily wrapped up, Paul found himself moving into happier times. It was Paul's wife, Jackie, who finally decided, for the good of all concerned, on divorce. To everybody's credit, this was done with a minimum of fuss, and the children of the first marriage were never exposed to the tug-of-love that too often becomes the nerve-wracking aftermath of divorce.

Free at last to marry, Paul and Joanne headed for Las Vegas. The ceremony took place in a gambling hotel towards the end of January 1958, but they did not stay long to savour the desert sunshine. After the crackle of summer lightning över Faulkner's emotional swamplands they wished to hibernate in the winter dreams of Dickens' country.

'We decided to spend our honeymoon in London,' Paul told me. 'Everyone warned us against the English winter but we were determined to go there just the same. After spending a few days in a little hotel in Greenwich Village we reached London early in February. We stayed at the Connaught, in Mayfair, one of the nicest, friendliest hotels in the world.

'The weather there was every bit as bad as they had said it would be when we first arrived but then there was one of those premature springs which I believe happen every so often in Britain. Anyway, the weather was marvellous. There were no tourists to speak of and we would get a car and head off into the country till we were literally lost. Hundreds of miles from London and checking into country inns at nightfall—there's a lot to be said for a winter honeymoon.

'We even got beyond the border into Scotland. Unfortunately, we didn't get right up to the far north. But what we saw of it was delightful. Joanne and I made a pact to return to Scotland one day and travel up as far as we could go, to Skye and the outer Hebrides. We'd go there in midsummer and see the midnight sun.

'This was a happy time. It felt good, being married. When we were not out exploring the countryside we'd take long walks in the London parks, sit in little pubs, and there was always the theatre. I have loved London ever since. It's probably the last of the civilized cities—with San Francisco.'

The newlyweds revived old friendships in London and met new, congenial people. Unlike Hollywood, where the movie colony tends to live an inbred existence cut off from the worka-day world, London was a cross-section of all human life. It was the centre of government. Parliament, the Law Courts, theatres, museums, shops, all reflecting the teeming activities of

73

a metropolis where life was not disrupted if a picture failed to gross a million in the first six weeks or Jack Warner put a star on suspension.

People like the Ustinovs, the Ken Tynans, Olivier, seemed to enjoy a social life that embraced current ideas and leisured activities, which had little or nothing to do with whether their latest film was boffo in Cincinnati or Zsa Zsa Gabor had found a new protector. There was less trivia, more wit, and a wry, humorous attitude towards current events which appealed to the academic in Paul and the literary and artistic interests of Joanne. Why, even the ballet was taken in its stride, something to be cherished without being turned into an élitist cult or seasonal ritual.

Having made one false start in marriage, Paul privately determined that for the rest of his life he would build something of substance from this second chance.

He was later to say of his failure to stay the course with Jackie, 'I felt guilty as hell about it, and I will carry that guilt for the rest of my life.' But he had taken this irrevocable step and would handle its consequences with style.

In a way, his children by Jackie had from their earliest days accepted their father's commuting between their home and his place of work. Tactfully helped by their mother, they soon adjusted to the fact that Paul's second marriage had in no way diminished his affection for them and they became used to the idea of having two homes instead of one, with Joanne as a delightful addition to the family, as it were.

They were also mercifully spared the financial hangups which can traumatize a family as effectively—often more so—as an actual divorce. Children of broken marriages do not inevitably become suffering victims, and many have found themselves better off than their schoolfellows lumbered with good, 'Christian' parents who hate each other's guts. Marriage is a relative blessing, whereas love is for real.

On returning to Hollywood, Paul found himself involved in a curious venture. The idea of starring in a motion picture based on Gore Vidal's *The death of Billy the kid* was promising. Vidal, who became a great friend of the Newmans, was building

74

a solid reputation for himself as a writer of striking originality with a prose style as gem-clear as Scott Fitzgerald's.

The portrait of Billy, as drawn by Gore Vidal, was arrestingly alive, something which could have been played to perfection by James Dean, had he lived.

Television director Arthur Penn was assigned by Warners to translate Vidal's quirky videoscript into a meaningful feature film, with Leslie Stevens doing the screenplay. Paul was encouraged by both director and writer to talk-out his own ideas of the part during the preparatory stages, and for a while this seemed like the inauguration of a more enlightened policy from the top.

But the brass could not leave well alone, and soon the project became bogged down with ambiguities created by having too many people looking over too few shoulders.

Round about this time I remember meeting Joanne at a promotional cocktail party given by Fox at their studio. Settling down in a corner with a mandatory highball, I listened attentively as, in full spate, Joanne regaled me with pungent accounts of the latest perfidies of producers and the iniquities of the middlemen who, she claimed, were running the business into the ground.

Cassandra-like, she predicted that within a few years this vast studio complex in which we were sitting would disappear and be replaced by supermarkets and apartment blocks and hotels. These days the towering monstrosities of Studio City prove the accuracy of Joanne's prophetic vision of the 'fifties, but more to the point at the time was her chilling prediction of the impending decline of feature film production. To cheer her up I remarked that, from all I heard, at least Paul was involved in an interesting project at Warners.

'*Billy the kid?*' she said witheringly. 'Yes, it *had* certain possibilities, but now nobody knows where it's at. It's beyond belief, even when these people are on to a good thing they have an uncanny capacity for lousing it up. Paul's going out of his mind trying to put some kind of individuality into his part, but it sure is heavy going. This industry will only save itself by its bootstraps if the old men who insist on running things will

75

begin to trust the creative people, instead of interfering at every stage of production and causing only confusion.

'Look at the way Kazan had to fight to shoot *On the waterfront* in New York. Harry Cohn wanted him to make the entire film in California, using the docks down at San Diego for location scenes. Why? So Cohn could keep a constant eye on what was going on instead of having to rely on his spies in New York to keep him informed. Kazan could argue till he was hoarse that the script was based on a situation that was unique to the New York waterfront, Cohn still wouldn't see the point. It was only when Kazan threatened to walk out on the project and sue the studio that he was permitted to work in New York. Everybody's dead scared, it's incredible.'

Studio employees hovering in the offing pretended not to be listening, but their proximity did not daunt Mrs Newman, who, without prompting from me, went off onto another tangent which brought her criticisms back to her home base, the Fox setup.

In this film city of fear Joanne Woodward was a jet-age Joan of Arc, frequently burnt at the stake by proxy. She and Paul were to become a rallying point for similarly frustrated, equally talented actors, writers and directors. In an industry where even world-famous stars found it expedient to mind their p's and q's, the battling Newmans were blasting off in all directions, and undoubtedly making themselves some powerful enemies in the process. They just didn't seem to give a damn, as long as they managed to keep their own priorities right. What were these priorities? Honesty, integrity, and a crying need for a time-and-motion study of Hollywood's corporate structure.

Paul's portrayal of Billy the Kid eventually reached the cinema under the title, *The left-handed gun*, and much of the intensity and thought that had gone into its making came across splendidly. It was certainly worth the effort, but mass audiences were not yet ready for a Western which tampered with their traditional concepts of a genre whose rules were laid down by the likes of Tom Mix and Hoot Gibson. Even the success of such breakthrough movies as *Stagecoach*, and later *Shane* and *High Noon*, drew heavily on traditional values. Paul's

76

Billy did not do too well at the box office, which may have justified the studio's doubts about the whole project, but one wonders how the story would have fared had the principals involved been allowed to work without studio interference.

The reactions of the two critics quoted below gives some indication of the general ambivalence towards this film when it first reached the public. Today it is something of a cult phenomenon and some commentators have seen in Paul's Billy the Kid intimations of the later and infinitely more popular Butch Cassidy. But art is short in Hollywood, and the immediate cash returns on this courageously original attempt to improve on a worn-out formula were sufficiently small to prove the 'enemy' right.

Howard Thompson in the *New York Times* led the baying pack: 'The sad thing is that some television people have tried to make a Western that's different. And by golly, it is,' he sneered, then rounded on the principal actor. 'Poor Mr Newman seems to be auditioning alternately for the Moscow Art Players and Grand Old Opry, as he ambles about, grinning or mumbling endlessly.'

Variety was more enthusiastic. 'A smart and exciting Western paced by Paul Newman's intense portrayal of The Kid. The best parts of the film are the moments of hysterical excitement as the three young desperadoes rough-house with each other as feckless as any innocent boys and in the next instant turn to deadly killing without flicking a curly eyelash . . . Newman dominates the picture.'

By the time these notices appeared Paul was facing his biggest challenge yet: the pitting of his talent against the professional guile and fatal, flamboyant beauty of Elizabeth Taylor in her remarkable role of Maggie the Cat.

8

Brat on a hot tin roof

'I really got them bugged out there, they really scratch their heads about me.'

The gossip merchants along Sunset and down on Restaurant Row licked their prurient chops, figuring they were in for a field day when it was announced that Paul Newman's leading lady in *Cat on a hot tin roof* was to be the concupiscent Elizabeth Taylor, playing Tennessee Williams' steamiest wanton to date, Maggie Pollitt, Maggie the Cat.

Their hopes were dashed when shooting began. What other actor, they grouched, could work in close proximity with Hollywood's homegrown hetaera, this star of stars in the grand manner of Theda and Gloria, then shamble off home each night and watch boxing on television?

Well, Newman could. With Joanne to go home to, they could have starred him simultaneously with Bardot, Loren, Monroe *and* Taylor, and he would still casually have stuck his chewing gum behind his right ear for each camera clinch, burned up a few more yards of film with perfectly simulated actor's passion, then slouched back to his dressing room to study his next lines or read the baseball reports or the latest intelligence from Wall Street and Washington.

Miss Taylor was, in any case, embroiled in her tempestuous marriage with Mike Todd. This did not deter the gossips, who fastened on any drop in the emotional graph of the Todd marriage on the assumption that two such strong characters simply would not allow the one to dominate the other.

It was pointed out that Liz's marriage to hotelier Conrad Hilton's heir, Nicky, had lasted only a few months since Liz had refused to tolerate her husband's interests in gambling and sitting up till dawn playing cards and rapping with his bachelor pals. The gossip mongers explained (in print and ad nauseam)

78

that the Taylor marriage to British actor Michael Wilding had only lasted 'because of the children' and Wilding's gentlemanly refusal to play the dominant male. The Todds' amiable tendency to stage many of their brawls in public further encouraged the Greek chorus—headed by Hedda and Louella—to keep a permanent look-out for the slightest fluctuations between the two.

Since Paul and Joanne also had no reservations about agreeing to disagree in public, the smaller-minded read storm warnings into the slightest sign of turbulence.

If Paul was overheard to say, 'I think the Los Angeles Dodgers have got the skids under them this season,' and Joanne replied, 'Oh, I don't think so', it would be enough to encourage any one of the hundreds of tip-off men in or out of the studios to inform the columnists that the battling Newmans were at it again.

This would be scarcely worth mentioning if it were not so much part of the climate of Hollywood at that time, when the columnists still wielded a power over the movie makers which younger people will find incredible.

In their heyday, Hedda and Louella claimed a combined readership totalling 75,000,000. More than six hundred newspapers printed Louella's column alone, and at the beginning of World War II, when paper shortages forced the Honolulu *Advertiser* to reduce its content by one-third, the editor wrote Hedda to assure her that her column was indispensable.

At the time of *Cat* there were still around four hundred columnists accredited to newspapers and serious journals as well as fan magazines, covering Hollywood, and a separate contingent (nicknamed 'the Bedouins' by the *Daily Mirror's* witty Lionel Crane), served foreign countries ranging from Britain, France and Germany to Beirut and Luxembourg.

Extraordinary perks and privileges were afforded the native gossips headed after the Gruesome Twosome—by Sheilah Graham, Radie Harris, Edith Gwynn, Sidney Skolsky, Army Archerd, Mike Connolly, Jimmy Fidler, Jimmy Starr and such colourful general newshens as Florabel Muir and Adele Rogers St John. Florabel affected outrageously outsize hats before Hedda turned gossipist, and Adele was the most literate of the lot.

In his introduction to his book, *Hedda and Louella*, editor George Eells describes the background of fear and intimidation against which the more powerful columnists thrived.

'In a society where everyone was either on the way up or on the way down, Louella and Hedda shared a determination not to lose footing. It earned them a few devoted friends, many collaborators and a host of enemies.

'Who were these women, these phenomena?

'To find out, one must know first that there were two Hollywoods. The first was lit by arc lights and inhabited by stars. The second generated the power to produce the illumination. It was the Hollywood of the moguls. In their day, Hollywood moguls functioned as despots. They ruled by will, made policy by whim and hired out of pique.

'When agent Charles Feldman became a rival for the affections of the glamorous Jean Howard, Louis B. Mayer simply barred him from the lot. That was Metro-Goldwyn-Mayer, the Rolls-Royce of the studios.

Mogul Herbert J. Yates habitually thought up and assigned 'Box-office' titles. One grim morning he handed writer Gertrude Walker a piece of paper upon which she found "Sing, Dance, Plenty Hot". She protested that was a review, not a title. Yates gave her a choice of writing the script or checking off the lot. That was Republic, the jeep of the studios.

'Whether a tycoon headed MGM, Republic or some other studio, he ruled. Should an employee seriously offend a tycoon, he might be unofficially blacklisted throughout the industry. Only a star of enormous box-office appeal could sometimes give the back of his hand to a tycoon.'

Eells cites as an example a highly popular screen juvenile who was once reportedly called into Mayer's office and informed that so much gossip was circulating about him and a male companion of several years' standing that the juvenile must get rid of his friend. The juvenile refused. Mayer insisted. The juvenile regarded the studio head coldly, then asked: "Mr Mayer, what would you do if I told you to get rid of

80

Mrs Mayer?" Then he walked out. There were no repercussions.

'Louella and Hedda linked these worlds,' Eells explains. 'Just as they became "star" columnists, so were they "star" adventuresses. Hollywood abounded with adventuresses on many levels. These were vivid, unconventional women, who thrived amid power, glamour and wealth. Their pasts were often veiled in mystery. Even close friends could guess at their ages, what their origins had been or how they had become connected with the industry. In the telling, their lives were reshaped to conform with what *ought* to have been. In the case of some, details seem too improbable for fiction . . .

'Adventuresses then were both respectable and raffish. They might be scenarists, story constructionists, playgirls or reporters. It was Hedda's and Louella's personal styles that put them in such company. Otherwise they might have remained hardworking, respected professionals comparable to Grace Kingsley, Florabel Muir, Agnes Underwood, Ruth Waterbury, Katherine Albert and Jane Ardmore—to name a few.

'It was not to be. They were phenomena, the likes of which we are not likely to see again. Both columnists were relentless in demonstrating their influence. During her lifetime, Hedda used to point dramatically at her home on Tropical Drive in Beverly Hills and chortle: "That's the house that fear built."

'Hedda wasn't kidding. Although her ashes are interred at Rose Hill cemetery in Altoona, Pennsylvania and Louella spent her last years rocking aimlessly back and forth in a Santa Monica rest home, their names still evoke real, if irrational, uneasiness among some Hollywood veterans. Judging from the responses I received when I began researching this book, I might have been preparing an exposé on the CIA or a Mafia chieftain.'

Paul Newman arrived on the Hollywood scene at a time when the gossipists still had the power to wound, if only in the preconditioned minds of the old guard, and it is to his credit that he never attempted to ingratiate himself with any of the more venal columnists. If he felt he had anything worth saying he would save it for the better feature writers—Al

Morgan, Joe Hyams, Rex Reed—or restrict his comments to heavy-handed stabs at humour or sly send-ups which frequently went above the interviewers' heads and got quoted straight.

There was a time when Paul refused to talk to anyone if it meant being quoted, a justifiable reaction to the period before his marriage to Joanne when some of the more persistent gossips pressured him into a state of stubborn non-communication. He only began to mellow again after marrying Joanne, and though he showed a stoical indifference to what the gossips were saying, he was helpful and courteous to bona fide interviewers.

'I never go out of my way to read what's written about me,' he says, 'unless I'm interested in the person who's writing it.'

As Brick, the impotent, alcoholic anti-hero of *Cat on a hot tin roof*, Paul gave an insightful performance of a man who was the antithesis of his own private personality. Then half-way through production Mike Todd was killed in an aeroplane crash and the widowed Elizabeth needed all the strength and stability of her co-star to see her through the rest of her performance.

This was a real test of her acting resources, and despite the shock of her bereavement, perhaps to some degree *because* of it, she turned in the best performance of her career to date. She would almost certainly have won an Oscar for *Cat* had not voters been scared off by her precipitate rush to marry singer Eddie Fisher.

Again the power of gossip had triumphed over art. In an impetuous moment Elizabeth blurted out to Hedda Hopper, 'Mike's dead, Eddie's alive', which, added to the implication that she had broken up Fisher's storybook marriage to that all-American peachorino, Debbie Reynolds, was enough to place her into the category of that other 'scarlet woman', Ingrid Bergman.

Miss Taylor was, at least, in good company, and her private (sic) life did not hurt the box office either. But the brave men of Hollywood chickened out when it came to recognizing her rare gifts as a screen actress in a quality motion picture. Only after she had lain at death's door in a London hospital—thus making the celluloid sacrifice, in Alexander Walker's propitious phrase—was she awarded an Oscar. Ironically she was thus honoured for playing a hooker in *Butterfield 8*, which, when she saw it for the first (and last) time in a studio screening room, so incensed her that she tore off her stiletto shoe and hurled it at the screen.

In *Cat* Paul demonstrated that his appeal as a male sex symbol did not rest entirely on his rapport with Joanne, and that he could trade acting 'know-how' with the most skilled screen performer of her generation.

Once again Liz had pulled off the trick of rendering a male star a woman's most potent gift, sharing with Garbo the power to make the men in her screen life transcend themselves. In 'real life', this gift was later to work wonders with Richard Burton, who, but for his fortuitous marriage, might have been relegated to the secondary ranks alongside such fine British actors as Stephen Boyd, Stanley Baker, Richard Johnson and Robert Shaw. Mr Burton has reason to be thankful for the lucky stars which guided him towards the greatest star of the post-war cinema, in or out of Hollywood.

Paul Newman, on the other hand, has never felt any compulsion to assert his hegemony in the marital field. He has frankly said of Joanne, 'Without her, I'd be nowhere—nothing. She really opened me up.'

The opening-up process has, among other things, made him foolproof in his dogged resistance to the wiles and blandishments of other women. In a profession where some of the world's most glamorous women have been known to encourage the attentions of spindly nonentities in the pursuit of their professions, and where popular male stars can arouse the rutting instincts of duchesses and grande dames listed in the Social Register, as well as shopgirls, Paul has managed to navigate the more dangerous channels with much adroitness. Even the fevered imaginations of the scandle-mag fiction writers have been hard-pressed to find anything more 'scandalous' than the occasional teeny-boppers random attempts to be photographed with him or to track down his whereabouts on a movie location—an international sport with which anyone connected with the communications media will confirm as an occupational hazard. It is one with which Paul has always coped with polite composure.

When *Cat on a hot tin roof* was released, Paul's performance hit cinema audiences in the collective gut. Some of the critics took director Richard Brooks to task for having watered down Tennessee Williams' original text, particularly the homosexuality between Brick and his dead buddy, Skipper, overt in the play but only hinted at on the screen.

Judith Crist complained that as a result of the stage theme of homosexuality being dropped 'Mr Newman's Brick is now a weakling who prefers the bottle to his beautiful wife'. Hollis Alpert, though disappointed, admitted that 'even though the plot has become rudderless, the movie still has some exceedingly well-drawn characters to offer . . . Paul Newman is adequate as Brick, even though the character is now virtually a static one.'

Once more it was left to the extreme ends of the critical spectrum to provide some form of consensus which reflected the response of the massed audience. Ron. in *Variety* said: 'Newman again proves to be one of the finest actors in films, playing cynical underacting against highly developed action. His command of the articulate, sensitive sequences is unmistakable and the way he mirrors his feelings is basic to every scene.' Bosley Crowther in the *New York Times* magisterially summed up: 'Mr Newman is perhaps the most resourceful and dramatically restrained of the lot. He gives an ingratiating picture of a tortured and tested young man.'

Shortly after their return from honeymoon Paul and Joanne found themselves a flat in an old apartment house in New York's East Eighties. There was nothing about it to suggest that it was occupied by film stars. It boasted an unexceptional entrance foyer, a living room, a dining-room, study, master bedroom, library, bedrooms for their anticipated children (who didn't take long to arrive) and for the use of Paul's elder children, a maid's room and a walk-through kitchen. It was tastefully but not lavishly furnished. The wall of the dining-room contained two Chagall prints next to a dollar fifty Mexican poster.

There were, however, two distinctive items of furniture. In the living room stood a coffee table made out of half a blacksmith's bellows. The master bedroom contained the Newman's pièce de résistance. 'It was not just *a* brass bed,' a friend recalls, 'it was *the* brass bed of all times'. It was bought in New Orleans and, according to Paul, it had previously seen service in one of the city's most famous bordellos. Paul would tell visitors: "Tennesse Williams considers it the perfect example of Southern decadence and is hoping that sooner or later I'll sell it to him."

With the arrival of Elinor Theresa followed by Melissa, the household was increased by the addition of a maid named Tressie ('She's maid, nurse and boss,' said Paul. 'She allows us to stay here') and two chihuahuas—El Toro and Little Brother, both of whom were more or less housebroken when they arrived but managed to get into the most frantic hassels whenever they heard a car back-fire in the streets—the legacy, no doubt, of an ancestry, traceable through scores of Mexican revolutions. Paul, Joanne and Tressie divided the cooking chores between them, Paul always insisting that he cooked the best hamburgers in town.

It was rare to find the Newmans, when in New York, on view at Sardi's or 21. Paul would more likely be found at an unpretentious actors' hang out on Eighth Avenue called Downey's.

'They won't let you into Sardi's or the other places without a tie,' Paul would explain, seriously. 'Since I don't see much point in wearing ties except for unavoidable formal occasions, I just don't bother to think about places where they insist on making you borrow a tie from the doorman for the privilege of eating there. I'd rather eat at home anyway.'

He would have settled for the Automat if he could, but by this time there was the problem of his collecting a crowd around him if he went into a popular public eating place. So he stuck to bars where the regulars left him in peace, and patronized out-of-the-way restaurants that treated him like 'family'. Most of the time he'd move around New York wearing slacks or chino pants, open-necked shirts, a sports coat, dark glasses and a cap. Whenever he could he'd ride a motor-scooter.

'It's not an affectation,' he told Al Morgan. 'The other day I took a cab from my apartment to class (at the Actors' Studio) and it took me forty minutes. I can get there in ten on the scooter. It makes sense and it's practical.'

Another advantage of the scooter was that he had no trouble with autograph hounds while riding around Manhattan. Togged out in cap and dark glasses, he was almost unrecognizable. If cornered he would as likely as not sign his name as Marlon Brando. 'There must be hundreds of my scribbles around passing for Marlon's signature.' These days he rarely signs autographs in public, having learnt from experience that to sign one is a signal for a stampede. Politely but firmly he just explains this point to the autograph seeker, and the more sensitive ones understand perfectly.

Joanne would often go along with Paul, riding on the pillion. 'It took a while to teach her how to lean on the curves,' said Paul, who for more formal means of transportation would drive a Volkswagen. 'Somehow,' Paul told Morgan, 'the scooter bugs the Hollywood crowd more than anything else, even more than the way I dress. Don't think there aren't pressures on me to dress up, shut up and get off the scooter. I know I can jeopardize my position. I frankly don't give a damn. This is the way I see it. It's my own business.'

He was beginning to feel very strongly about his own identity. 'I'm two people. I'm me . . . Paul Newman. And I'm Paul Newman, the actor. The first one is not for sale. When they hire the second one, I do the best job I can but they have no right to tell me how to live, how to dress or how to think.' By Hollywood standards he was an out and out nonconformist. 'I really got them bugged out there, they really scratch their heads about me.'

A cause for head-scratching around this time was occasioned by his decision to accept a bit role in the motion picture anthology of Ernest Hemingway's Nick Adams stories, *The Adventures of Hemingway as a young man.*

'They screamed at me out there. I was cheapening myself by playing a bit part, they said. I was a star, I couldn't play a bit. You know why I did it? It was the part of a forty-five-year-old, punch-drunk fighter. It was a good part and I wanted to play it for that reason alone. But I had another reason. It was the part I'd played some time before on TV, the bit I'd taken over from Jimmy Dean. I wanted to do it again for myself. I wanted to sit down and look at the kinescope of the TV show and then look at the movie and see what I've learned about acting over the years.'

He was bothered that he could not find a suitable play to get him back into the New York theatre. 'I can't find one,' he complained. 'I read scripts by the car-load. I'll tell you, though. If I do find a play and I think it belongs off Broadway rather than on, I'll do it there for peanuts. To hell with the loot.'

Unconsciously Paul was moving with the times. Along with Brando, Clift, Tony Franciosa and other so-called nonconformists, he was creating the right climate for the nonconformist deluge which the young were to spring on the square world during the 'sixties.

Just as Kerouac, Ferlinghetti, Ginsberg, Corso, and the rest, had been defining attitudes and setting the stage for what were to become the commonplaces of protest and counter culture, Newman, by insisting on doing his own thing, and with his widely noted contempt for the perks and privileges of his star status, was making it just that bit easier for the kids on the brink of social and aesthetic awareness to switch on, tune in, and freak out.

Having hit the heights in the Faulkner and Williams stories, he now plunged into the depths with a succession of parts which simply did not work for him. He made a gallant stab at comedy with Joanne in *Rally 'round the flag boys!*, produced and directed by Leo McCarey from the novel by Max Shulman.

They just about scraped through, but the public were not quite prepared to see the tragic anti-hero or tough hustler of recent films transformed into a rabbit-livered commuter just like any other white-collared slob on the Penn Central special to New Haven.

87

The delectable Joan Collins provided some lively competition for Joanne's sexy matron, but Paul had a long way to go before he could even begin to approximate the light touch of a Cary Grant or, for that matter, a Jack Lemmon or Tony Curtis.

Bosley Crowther in the *New York Times* let them off lightly, saying: 'As crazy a lot of sheer farce madness as had been put on the screen in some time pops out in [this picture] and what's more, it's played by two of Hollywood's most formidable young dramatic stars, Joanne Woodward and Paul Newman. How's that for crazy, man! For all the apparent odds against her, Miss Woodward makes a cheerful farceuse, on the order of the late Carole Lombard, and Mr Newman plays it broadly for laughs. It's no epic. But it's good for laughs.'

The young Philadelphians, shown in England as *The city jungle*, is one of the few Newman pictures the present writer has not been able to see, and must make do with the following terse comment from *Time* magazine. 'For a moment there, it looks as if the picture is going to make an honest if not very original point. But before anyone can say Fish House Punch, the script gives the hero a splendid opportunity to save his soul without losing any money.'

Paul seems to have made his presence felt, however, and as the admirable Lawrence J. Quirk wrote in *Screen Slants*: '*The young Philadelphians* is about as archetypal a Paul Newman picture as can be devised, at least in so far as it showcases one of his emerging screen incarnations, namely the young-guy-on-the-make . . . Of course, it's pat, thin stuff for much of the time, and the courtroom pyrotechnics towards the end are contrived to the point of the outrageous—but who really wants to turn cinematic purist and start splitting hairs on this or that when Paul Newman is engaging us mightily with his entertaining manœuvrings onwards and upwards. And despite the hefty support he gets from a slew of accomplished performers, it's Mr Newman who succeeds in making this picture look more solid and craftsmanlike than it actually is. Who said films were primarily a *director's* medium?'

Saved by the gong, or rather the star. This was not the first time that the presence of Paul in a picture had given it a distinction it would otherwise have lacked, and its director would not have deserved. And in his next venture, *From the terrace*, he in fact turned what could have been a rather trite 'women's' picture into something far more important dramatically.

In this the usually sympathetic Joanne plays a really vicious bitch of an heiress, with all the exasperating sham-sensuality of the leisured nympho, okay for a one-night stand but hell to live with or be married to. It really is a remarkable performance within so conventional a framework, and Paul's carefully understated responses are the work of a mature and thinking actor.

His growing love for the gentle, undemanding Natalie Benziger, played to perfection by Ina Balin, is a devastatingly accurate dramatic statement, and a vast improvement on the corny old helpings of highly spiced ham that Hollywood had been serving up for years to represent a situation long done to death by such monstrosities as *Back street*.

The penultimate scene in which Paul turns down a great future in Wall Street to seek out Ina is a high moment of commercial cinema. At a certain level the whole exercise is simply a preposterous cliché, but the concentration of thought and feeling which the principals brought to bear on their roles lifted a merely slick story into some cinematically sublime moments.

Paul could now be considered to have joined the ranks of the great dependables—Peck, Heston, Wayne—the staples of a cinema which still relied on a star system. But could he achieve more? This was the question he was asking himself on the day he stormed into Jack L. Warner's executive suite and demanded that he be allowed to buy his way out of his contract.

'I had to find out just how far I could go as an actor without commitments to any one particular company,' he told me wryly. 'It cost me half a million dollars and kept me poor for several years. But I was free at last to make my own decisions. If I failed in anything it would be *my* failure, no one else's. All things considered, it was the best financial transaction I ever made.'

Now he faced another challenge. Stuck in the sands of Israel working on *Exodus* under the jackboot of Otto ('The Great') Preminger, he would be hard put to create a convincing character under gruelling and sometimes exasperating circumstances.

9

Grand tour with fotofloods

'One of the nicer things about being an actor, is getting
around the world and meeting people you wouldn't ordinarily meet if you stay at home and mind the family store,
as I might have done, or settle for a steady job.'

Paul's first visit to Israel for location work on *Exodus* promised
to be rewarding, not only as the experience of a new country
but also as some kind of a homecoming. Otto Preminger's
plans for a grandiose screen version of Leon Uris' massive
novelization of a part of the heroic struggle that went into the
creation of modern Israel was a project close to Paul's heart.

It was a chance perhaps to pay his tithes to the ancient
forces which had shaped his father's gentle philosophy and
indirectly helped to form Paul's own rough-and-ready humanism, with its total freedom from the more virulent prejudices.
A closer look at the city of David, a spiritual confrontation
with the promised land of Moses—not that Paul would have
put it so fancily.

On arrival in Tel Aviv, followed shortly by Joanne and the
children, Paul soon found himself heavily involved in Preminger's production treadmill. Impetuous, imperious, at times
more like a Prussian Junker than a civilized Viennese Jew, Otto
can be an infuriating taskmaster. He also can be the most
charming fellow in the world when the moon is in the right
quarter.

I remember having to 'phone him one morning from my
home on the beach to cancel a luncheon appointment in
Hollywood, having been laid low by some virus. In my en-
feebled state it took me nearly half an hour to prevent him from
sending his personal physician down to check me out, and for
the next twenty-four hours a steady barrage of get well messages
and gifts was showered upon me from the greatness of Otto's

heart. Never have I been more compelled to clamber out of a sick bed and present myself bright and shining for a later lunch date. Many others can testify to Otto's deep concern for his fellow creatures.

At other times, he is capable of unwitting cruelties and riding roughshod over everyone in sight. Marshalling 'Otto's Army' into battle positions for his cameras was a task of DeMille proportions, and not since the legendary Cecil B. had set up his Hollywood legions on the other side of the Nile and stunned the Sphinx into cockeyed stupefaction, had the Middle East been so overrun by Californian hordes.

Paul's primary concern was to try not to get lost in the shuffle. A miniaturist, who likes to work close to the lens in an atmosphere of dramatic intimacy, he found himself meandering through huge set-pieces where much of his work could have been done by a stand-in listening to the racing results on a transistor radio.

Some of the scenes aboard the escape ship *Exodus*, perilously carrying Ari-Newman's refugees from Cyprus to Haifa, promised—at least in Dalton Trumbo's original script—to offer him some of the emotional scope, of a Tennessee Williams situation. Yet even these seemed to die the death in actual translation onto film, and after a while the ritual of sitting through the latest 'rushes' became an increasingly painful experience.

There are times when an actor knows he has got himself into a situation over which he has no personal control, and though Ari Ben Canaan was a cut above Basil the Slave it was a time of considerable frustration for Paul. He nevertheless went through the motions stoically enough and, like a prize-fighter under pressure, sought wherever possible for suitable openings to score dramatically. They were few and far between, but the film shows occasional flashes of dramatic tension which would have greatly enhanced Paul's performance had he been able to build these up into a consistent pattern.

Paul was not a lone sufferer by any means, since the impressive cast list included Eva Marie Saint (dressed by the upcoming Rudi Gernreich), Ralph Richardson, Peter Lawford, Lee J.

Cobb, Hugh Griffith, Gregory Ratoff, Felix Aylmer, Marius Goring, Victor Maddern and Joseph Furst. The hot desert winds, the sometimes remote locations, the actual hard graft that went into the simulations of tough guerrilla warfare did not help to sweeten the frayed dispositions of these highly individualistic performers . . . and throughout the normal hazards of a tough location there was the constant 'voice over' of 'Panzerfuehrer Preminger' urging them all onwards and upwards to heights of bathetic kitsch.

Whenever Paul and his family could get away for a few hours they would explore the countryside, never failing to be impressed by the shrines and symbols marking man's historic religious impulses through the three mainstreams of Christianity, Judaism and Islam.

Even more than Athens, Jerusalem is a city of clear light, and as the cocks crowed over the domes and minarettes, Paul would stand on his hotel balcony at dawn and carefully build up his considerable reserves of energy to deal with the day's working problems. Dogs barking across the valley in which Jerusalem is cradled would be echoed around the slumbering hills. Solomon's Stables, the Church of the Holy Sepulchre, the Dome of the Rock . . . Paul's eyes would search across them and seem to be staring into the heart of life's mystery.

The Mandelbaum Gate was still in use as a means of access to many of the important Christian shrines, which seem to have proliferated in the territory then belonging to the Hashemite Kingdom of Jordan. As a world-famous actor, Paul was free to wander where he wished, enjoying cocktails in the American Bar atop the Mount of Olives, listening to the click of Japanese cameras in the Garden of Gethsemene, or taking the road to Bethlehem where it is still possible to see ragged families living in caves as they did when the apostles trod this same road.

But Paul sensed constraint in these surroundings, a feeling of tension which curtailed his trips and cast an added pall over the already gloomy atmosphere of the unit. While Preminger's team was stolidly accumulating reels of film for his epiphany in Technicolor and Super-Panavision of a nation's steady climb to hard-won autonomy, everyone was uneasily aware of the underground stirrings and rumblings of real life antagonistic factions surreptitiously training and accumulating arms in preparation for future bloody confrontations.

On the Via Dolorosa rabbis, Catholic priests, Armenian monks mingled with German wandervögeln and Baptists from the Bible Belt . . . and in narrow streets Arab eyes observed the passing pilgrims. Beneath the shimmering Moslem symbol of the Dome, tough young undercover Israeli guerrillas grimly counted the bullet nicks in the Wailing Wall. And vowed to avenge the blasphemy.

It is at such times as this that Paul questions his role as an actor and wonders what his carefully acquired skills are worth when measured against the achievements of such men as Moshe Dayan, Ben Gurion, or a great soul like Golda Meir—or nearer home, to men of the calibre of Eugene McCarthy, Ralph Nader or the most obscure civil rights worker, doctor, or country schoolmaster.

The unease that was so much part of a mood that went into the making of *Exodus* was reflected in the critical reaction to the finished product. Bosley Crowther spoke of a 'massive, overlong, episodic, involved and generally inconclusive "cinerama" of historical and pictorial events . . . an ambiguous piece of work . . . so much churching around in it that no deep or solid stream of interest evolves'.

Hollis Alpert pointed out that if the picture 'had been allowed to end forty or fifty minutes before its full running time, I suspect I would have left my seat with fewer mixed feelings . . . but Preminger relentlessly insists on going on, and the more he does, the more the lack of dimension of the characters becomes apparent. Figures who, up to then, had been heroic in size, become longwinded and lose our interest, even though they are played by such capable people as Paul Newman and Eva Marie Saint'.

In the aftermath of recriminations and counter-recriminations which followed the release of *Exodus*, Paul remained resolutely silent. He was above the level of backbiting which exists 'below stairs' in any profession. I cannot resist recording a small observation of my own during the screening of the gala première of *Exodus* in London. I happened to be enjoying a few drinks with Francis Bacon and Colin MacInnes in Muriel's Club, in Soho, when one of the key production executives of the film wandered in from the nearby cinema where the credits had just started to roll before a distinguished audience. The poor fellow had obviously been priming himself for the ordeal for several hours, and as his rapid orders for large shots of Ricard multiplied his tear ducts sprang a leak and he slumped over the bar, sobbing, 'They blew it. They had everything going for them, and they blew it. Goddammit, they had the whole of Israel ready to help them out. It could have been a great, great picture . . . but no, they just blew it.'

After more than an hour of this, the unhappy man straightened his black tie, buttoned up his Tuxedo, and wandered out in the streets looking for someone to sell him a gun with which to shoot Otto Preminger. Even the sophisticates in Muriel's, that night, knew that they had been witnessing that rarity in the picture business—a moment of truth.

By this time Paul was happily engrossed in the meaty role of Eddie Felson, the curiously dignified pool shark of *The hustler*, the shooting of which took place mostly in New York. Here he had the advantage of being directed by one of the masters of the neo-realistic school, Robert Rossen, a man of great courage and commanding authority. He also had the advantage of being coached in the subtleties of shooting pool at championship level by perhaps the greatest professional of all time, Willie Mosconi.

'I had a good feeling about this one right from the start,' Paul told me. 'When I was preparing for the part, most of the furniture was removed from our dining-room to make way for a billiard table. I then spent many happy hours at home playing with Mosconi. What I called a perfect way to rehearse a part, wouldn't you agree?'

Once again his Ivy League personality was submerged in the portrayal of a misfit from the wrong side of the tracks, a soul-brother of the young Rocky Graziano or the barn-burning Ben Quick—a mid-century urban Billy the Kid restricted by the proliferation of the corporate state to sleazy pool halls and transient, cash-on-the nail apartment houses.

There was also another of those dour, dipsomaniacal floozies that are always so readily available to the itinerant American male (usually himself on the lam from another such woman and only one jump away from the nearest alimony jail) who have become a staple commodity in the realistic cinema, and which Joanne was one day to play in *W.U.S.A.* Here she was played with a touching, derelict conviction by Piper Laurie, as the crippled semi-hooker, Sarah Packard.

Another asset was the inspired casting of Jackie Gleason as Minnesota Fats, 'the champion poolplayer of the fifty states', and the introduction of an actor who was to become one of the great performers of the century—George C. Scott, bringing his dangerous, elliptical brand of cold menace to the part of Bert Gordon, the ruthless matchmaker who pits Eddie against the jungle cunning of Fats.

The hustler has become a classic, and it has been said that on its completion Rossen—a very sick man—told friends he could now die in peace, knowing he had left his indelible mark on the best thing he had ever done. This from the man who directed *All the king's men.*

The Newmans were working in New York, among friends, before the lights began to dim on the Main Stem and the warrens around Times Square became Rat Alley. They had moved further downtown to a bigger apartment on Park Avenue, and their home became the *salon* of what was later to be called Radical Chic. This was the period of great liberating ideas. The 'sixties were not yet in full swing and we were witnessing the dying fall of the Eisenhower age of innocence when the old *Saturday Evening Post* concepts had not yet been put to the test and the intellectuals were waiting for a sign, a rallying force, which eventually materialized with the New Frontiersmen of John F. Kennedy.

The hustler was filmed just before America was caught up by a cultural revolution, the effects of which are still reverberating throughout the country. The Newmans were still rebels without a cause—or with limited objectives—and though their intellectual sympathies were to be engaged by the general reshaping of traditional ideas, as actors they would long continue to work within the traditional dramatic frames and conservative story values through which they had achieved artistic maturity.

In pictures like *The hustler, Hud, The outrage, Harper, Hombre, Cool hand Luke,* and even in *Butch Cassidy and the Sundance kid* and *Winning,* Paul would be perpetuating a screen-acting genre established by Muni, Bogart, Garfield, Brando, Dean and McQueen, in which the star performer establishes the stance of the existentialistic loner in a world where blood is argument and nobody wins forever.

Paul's protype role over the years has all the characteristics of Muni in *I am a fugitive from a chain gang,* of Bogart as Duke Mantee, Garfield in *Body and soul,* of Bogart again as Philip Marlowe, of Brando as Kowalski and also Terry Malloy, of Dean in his only mature role of Jett Rink in *Giant,* of McQueen as the Cincinnati Kid and Bullitt the rebel cop.

Newman is the screen rebel in transition from the simple verities of Bogart's Marlowe to the complex moral ambiguities of his most incisively 'committed' role, that of Rheinhardt in *W.U.S.A.* This film must eventually find its place beside Chaplin's *Modern Times,* as a definitive artistic commentary on a nation's malaise.

When *The hustler* was shown in New York, *Time* was considerably impressed by 'a clutch of phrases ("I got oil on my arm") that breathe the smoky poetry of the pool-rooms and ring true as a struck spittoon.' Bosley Crowther asserted that, 'It crackles with credible passions. It comes briskly and brusquely to sharp points . . . Paul Newman violently plays with a master's control of tart expressions and bitterly passionate attitudes.' 'Paul Newman is always a dominant figure in any scene,' observed Alton Cook, 'but there is something extra this time in his intense ardour as the man who treats a game with religious zeal that at times mounts to mania. His standard is high but he has surpassed it this time.'

Best of all, perhaps, was Paul V. Beckley's comprehensive yet succinct assessment of the film, the star, and the director. 'The writing, the directing and the acting all have that kind of intense unanimity that convinces you everyone involved understood and felt what they were concerned with . . . I'm not sure Paul Newman has ever looked more firmly inside a role . . . Rossen has been at pains to avoid that overemphasis that is so often fatal to any emphasis at all. His movie is all of one piece. Its effect is built not alone out of the crises of the characters but of their quiet moments too, and these add much to the general impression of everything moving from first to last inevitably and rightly.' As in the Greek classical ideal, he might have added, for there is an almost Orestian inevitability in Eddie Felson's progress within the perimeters of urban doom.

People were beginning to notice Paul's uncanny flair for getting under the skin of some of the sleaziest characters ever created by modern fiction, and there were some in New York and Beverly Hills who were convinced that he periodically took off from his cosy domestic scene, and in the manner of one of the more decadent late-Victorian fictional characters (Dr Jekyll, Dorian Gray) plunged into the Bohemian underworld and practised nameless vices to nourish his actor's art.

Nothing can be further from the truth, even though these rumours were rife along Sunset Boulevard to the author's certain knowledge as late as 1973, and the real explanation is so simple that it always fails to satisfy the sensation seekers.

Paul has the eye of a novelist. The phrase, 'I am a camera' might have been coined for him alone. Before he became famous he would sit for hours in bars, cafés, diners, the Automat, watching people's mannerisms, the way their posture would change with their shifting emotions, their reactions to their surroundings and so on. He also has an acute ear for the way people talk, and is quick to notice how features change to accommodate a regional drawl, a Yankee twang, a Germanic upper lip, an under thrust French lower lip, the grin of a Japanese, the lilt of a Connemara brogue, the strained sibilants of a Mexican customs official, the growl of a Bowery cop, the pasta-rich laughter of a restaurateur in Little Italy.

Even now that his notoriety makes it difficult for him to move around freely in public places, he will single out a face, a voice, a gesture, as he goes through the formalities of a cocktail party or restaurant meal, and file them away in his memory-bank for future use either in one of his own characterizations or as a director concerned with bringing out the best in other actors.

Like a trained writer, Paul doesn't make a production out of his ability to observe and record selectively. It's a flair, an instinct. Brando has it, and so do actors like Henry Fonda, Alec Guinness, Paul Scofield. More extrovert actors only observe other actors, the thoughtful ones take pains to study *people*.

There is also the matter of empathy. Away from the studios and the theatre, Paul leads a comparatively normal existence. His family is usually with him no matter what home he is temporarily occupying. There are the many friends he has made at his auto clubs, wartime buddies who drop in, specialists in various fields. Businessmen, mechanics, academics, the not always famous writers and their wives and children, he finds time for all of them once they have attracted his friendship.

Finally, there is his tolerance of 'characters' and oddballs providing they have talent as well. The late Laurence Harvey was always a welcome visitor at the Newman home, with his West End mannerisms and camp determination to outrage the squares and bait the pompous.

Tennessee Williams, Gore Vidal, Tony Perkins have been colleagues and co-workers living in that wifeless and childless world of bachelors which Paul's acting roles occasionally call upon him to comprehend if not to enter.

When the shy Perkins took the plunge and became a husband and father, it was to friends like the Newmans that he turned for the kind of Doctor Spock advice that could only come from people who were bringing up several children in every conceivable age range from infancy to early adulthood.

All types of human life have flowed, and continue to flow, through the Newmans' circle, giving them food for thought, material for study, and a growing awareness of the diversity of their fellow creatures . . .

Both Paul and Joanne have reason to be thankful for never

having been tempted to live in ivory towers, and their solid connection with the workaday realities shows in the flawless veracity of every move and gesture they make on the screen.

By now, Paul had managed to spend a considerable part of his time away from Hollywood. He had made another sortie into the New York theatre in Elia Kazan's staging of Tennessee Williams' *Sweet bird of youth*.

When he walked on to the boards of the Martin Beck Theater, on 9 March 1959, as Chance Wayne, gigolo to a washed-out movie crone played by Geraldine Page, he gave the audience a glimpse into that elusive other, buried life which lies within the 'wholesome' Paul Newman—until he conjures it up for one of his all-too convincingly sleazy roles.

The audience was suitably electrified and the critics gave him the best notices of his career to date. While pointing out that it was hardly a noble play, Brooks Atkinson conceded his acceptance of its 'overtones of pity for those who are damned. Although the old harridan from Hollywood is a monster, she is no fiend; she knows what she is doing and why. Although the young man is a monster, he represents the seamy side of the American dream. He means to take whatever he can snatch; he is the perpetual adolescent, steeped in gaudy illusions of success and grandeur. . . . In the central roles, the acting is magnificent. Miss Page is at the peak of form and Paul Newman's young man is the perfect centerpiece. Although he has a braggart, calculating exterior, he is as immature as an adolescent; brassy outside, terrified and remorseful when he stops strutting. . . .'

Robert Coleman recorded in the New York *Mirror* that: 'Paul Newman etches a frightening portrait of a small-town hotshot who hasn't the stuff to be a big-shot. His disintegration, when he finally faces up to reality, has genuine emotional impact. Newman, as well as the audience, was moved by the concluding passages of the play. There were tears in his eyes as well as in those of many outside.'

The ending of the play has Chance Wayne, abandoned by his Hollywood crone when she thinks she has a chance of making a comeback, sitting in his motel room in a state of near-catatonia, waiting for the local bully-boy (Rip Torn) to arrive with his heavy mob and carry out a threatened ritual castration. For despite his dependence on the elderly actress, Chance had come back to his home town to win back his girl, Heavenly Finley, daughter of a corrupt political boss. But he has infected her with syphilis and made her pregnant.

If tragic implies an inevitability of fate, as Aristotle would have it, *Sweet bird of youth* comes as near to tragedy as anything achieved in the post-war American theatre. What Hollywood did with it later, with director Richard Brooks assuming the mantle of deus ex machina, will be touched on later. But once again Broadway had served to prove to Hollywood that in Newman they had call upon the services of an actor of the highest calibre, and once more this actor had drawn on the hidden reserves of his astonishing emotional-bank to provide the ailing theatre of New York with one of its most memorable acting achievements

Newman had worked so hard at his craft that there was a widespread tendency to take his screen performances for granted, not realizing his mastery of 'the art that conceals art' which separates the few truly great screen 'actors' from the merely good-looking 'reactors' whose names would fill the Beverly Hills telephone directory.

Thanks to the theatrical genius of Tennessee Williams, caught just before it so tragically went sour, this actor who was in the habit of telling Hollywood where and how it was going wrong, was once more given the opportunity of laying his talent on the theatrical chopping block and proving himself capable of putting his money where his mouth was.

Compare the following: 'It will be a very long time until we see a more moving portrayal than that of Paul Newman.' 'Newman . . . is very good indeed . . . It is too bad that such excitement is doused so often by the watery and melodramatic sequences that recur rhythmically as though devised to offset the corrosive effects of the film's high moments.'

The first quotation is from John McClain's notice of the stage play in the New York *Journal-American*, the second from

Paul V. Beckley's review in the *Herald Tribune* of the film version some two years later.

It is curious to remember that in 1962, when *Sweet bird of youth* was filmed in Hollywood the puerile restrictions of the Production Code were still inhibiting directors from filming without the tinkerings and tamperings of a self-imposed censorship.

It was left to buccaneering characters like producer Joseph E. Levine to open up the censorship restrictions by means of what Alexander Walker refers to as the technique of Auditory Sex, which consists of putting into the dialogue the sexual implications that the censors would not allow to be put explicitly into the visuals.

'The sex in a Levine film,' Walker observes in *The Celluloid Sacrifice*, 'is strictly for the ear, not the eye, though publicity must suggest that the eye is catered for, too. In *The carpetbaggers* and *Where love has gone* lust, lechery and perversions are continually being implied by the characters—but by word rather than deed.'

Examples: 'What do you want to see on your honeymoon, darling?'—'Lots of lovely ceilings.'

'For once the hero is going to let the heroine show herself properly grateful.'—'Properly?'

'My films add dignity and culture to the movie industry.' —'And three starlets a week to your bed.'

'The fans write in for her autograph. If only they knew that just by pushing her doorbell they could get everything.'

'You have only one concept of love, a vile and sinful one.'— 'If you're dying of thirst you drink from the nearest mud hole.'

On such gems of the scriptwriters' craft was built a new climate of freedom in the American cinema, and not on the poetic works of Tennessee Williams, who was reduced to writing long memos to the directors of 'his' pictures, in which he pathetically tried to draw their attention to passages in the scripts where an insight had been distorted, a meaningful phrase bowdlerised or obliterated altogether.

Invariably, the memos were ignored, and at one time the playwright was barred from the MGM studios. (Around this time Orson Welles was turning down good money—which he certainly needed—rather than have a film of his undergo the notorious MGM cutting-room treatment from which all but the least recalcitrant directors were also barred.)

The Production Code stood firmly against the direct depiction of various kinds of sexual relationships, yet permitted the cliché treatment of the same relationships simply for commercial entertainment.

Thanks to such dubious liberators as Joe Levine, the guardians of the Production Code and the prognoses of the Legion of Decency were forced into a defensive position for the first time in more than thirty-five years. Soon the cowards of the cutting-room floor were making fortunes out of various forms of pornography leading up to the implicitness of *Deep throat*. But this break-through made it equally possible for the achievement of such masterly works as *Cabaret*, *Last tango in Paris*, and Nicolas Roeg's *Don't look now*, in which Julie Christie and Donald Sutherland come full circle to the high romanticism of Garbo and a presentation of sexual congress as aesthetically impeccable as Rodin's *The kiss*.

Art, like life, is in a state of constant change while yet returning again and again to certain primary images; and the work of Paul Newman seems to be more a constant return to, and reshaping of, a prototype image viewed from shifting angles and in varying gradations of light. So despite Brooks's pussyfooting approach to the central figure of Chance Wayne, and his bowdlerised script, Paul retained enough of the overtones of his stage performance in his screen projection to 'get by', as it were, and further consolidate his name as an actor of growing stature.

But it was left to Bosley Crowther in the *New York Times* to once again assume his by now stock role of the American motion picture industry's Jimminy Cricket in this period of moral confusion and hesitancy before the floodgates opened. A period when, in Murray Schumach's telling phrase, 'Money (was still) Hollywood's guiding light in living with censorship.'

'It is ironic that the work of Tennessee Williams, who is allowed to be the most powerful and prolific playwright (if not the most pleasant) writing for the American theatre today, has tended more and more to be unsuitable for translation to the screen—at least into the kinds of motion pictures that are conventional with Hollywood.

'We mean, of course, those pictures in which ugliness and violence are toned down and the logic of predestined frustration is hoisted into the illogic of some sort of halfway happy end . . . the total point of the play's conclusion in the emasculation and utter debasement of the principal character has been destroyed. Mr Brooks had altered the ending so that the fellow is only beat up and kicked a bit by the brother of the young woman he has violated and then is oddly allowed to run off with her.

'In short, to satisfy the Hollywood hunger for the romantic ideal, Mr Brooks simply has reversed the play's cold logic. He has turned defeat into victory. This tampering . . . knocks the final punch out of the picture and reduces what might have been a really cruel sport of honest cynicism to a weak splash of phony hope.'

Ever since Nahum Tate arranged a happy ending for King Lear the producers of popular dramatic entertainment have doggedly tried to improve upon art by tagging happy endings on to the most uncompromisingly stark material, and it must be remembered that Mr Brooks was working in the studios that had produced the saga of Andy Hardy. As Lawrence J. Quirk wittily summed up: '. . . Brooks meddled and tampered as he had in *Cat on a hot tin roof* and reinforced his burgeoning reputation as Chief Castrator of Honestly Cynical Stage Art by changing the ending around so that the hero, Chance Wayne, is merely beaten up, rather than castrated.

Long before the term 'the jet set' became common coinage, the Newmans, in their determination to treat Hollywood simply as a stopover place to work when a film production demanded their presence there, were constantly jetting back and forth between New York and the West Coast, and New York and Europe. Not that they could in any way be identified with the pinheads who were to make up the 'set' in the following years, inheritors of the Bright Young Things of the 'twenties or the

Café Society of the 'thirties. Like most serious actors of the day they were turning the studios of Pinewood and Shepperton, of Bouloigne-sur-Seine, and Ciné Citta, into the far-flung outposts of Mother Hollywood and, in many cases, the attractive alternatives to the threatened white elephants in Culver City and Burbank.

Picture-making was 'going international' and directors like Wyler, Wilder, Huston and Preminger were increasingly filming their screen stories in the actual locations. Partly to compete with the actualities of television, partly as a means of tax relief or the use of frozen assets, this practice was also to provide a welcome treat for cinemagoers who were now encouraged to feast their eyes on the diverting background scenery of the South of France, Sicily, Tunis, Greece, Tuscany, and the great capital cities recovering from the ravages of world war.

Pleasant narrative trifles were given gratuitous depth in films like *Three coins in a fountain*, *Bonjour tristesse*, *A certain smile*, *Roman holiday*, *The reluctant debutante* and *Boy on a dolphin*, and doubtless enjoyed more substantial box-office returns than if they had been shot against fake Hollywood sets.

Paul and Joanne were, in any case, predisposed towards Europe. They had artiste and writer friends in most of the capitals, London was almost a second home, and when they went to Paris to film *Paris blues* they considered it something of a second honeymoon as well as a chance to work with a bunch of congenial fellow-artistes for whom they had considerable respect.

Paris blues was produced by Marlon Brando's Pennebaker company and the music composed by Duke Ellington. Paul and Joanne were 'paired' with Sidney Poitier and Diahann Carroll as expatriate Americans working as musicians or vacationing in the Paris of the late 'fifties, which happened to be a very good Paris indeed. A city which had shaken off the miasma of war and military occupation, it was not as yet brainwashed by De Gaulle. In some ways it resembled the Paris of the middle 'twenties when Hemingway was collecting material for *The sun also rises* and there was a springtime air of expectancy along the boulevards and on the terraces. Any city that had just hatched the young Bardot couldn't be all bad anyway.

Louis Armstrong also had a part in the film, and with Martin Ritt directing there was an added feeling of buoyancy on the set when the Newmans checked in for a preliminary runthrough of the script with the principals. The two girls, Joanne and Diahann, were visiting Paris on a two-week vacation according to their film roles. Off duty, they found a great deal to explore and a convivial host of friends to keep them up late at night.

Moustache, who played drums in the picture, ran his own restaurant on the Left Bank, where he would start knocking the daylights out of his skins shortly after midnight and keep the place jumping till early dawn. Paul and Joanne would also patronize the good jazz clubs which then proliferated throughout Paris. Bechet was still alive and playing his heart out and there was always something good going on at the Blue Note and the Club de St Germaine near the great cafés of the Boul' Mich', the Flore and Deux Magots, where you could still see Picasso, or Sartre, or Cocteau in full conversational spate.

They would go up to the rib joint in Montmartre where the novelist James Jones liked to hang out, and characters like Bill Marshall and Lobo Nocho and Mezz Mezzrow would drink cheap wine and eat New Orleans-style gumbo and black-eyed peas. Paris was still a great place for enjoying gastronomically simple dawns, with hot dogs at Morgans or onion soup at Les Halles.

For less respectable people than the Newmans there were the cafés in the Arab quarter where you could always find a good hash connection, or pick up little trifles at the Flea Market. You could go out and hear Beethoven played at Royaument Abbey or recreate the world of that splendid monarch, Louis XIV and watch phantoms flicker across the sunlit lawns of Versailles to the music of a ghostly gavotte.

It was Paris as it should always be, unspoiled by the greed of the tourist rackets, basking in that brief, bright interregnum between the Liberation and the present long night of inflationary chaos and political claustrophobia.

Though the critics didn't quite know what to make of *Paris blues,* many ordinary cinemagoers have since found it an accurate evocation of a certain period that held a promise of good things to come. In an odd sort of way, it said things to people who believed in an America that died at Dallas on 22 November 1963.

'They're making the grand tour, complete with klieg lights and fotofloods,' a publicity agent remarked as we watched a night scene being set up near the Gare du Nord one chilly dawn. 'Can you imagine Joanne and Paul as Hollywood stars before the war? The only times they would have come to Europe then would have been on royal visits—like Doug and Mary, or Charlie Chaplin—and they wouldn't have seen anything, really. Yet these two have had the whole of Paris wide open to them, and they're managing to enjoy it just like any other well-heeled travellers. Three cheers for democracy.'

When I later mentioned this to Paul, he said: 'You're right. One of the nicer things about being an actor, is getting around the world and meeting people you wouldn't ordinarily meet if you stay at home and mind the family store, as I might have done, or settle for a steady job.'

What the Newmans learnt yet again from this venture was never to underestimate the importance of a script. Perhaps there had been too many hands at work on the screenplay based on a novel by Harold Flender. Get the script right, and you're half-way to the realization of a good movie. The credits of *Paris blues* included: 'Screenplay by Jack Sher, Irene Kamp and Walter Bernstein. Adaptation by Lulla Adler.' Then there was talk of a 'script doctor' having been flown in from London, who worked for a few days in Paris fortified against the indignities of his task with strong liquor and a fluent command of the stronger Anglo-Saxon cuss-words.

The crux of the picture's failure, according to *Variety*, was 'the screenplay's failure to bring any true identity to any of these four characters. As a result, their relationships are vague and superficial. Furthermore, except for sporadic interludes, none of the four players can achieve clarity, arouse sympathy, or sustain concern. This is especially disappointing in view of the acknowledged calibre of performers such as Newman, Poitier and Miss Woodward.'

Still, they had Ellington and they had Satch. They also had that particular Paris, one which is unlikely ever to be seen again. The Newmans further cemented friendships with Sidney Poitier and Diahann Carroll, friendships which—especially in the case of Poitier—were to bring about solid alliances in the production field later on and lead to the making of several memorable films, not necessarily with the stars included. But that was in the distant future.

In the air-conditioned production offices of Hollywood, a growing number of executive whizzkids were impatiently awaiting the return of the Newmans to the Coast where a mounting pile of projects awaited their joint scrutiny. As far as the travelling couple was concerned they would from now on be more favourably disposed towards scripts based on away-from-it-all locations.

Newman (far right) in a scene from the 20th Century-Fox dramatic western *Hombre*. (*Copyright 20th Century-Fox*)
Previous page: Paul Newman—a characteristic shot (*Kobal Collection*)

Above: Paul Newman and Joanne Woodward in a scene from *WUSA*. (*Copyright CIC*)
Left: Newman plays a tough, hard-living logger in *Sometimes A Great Notion*, a Universal/Newman-Foreman Production. (*Kobal Collection*)
Right: Another scene from *WUSA*, a Stuart Rosenberg, Paul Newman, John Foreman Production. (*Copyright CIC*)

Paul Newman and Robert Redford star as the roguish pair who roamed the west in the 1880's in *Butch Cassidy and the Sundance Kid* (*20th Century-Fox*)

A scene from *Butch Cassidy and the Sundance Kid*, produced by John Foreman and directed by George Roy Hill (*20th Century-Fox*)

Paul Newman and friend in Greece (*Central Press Photos Ltd*)

Paul Newman and Joanne Woodward (*Central Press Photos Ltd*)

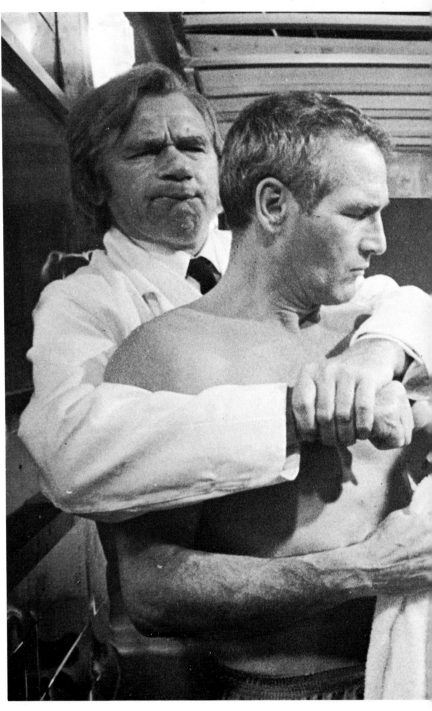

Newman in a scene from *The Mackintosh Man* (*Copyright Warner Bros.*)

Newman and Dominique Sanda—another scene from *The Mackintosh Man* (Copyright Warner Bros.)
Top: The Mackintosh Man (Copyright Warner Bros.)

ewman and Redford on the set of *The Sting*—a chat between scenes! (*Photo-
ıph by Cyril Maitland—Camera Press Ltd*)

p: Those blue eyes still twinkling—Newman in *The Sting* (*Photograph by Cyril
aitland—Camera Press Ltd*)

xt page: Newman in a typical stance—again with Redford in *The Sting* (*Photo-
ıph by Cyril Maitland—Camera Press Ltd*)

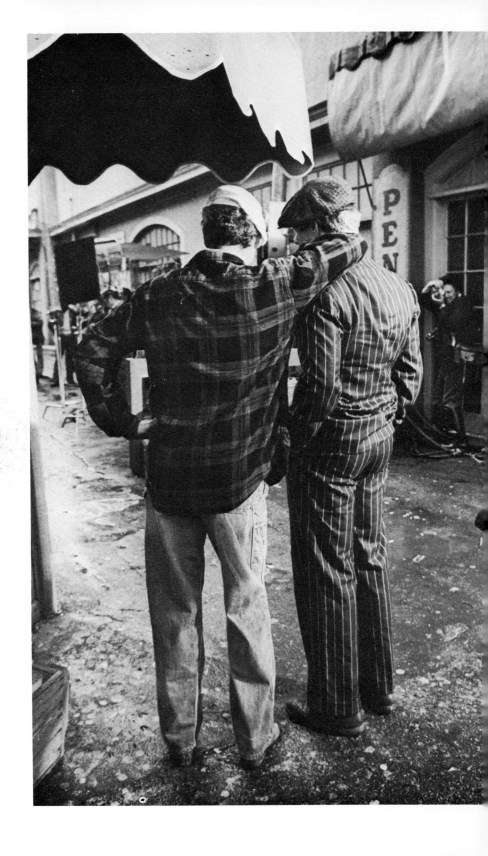

10

The movie is the message

'What do you think is more important to get across in a movie—emotions or a message?'

Gradually an image was forming, a pattern taking shape and substance. Paul was to find himself in a series of pictures in which he would project the personality of the stoic loner going against the grain of his environment, the archetypal American dream male walking into a situation and setting things to right according to *his* set of unwritten rules before moving on to the next town, the next confrontation, the next challenge. He was the Chandleresque Harper in *Harper*, the cynical Hud of *Hud*, the inscrutable Indian of *Hombre*, the cheerfully masochistic chain-gang prisoner of *Cool hand Luke*, a proliferation of H's which—since *The hustler*—did not necessarily add up to financial happiness.

Shortly after *The hustler*'s hit release on the circuits, people were saying that nearly everyone connected with the picture was making a lot of money out of it except Newman. The deal with Warners to release him from his contract was obviously a long-term crippling factor, but there was also too great a diversification of interests going on regarding some of the deals he was making, and this helped to make his cut in the profits negligible when—eventually, sometime a year or two later— it reached his bank. He was a money-spinner but not enough of it was spinning his way.

Steadily and determinedly, as a *Time* write-up puts it, he had been finding needles in the Hollywood haystack and using them to sew up good parts in reasonably interesting pictures, which became all the more interesting for his presence. 'He has found too many needles,' the report concluded, 'to have done it without a magnet.'

Newman's magnetism as a performer seemed hard to analyse

if easy to name. He embodied the man of the moment. His characters had brains, self-assurance, wealth or the seeming ability to get it, a calculating glint in their eyes, the ambition and thrust of a jet engine, a nice awareness of their own nastiness and yet, in keeping with almost every previous model of the basic Hollywood design, an underlying boyishness that popped out, sometimes unbidden, like a giggle from behind a Halloween mask.

His magnetism as a star stemmed from rejecting many things a standard star had come to mean. He consistently knocked the system. Hollywood studio executives were 'used-car salesmen at best'. He pulled few punches about himself: 'I sense my work is becoming repetitious.'

'He lives a hilariously cockeyed variation on the theme of sound mind in sound body,' *Time* reported, 'eating health foods and going through concentric circles of Hades with saunas and gymnasium torture machines so that he can smoke too many cigarettes and swill too much beer. It is a process of robbing Paul to pay Paul, and it is very trying. Newman had a lot of toughening up to do, for example, for *Cool hand Luke*, in which he did the roadwork scenes himself. "My next picture I want to be easy," he said. "Not even costume changes. Only from tails to tux."

'If his casual youthfulness is studied, he has studied it well: his clothes, his cold Coors beer in the dressing-room refrigerator, his easy camaraderie with people he likes. Things that move him. He is nuts about the internal combustion engine in all its noxious forms. He wears an electronic watch whose works, unlike those that impel a Newman performance, are conspicuously visible. Yet he cares about quality, too, and the state of the art that is so often practised as a craft.'

This impression of Paul shortly after he had entered his forties neatly draws together the opposing forces in his make-up to present a somewhat bland surface personality. This kind of personality can be best explained in the terminology of Thomas A. Harris, popularizer of the *I'm OK—you're OK* school of psychology.

One could say with Harris that Paul, no doubt through

analysis, had resolved his major Parent–Child conflicts and achieved a fully emancipated Adult. It is through the emancipation of his Adult that he was able to come to terms with almost every challenge Hollywood offered as well as reach out to other areas of knowledge about his place in the universe, about society, and about other people, which is the prerequisite of the well-rounded personality and can be found in actor philosophers like Peter Ustinov, Rod Steiger and the later Brando.

Rarely though has Hollywood thrown up such a perfectly controlled personality. The tensions are there, the flashes of anger and frustration, but he never allows them to get out of hand or deflect him from his immediate purpose.

Before his most recent phase, which began some time after his proficiency as a director had been confirmed by the success of *Rachel, Rachel,* he almost made a virtue out of his ability to discuss and analyse his problems from a detached standpoint, almost as if he was analysing one of his screen or stage characters.

'I have a recurring nightmare,' he told Peer J. Oppenheimer, who may have taken him a shade too seriously, 'in which I always dream that the whole bottom is going to fall out of my career, that I will have paid several million dollars in taxes and will have no annuity to live on in my later years.'

This nightmare, he explained, was built upon a feeling of guilt. 'Because acting comes easily to me and because I've been fortunate enough to have made pictures that turned out okay, it is very difficult for me to comprehend why the rewards should be so extraordinary. That's why I feel it might all come to an abrupt end. And if it did, I would have to adjust to new circumstances. It isn't just the money, but the fact that I've become accustomed to a certain kind of living and recognition that may be totally destroyed. I worry so much that I'm lucky if I get five hours sleep at night—even between films.'

An actor talks as the mood takes him, and Paul was obviously going through a phase which was causing him moments of uneasiness. Until he was well into his forties he had no real sense of security and for years he insisted that in spite of comparatively high earnings he was by no means a wealthy man. 'I've never been able to make the kind of investments that people think I have. Sure, I have a business manager, and a good one. But, nevertheless, the money is always going out for some reason or other apparently faster than it is coming in.'

To achieve some kind of financial balance he began to form partnerships with producers and directors, one of the most successful being with director Martin Ritt. But it is virtually impossible for a star and a director to work in tandem all the time, with so many offers reaching them from different sources, and it was not until he and John Foreman got together and formed the Newman–Foreman production company that real stability was achieved creatively and financially.

Slowly he began to build confidence in his ability to select roles for himself which allowed him to develop without getting grotesquely out of character, yet he remained diffident about going too far out and retained a certain amount of awe for his distinguished Actors' Studio senior, Brando. While for many years, indeed, for the entire decade leading up to Brando's phoenix-like revival as the Godfather, Paul's pictures were, by and large, more successful than Marlon's, he still tended to trust Brando's judgment above his own.

Producer Ronald Lubin said: 'After Paul read the script of *The outrage*, he felt it wasn't right for him and suggested I give it to Brando. So I sent it to Brando in Europe. He loved it but wouldn't commit himself until he got back. Because of other commitments, I didn't dare hold up the start of the film. But when Paul heard how much Brando liked the script, his whole attitude changed and he accepted the role.'

But he was learning to evaluate his own importance as a star in relation to the potential success or failure of a production, and began to leave his normal diffidence at home when he was drawn into negotiations and the planning of budgets. 'Once a picture is half-finished,' he observed shrewdly, 'the star is the only person who isn't expendable. The director, the producer, anyone else can be fired. The actor, then, operates from a position of great power. He shouldn't take advantage of it, but he often does.' He is too straightforward a man to play games with producers, but he also learnt to protect himself against exploitation and financial loss.

He was also acutely aware that audiences were changing with the shift of the times. 'You can't dissociate pictures from the thermonuclear bomb, and you can't dissociate them from the upper classes' need to assume the energies of the lower classes of seventy-five or a hundred years ago. In those days you planted a potato, and if it died, you died. Cause and effect were clear. Now a man works for a corporation. It's all interpersonal, interrelated, and very complicated. He can't see how he affects what's happening.

'So when it comes to leisure he wants it clear and simple. That's why people started taking entertainment—TV, movies—like dope. It was a functioning, operational opiate. Well, a segment of young people have learned to kick drugs . . . and I think that a satisfactory majority of adults have now kicked the entertainment opiate. They no longer watch TV as if it were a strange, hypnotic creature. They're ready to experience again.'

With the added responsibility of becoming his own production boss, and as it were investing his own money in his own talent, he read through hundreds of scripts which called upon his own instinctual powers of analysis and demanded greater self-reliance than ever before. He refused to fall into the trap of singling out stories with an easy message which might have made money-spinning concessions to mass audiences while lacking overall integrity.

When asked, 'What do you think is more important to get across in a movie—emotions or a message?' he replied without hesitation: 'Emotions, very definitely.'

Successful comedy still eluded him; although there were several near-misses he was nowhere near to becoming another Cary Grant. He had too much natural authority to lend himself to the indignities of slapstick, and his forays into light comedy nearly always seemed slightly off-key.

It is not for me to comment on the lighter movies Paul made in the early and middle 'sixties, beginning with *A new kind of love* and continuing with *What a way to go!* and *Lady L, Torn curtain* and *The secret war of Harry Frigg*, except to say that *Torn curtain* seemed more of a thriller when I saw it the second

113

time around on the small television screen, and both Newmans radiated considerable charm in *A new kind of love*, which also seemed to improve when transmitted on television (which says little for either of these films since TV is always more effective when relaying trivia than art).

Regretfully, I share with most Newman fans the common failing of not liking it overmuch when he steps too sharply out of his heroic mould, or tough anti-heroic persona, and traipses through comedy routines somewhat in the manner of Abraham Lincoln doing the Watusi.

Despite Frank Sinatra's evocative handling of the title song, *A new kind of love* was a sad travesty of the finer feelings that had gone into the making of *Paris blues*; and, while it was a delight to see Joanne, for once, in a transformation part which allowed us to see how glamorous she is when unconstricted by the demands of a drab role, it would have been embarrassing to have dragged a Martian into the cinema and asked him to assess the talents of this distinguished acting couple on the strength of their appearance in this picture.

No, it is better to draw a veil over these torn curtains and secret wars, and concentrate instead on the relative virtues of *Hud, Harper, Hombre, The outrage,* and *Cool hand Luke*.

One of the best things to emerge from Paul's partnership with Martin Ritt was the creation of Hud, developed from a character in Larry McMurtry's novel *Horseman, pass by*. Still privately smarting from the bowdlerizations of Tennessee Williams and the cool reception of *Paris blues*, Newman and Ritt gave writers Irving Ravetch and Harriet Frank Jr. the green light to tell the story of Hud straight. 'Hud is a no-good shit-heel without an ounce of feeling for others,' Paul insisted, 'and must not be allowed to play for the audience's sympathy.'

Paul spent weeks beforehand working on a cattle ranch in Texas, where the story was located, and again insisted that there be no concessions made towards him as he took his turn as a cattle wrangler, ranch hand and saddle tramp living in the bunkhouse and sharing his meal with the rest of the hired help. By the time he was ready to go in front of James Wong Howe's probing cameras with co-stars Melvyn Douglas (playing his father) and Patricia Neal (housekeeper at the family ranch) and Brandon de Wilde (impressionable nephew) his hands were calloused from roping steer and he had acquired the loping, stiff walk of the practised cowhand. He had also developed a built-in sneer which, as Hud, he maintained throughout the 112 minutes of the movie when it was finally cut to the bone.

This dedication and scrupulous honesty paid off, with critics falling over themselves to hail this as the best American picture since *The hustler*. By refusing to compromise, Paul had struck another blow against the restriction that Hollywood's power élite still insisted on imposing. Bosley Crowther summed it up best when, in the *New York Times*, he wrote:

'While it looks like a modern western and is an outdoor drama indeed, *Hud* is as wide and profound a contemplation of the human condition as one of the New England plays of Eugene O'Neill. The striking, important thing about it is the clarity with which it unreels. The sureness and integrity of it are as crystal clear as the plot is spare . . . with a fine cast of performers, he has people who behave and talk so truly that it is hard to shake them out of your mind.

'Paul Newman is tremendous—a potent, voracious man, restless with all his crude ambitions, arrogant with his contempt and churned up inside with all the meanness and misgivings of himself.'

Arthur Knight added: 'In this age of heel-heroes and beasts that walk like men, screen writers Irving Ravetch and Harriet Frank Jr have pulled a switch that is both commercial and commendable. Working with a few lines from a novel by Larry McMurtry, they have created Hud, a charming monster who demonstrates by inversion that such old-fashioned virtues as honesty, loyalty and filial duty are still highly cherishable.

'There can be no two thoughts about Hud: He is purely and simply a bastard. And by the end of the film, for all his charm, he has succeeded in alienating everyone, including the audience. Always excellent with actors, the director has drawn memorable performances from his small, skilled cast. He uses Newman's considerable personal magnetism first to cover, then to reveal, the shallow, egocentric, callous nature of Hud. With his lean, muscular body and scornful smile, Newman's very essence is a threat poised over every scene. Alma, played with warmth and dignity by Patricia Neal, is the film's counterpoint of Hud.'

The outrage was filmed from a screenplay based on the Japanese film *Rashomon*, by Akira Kurosawa, from stories by Ryunosuke Akutagawa and the play *Rashomon* by Fay and Michael Kanin. Rod Steiger had played the bandit role on Broadway, with Claire Bloom. Paul took over the Steiger part for the film, with Miss Bloom in her original role and Laurence Harvey playing her husband.

Again Paul was working under the direction of Martin Ritt, with Michael Kanin adapting the script from his stage play; again a great deal of emotional power and passion went into the making, and it has always been one of Paul's favourite films. Once more, he went off on a preliminary research trip to get the feel of the location.

Paul and Ritt had decided to change the ancient Japanese setting of the story to that of old Mexico. For several weeks the actor toured the tequila circuit south of the border, living in crumbling adobes and hanging around dimly lit cantinas. Growing a thick stubble and speaking broken English he acquired what he considered a serviceable Mexican accent, but when the film was shown to the critics they seem to have been disconcerted by it.

Judith Crist complained that 'what should be a cogent, almost ritualistic examination and re-examination of the many facets of truth emerges as little more than a story told and thrice re-told simply to provide three performers with exercises in acting.

'Paul Newman emerges as a sort of junior-grade Leo Carrillo, spitting and spewing and wallowing in dialect and playing the villain, the lecher, the social outcast, the lover and the coward to the hilt for his own very private edification. Perhaps *Rashomon* cannot stand the transition from East to West or to modern times. As it is, *The outrage* emerges as a sententious theme with dull variations.'

Although *Variety* reported that 'Newman as the violent and

passionate killer . . . dominates the action', A. H. Weiler in the New York *Times* pointed out the basic flaw in his performance. 'Mr Newman's outlaw is perhaps played too broadly. From the top of his large sombrero to his matted hair, buckskin chaps and down to his large, jangling spurs, he is obviously a rough renegade seeking animal pleasures and self-preservation. But he also, it is revealed, is not a gent who commits murder deviously. He sounds like a parody of the Mexican villains in old movies.'

Harper helped to redress the balance, with Paul making his first (and so far only) foray into the world of the sleazy private eye pioneered to perfection by Bogart. With Lauren Bacall, Bogie's widow, as his co-star, he would have been in dire trouble if his performance had been less than perfect. Based on *The moving target* by Ross MacDonald, the best of the post-Chandler thriller writers, the film was one of the big commercial successes of the mid-'sixties. (In Britain it was released under the original title of the novel.)

Just as Sinatra was enormously successful as Tony Rome, the Miami private eye, without ever returning to the part, Paul refused to make capital out of the snug way he fitted into the sharp jacket of Harper and did not get anywhere near to this type of character again until *The mackintosh man* which touched on the sleazier side of the espionage game. If proof were needed that Paul Newman has never settled for the easy life of the matinée idol, *Harper* supplies it abundantly.

Richard Schickel in *Life* commended Paul, director Jack Smight and scriptwriter William Goldman for playing their film as straight as MacDonald habitually does in his deadpan thrillers. 'Goldman's script,' he went on, 'is full of snap-crackle-pop dialogue and he adorns the essentially simple plot (Harper is trying to find a kidnapped millionaire) with Byzantine twists and turns, around which nearly always lurks a grotesque and curious minor character. Smight has a good feel for the tawdry, *nouveau gauche* Southern California atmosphere.

'As for Newman, this is the kind of superficial role— plenty of action, jokes and manly sentiment—for which his superficial talent is ideally suited. *Harper* delivers us an unemotional memo on the way things too often are in our society, then shrugs and wisecracks. But in the prevailing conscience-less climate of American moviemaking, it is good to see a film with at least that much awareness of its social context, that much critical objectivity.'

It takes more than a superficial talent to play Eddie Felson and Hud, and Schickel's own rare lapse into superficiality was counterbalanced by Rose Pelswick's fulsome approval in the New York *Journal-American*, where she wrote: 'Paul Newman checks in just about the best performance of his career . . . developed in a mood that's remindful of the early Raymond Chandler's, this is a hugely entertaining thriller that manages to come up with suspense and excitement and comedy and yet never gets out of hand. Newman as the cynical and oh-so-hip Harper, is perfectly cast in the role, playing it cool no matter what comes up, tossing off flip lines and slugging it out with the best of them.'

My own pleasure in this film was enhanced by the presence of Shelley Winters giving us one of those delicious self-parodies to which she has become increasingly addicted. When I spoke recently to Robert Wagner, that master of dramatic under-statement, he assured me that he had more fun during the shooting of this picture, especially when Shelley Winters was around, than anything he'd worked in for a long time.

Hombre and *Cool hand Luke* followed quickly within a year with the unfortunate *Lady L* quietly slipped in between these two strong vehicles and *Harper*. Having also just tangled with Hitchcock in *Torn curtain*, Paul was hoping to get plenty of dramatic mileage out of *Hombre*, playing a white man brought up as an Apache in a story distinctly reminiscent of *Stagecoach*.

It was not to be. The role seemed strong enough on paper. His fellow passengers on the coach ride all treat him with varying degrees of bias, ranging from the mildly suspicious to the downright contemptuous, and these biases do not notice-ably alter when their main chance of survival lies in his resourcefulness after they've been pinned down by a gang of roving bandits. He extricates his thankless companions from their predicament but dies bravely in the last reel.

Again the trouble lay in Paul's stepping out of his most easily recognizable persona. Lawrence J. Quirk sized up the situation when in *Screen Slants* he wrote: '*Hombre* is a well-intentioned "western-with-built-in-think" (to coin a phrase, but it cannot escape an aura of *déjà vu*). Yes, it's all been done before, this business of a group of people of varying ethical and moral persuasions coming together via fortuitous circumstance. Such strong assets as Fredric March and Richard Boone try to lend conviction to the proceedings, some of which tax even their considerable talents, but the casting of Paul Newman as an Indian who *isn't* an Indian (he's a Caucasian adopted by Indians in early life) lends a strong impression that in attempting to reach out once more for a "versatile" image, he is again essaying a role that is ill-suited to his admittedly narrow but none the less deep talents.

'Give Newman a part suited to his chemistry and personality and he delivers, *in depth* (as in, say, *The rack*, *Cat on a hot tin roof* or *Hud*), but take him out of his proper milieu and Newman is invariably and automatically forced to resort to a variety of surface postures and gimmicks which only serve to highlight the fact that he is not a character, first; individual-personality, second; thespic type but rather an actor of more confined range who delivers with solid intensity when allowed to tap his own unique inner resources. This he does not—and cannot —do with a gimmicky part like *Hombre*.'

But in *Cool hand Luke* he was not only back in top form, but adding lustre to a film unique in its passionate social comment which never lost a moment of tension or riveting entertainment in the projection of its message. As Luke Jackson, who has been sentenced to two years with a chain-gang for unscrewing the tops from parking meters while on a 48-hour bender, he is, as Bosley Crowther put it, 'superb in this forceful portrait of a man born to lose . . . that traditional object of sorrow and compassion in American folk-song and -lore, the chain-gang prisoner, is given as strong a presentation as ever he has had on the screen.'

'Of course he is exactly right for the role of a rebellious prisoner in a concentration-camp-like Southern jail system (it would have been almost impossible to find anyone *more* right),' comments Hollis Alpert; 'yet this wouldn't have automatically guaranteed the emotional charge he generates. Newman manages a considerable gamut: he is funny at times, stalwart, submissive, defiant, pathetic, and eventually tragic. Obviously he and Stuart Rosenberg (another of the crop of youngish directors who have emerged from television prep school) worked in a harmonious relationship, notably aided by a good script. If there is such a thing as tasteful violence, this film has it. We are made to understand what is going on, why it is going on, and what is right or wrong about it. *Cool hand Luke* may not be humane but it is certainly human.'

Lawrence J. Quirk, not for the first time or last, had the final, succinct word. 'When Paul Newman is good he is very, very good, and when he is bad he is—miscast. He is certainly *not* miscast in this strong prison drama; in fact he is superbly in his acting element, and very, very good he is, indeed; in fact Mr Newman is simply wonderful here, and that Oscar he has long been outrageously denied for a slew of distinguished performances should certainly come his way for 1967 if there is any justice in the world.'

Paul was, meanwhile, preparing to go onto another tack altogether, a departure for which he had been unconsciously preparing himself for fifteen years or more.

'I've been playing non-heroes till I'm beginning to feel like a non-actor,' he said crisply. 'Film, they say, is a director's medium. Well, I don't know about that, but you seldom hear of directors going around saying they want to be actors.'

Now, in a curious way, without his having gone out of his way to get the job, direction was being virtually thrust upon him. Joanne had found this book, see, and a friend had written a marvellous script, but nobody in Hollywood wanted to direct it, see? Nobody amounting to a hill of beans wanted to touch it, see? But Joanne wanted to play the leading role, see? And someone had to direct her, see?

In the long run, Paul got the message. Took the hint, see? And that is how it came about that in the long, hot summer of 1968, Paul went to Danbury, Connecticut, and took on the challenge of directing his first full-length feature film—*Rachel, Rachel*.

11

Joanne, Joanne

'With due respect to some of the fine directors I've worked with, I just wish Paul could direct every movie I'll ever do again.'

Joanne Woodward

Hollywood's surprise event of 1968 was *Rachel, Rachel*, a low-budget movie directed by Paul and starring Joanne in a part the wiseacres had dismissed as impossible to bring alive on the screen. Commercially it's unviable, the Newmans were told time and again. Forget it, you've a hundred other properties to choose from.

Though it was Paul's first effort as a director, when the picture was shown the critics and public found it delightful—in Paul's words, they were really experiencing again. At the Academy Awards ceremonies it was nominated for Oscars in the following categories: Best picture, best actress, best supporting actress (Estelle Parsons), and best screenplay (Stewart Stern). The New York film critics named Newman director of the year and Miss Woodward, best actress. So did the Hollywood Foreign Press Association in its awards.

How did this miracle happen? Like most Hollywood miracles, much blood, sweat and tears went into its making. Telling it later to Joan Barthel of the *New York Times*, Paul humorously pitched his account in the form of a schoolboy essay.

'I spent my summer vacation in the town of Danbury, Connecticut. I directed my first full-length movie. Jesus, I really picked a corker. It is called *A jest of God*, and it explores the mind of a disturbed and neurotic young lady who has a very bland exterior but a very animated and colourful inner life. It is a terribly complicated film. I directed it barefoot.

'My wife Joanne is in it. She is brilliant. God, she's marvellous. We have the same acting vocabulary, and that made it a hell of a lot easier. I just gave her one-line zingers, like "pinch it" or "thicken it" and she knew what I meant. I can't think of any other actress that the experience of directing could have been better with.

'I think it's easier to direct if you're an actor because, good Lord, you understand an actor's problems, and you understand that certain transitions are difficult. Actors want to direct because they get fed up with the restriction of acting inside their own skin.

'You can only deal with your own experience, and after you play a certain number of characters you find yourself repeating, no matter how different you try to make it, whereas in directing you're constantly working with new people in a new framework. It is interesting to see how my experience and my imagination will work inside the framework of somebody else's personality. I don't care that my prestige is on the line; that's somebody else's problem.

'As an actor, it gets pretty bloody dull if you just sit back and play it safe. And it's very easy to play it safe by picking out things that have a built-in saleability, like major novels and Broadway successes. My wife's agent found this book. It was written by a Canadian author, Margaret Laurence, and it won the Governor-General's award, which is like our Pulitzer.

'We asked Stewart Stern, an old friend of ours, to write the screenplay. It was sort of a family affair: my daughter Nell is in it—as a parent I was against that, but as a director I thought she was great—and so is Frank Corsaro, who directed us in *Baby want a kiss*, and so is my auto mechanic. I had a marvellous crew. The first day of shooting I said to them, "I'm a virgin and I need your help," and they were so first-class I couldn't believe it.

'One problem was, where does the genuinely poignant end and soap opera begin? And another was, I had to mount the whole damned show in five weeks, and script revisions going on all the time. Once Stewart wrote an original hymn for it while we waited to shoot the scene. I said to him, "I want it atomic; I want crumbling cities, and I don't want it so damned square." So we did it as a tango.

'I really didn't find directing that much more difficult than acting, because as an actor you direct yourself anyway. The administration and production problems all came as a great pain in the rear, but as for the actual shaping of scenes—what the hell?

'I didn't get anywhere near as tired directing as when I act. As an actor you stop and start the motor all day; it's like running a hundred yards two feet at a time. When you're involved with every facet of the production—script, attitudes, lighting, make-up, wardrobe—you're constantly pumped up and you don't have an opportunity to slow down.

'Our movie is a small but hopefully, distinguished film. We had a seven hundred thousand dollar budget, and anything over budget came out of my pocket, my after-tax pocket, so it was twice as painful. My wife and I took no salaries at all, but if the picture ever goes into a profit position she and I and Stewart will split three ways. I must say, by way of applause to Seven Arts, which put up the money, that I had nobody breathing down my neck. They were willing to take a gamble.

'This does not have the size and the scale of a picture that you would expect a major company to do. But if people are willing to see something that isn't *The guns of Navarone*, and if they are willing to accept the conventions we used to get inside this woman's mind—fantasy, flashback, voice-over—it will be very successful, although I didn't go into it with the idea that it would be a blockbuster. The people who will not buy it, the people who will say "It isn't real", are the people who dismiss their own fantasies—like the times they've addressed the United Nations, or the times they've been to bed with Claudia Cardinale.

'I'll read the reviews as a producer, although as an actor I don't read them. The trouble with the reviews is you get a hangover from them. But the hangover of exhilaration only lasts an hour and a half; the hangover of depression lasts six months. I know when the work is good and when it's bad, and with a very, very few exceptions, I don't have that much respect for the critics anyway.

'This is the first real production for my company, Kayos

Productions, pronounced chaos—isn't that a hoot? I've always been interested in directing. I was a directing major at Yale, but it took me thirteen years to get around to it, although I directed a short several years ago. Yeah, I'd like to do more directing if I can find a script I like. I have always enjoyed the intellect of making films. My perfect movie would go like this:

'You get a marvellous, original idea for a picture. Then you get a playwright and you start working on developing the first draft. Then you start developing the second draft. Then you start thinking in terms of casting and location, then you work more on the production, more on the casting, then you actually cast. Then you set up the production and you start your rehearsal with the actors.

'You rehearse diligently and marvellously and you make all kinds of discoveries about the actors, about the nature of the manuscript, what changes are needed, what works, what doesn't work, what you need in terms of additional dialogue and new scenes. Then you rehearse for two weeks—you figure out your entire production team, the lights and the sound and so forth—and you work with the set designer and you go through all that.

'You finish your last day of rehearsal on a Friday afternoon at five-thirty, then you say WRAP, and everybody goes home, and you never shoot a foot of film.'

Well, that did not happen with *A jest of God*, which, of course, became *Rachel, Rachel*, because, it is said, someone along the line somewhere came to the conclusion that the word 'God' in a title was death at the box office. Of Paul's directing, actress Estelle Parsons said, 'I don't as a rule communicate too well with directors, but he's wonderful. It's all been so relaxed and easy.' Stewart Stern said, 'He's the only man I ever met who decides what makes him nervous—like directing a movie—and then, with his hands sweating and his feet sweating, goes right into it.'

Despite showing odd signs of tension, in general, he stayed cool and loose as he roamed the set, a casual figure in paint-smeared shorts, terry-cloth shirt, dark glasses pushed up on his head aviator-style, a can of beer in hand, declining either to bark to his crew—only a mild, 'You ready, gang?—or to pontificate to anyone in the manner of the old-style breeches-and-leggings and horsewhip type of director.

Asked later if it was true that no one associated with *Rachel, Rachel* expected it to be a popular success, Paul said: 'I thought the picture would have a small but loyal following. I had no idea it would break loose the way it has. Every studio in town had turned down the package. They thought the story was too internal, not enough happened.

'A lot of the men running the studios now are businessmen whose experience was in industry, large corporations. I can understand they'd look at something like this and have their doubts. But you'd think they'd defer judgment—that they'd say to themselves, well, I can't see it, but someone with a successful record believes in it, I'll take their word for it. They don't. The picture cost just over seven hundred thousand dollars and it's expected to gross at least seven million.'

Asked whether he thought it inevitable that an actor should graduate to direction, he said: 'There's a myth that movie stars all started out behind soda fountains or as car hops . . . that they're not very bright. What's so amazing about an actor directing? If a man did lithographs and then started turning out oils, nobody would be shocked. It would be considered a natural development in a painter. Movie-making is a community art-form, you all work together. Naturally, you learn something about each other's professional functions.

I think there's a place for a film like *Rachel, Rachel*. Just as Melvin Laird decides what to do about a new ballistic missile system, we all have our critical decisions. They're important to us. Our ruts, for instance. They're different from Rachel's but still ruts. We see the same people night after night, serve the same Scotch and water . . . Why not Bloody Mary's? Or Margueritas? Why should it be a sauna first thing in the morning, the *New York Times*, then a shower with an ice cube over each eyeball? Affluent people, especially, need to break loose, to live in primitive surroundings once in a while. . . .

'Might I some day express a political view in a movie? A bad Western is just a bad Western. A bad message movie is a disaster.'

John Cassavetes has said that when he's acting he wishes he were directing, and vice versa. Did Paul ever have this problem?

'No, because I don't like to act.'

Did he ever like to act?

'Let's say there are two phases of acting. I like the research, deciding how to approach a part. But the actual performing in front of the cameras—that's always been painful to me.'

Directing Joanne for the first time was a consummation of sorts, a translation of the regard and respect they have always felt for each other into the language of their craft. People can talk themselves blue in the face about the compatibility of auras or the chemistry of mutual needs, in the long run an intricate partnership like that of the Newmans must be seen to function successfully both in the private and public sectors of the liaison.

Okay, it works for them personally. But is it good for their art? The successful outcome of their struggle to put *Rachel, Rachel* onto the screen was also a vindication of their original hunch about each other, demonstrating that their marriage was working for them on the creative as well as emotional level. From here they would go on from strength to strength, *sans peur et sans reproche*.

'The film was clearly undertaken in a spirit entirely too rare in American life,' reported Richard Schickel in *Life*. 'That is to say, a star, Joanne Woodward, and a screenwriter, Stewart Stern, discovered a novel, Margaret Laurence's *A jest of God*, that was, to them, something more than a mere property. Instead, it was a difficult and delicate thing that challenged them as artists, something they felt they simply had to make.

'They apparently encountered enormous difficulties in obtaining the relatively modest backing they required, and it was not until Miss Woodward's husband, Paul Newman, put his plentiful clout behind the project by agreeing to direct it that they could go ahead.

'Everyone involved thereupon did his work with taste, conviction, and solid, sometimes brilliant, craftsmanship. Stern's script, despite a tendency to tell rather than show, rings with gentle irony and rueful truth. Miss Woodward demonstrates again that she is perhaps the only major female star of our day capable of genuine naturalism, submerging self and image in a subtle, disciplined performance that avoids showiness, excessive sentiment, self-consciousness.

'As a director Newman is anything but the bouncing boy-o we are accustomed to seeing on our screens. He has a sensitive, slightly melancholic eye for something most American movies miss—the texture of ordinary life. He displays, moreover, a feel for emotional nuances and a technical sureness; he is neither too radical nor too conservative. That is remarkable in a first film.'

Much thought, much concentration of thought and feeling had gone into Paul's first directorial effort. 'Directing his first movie, Paul Newman is off to an auspicious start in a new career', commented William Wolf. 'If he hasn't set the industry on fire, he shows a truth-seeking directness that stamps his film with conviction and honesty. He also possesses a key quality: he knows how to be lean and judicious instead of cinematically verbose.

'Joanne Woodward is a marvellous actress, and her husband obviously knows what she can do in a part and helps her to make the most in this one. *Rachel, Rachel* contains enough truth about people and loneliness to earn interest and admiration. There are many eloquent touches—flights of fancy into what Rachel would like to see happen and sequences capturing small-town Americana. Admirers of Paul Newman will now have an additional reason for their esteem.'

Shortly after the picture was completed, Joanne talked to the perceptive Rex Reed, the most gifted American show-scene reporter and commentator of his generation. On that particular bright summer day, 'with the California sun licking at the windows like tongues on an Eskimo Pie', she had something worth talking about and she unburdened her IQ of 135 thoughts into Mr Reed's attentive ears.

'Paul gets all the wonderful parts,' she weighed in, 'but I always seem to be the afterthought, like the backdrop who stands behind the pitcher. You know, even a bad movie takes two or three months out of your life, so I finally decided that if

I am going to take that much time out of a life I enjoy, it better be something I bloody well care about.

'For a script like that, I have to find it myself. Good things are seldom offered me. When I started, I just wanted to act. That's all I cared about. I did some good things, like *The three faces of Eve*, but I also did some things I didn't care about. Now the older I get, the more I realize that life is like cotton candy. Take one bite and it's gone. Life is too short to worry about the tiny dissatisfactions. They're a pain in the rear. I hate wasting time. Like the tourists driving around on Sunday afternoon looking at movie-star houses. They could get killed tomorrow and what do they have to show for it? They spent their last day on earth looking at Paul Newman's house. I refuse to fiddle away my life in dribs and drabs. One thing I say to the kids, "Tell me anything, get mad, yell at me, but *never* say you're bored."

'One day John Foreman called. He was our agent once and now he, Paul and I have formed a company. We've known him for years. He got me my first job fresh out of Greenville, South Carolina, in an old Robert Montgomery TV show. Anyway, he had read a review of *A jest of God*, and we got the galleys and decided to take an option on it. Paul couldn't believe we had done that. Then when he read the book I don't think he liked it much.

'Paul had no intention of directing it, but we couldn't get anyone else interested. Stewart Stern, who wrote the screenplay, and I went around offering ourselves to everybody but I'm afraid offering a package of the script and me was hardly like offering Elizabeth Taylor and Tennessee Williams.'

But somehow they did it. It wasn't easy. And they surprised everybody even more by turning out a thoughtful, provocative, moving film. Paul, who had rejoined his wife after a plunge into the pool, told Reed: 'I hope it's successful, not because of any financial reward—hell, both Joanne and I did it for nothing—but to prove to Hollywood you can make a film about basic, simple people, without violence and a band of Indians scalping the settlers.'

Joanne returned to one of her more dominant recurring

themes. 'I've been knocking Hollywood so long it's become a joke out here. I don't like it, that's all there is to it, and I don't really know why.

'Maybe I'm perverse. Life is pleasant here, but it's just not me. It will never be home. This house is not me. It's rented out all the time. The kids went to a school that was very proper, all straight A's and Debbie Reynolds was head of the Girl Scouts, you know what I mean? I couldn't wait to get them out of there.

'I don't like the way Beverly Hills looks. I loathe manicured lawns and I hate palm trees. We just sold this house and we're moving into a place with a prizewinning cactus and three of the biggest palm trees you ever saw in the yard and I'm having them all cut down and planting magnolia trees and rose bushes.

'People expect us to have big houses and servants and the whole *schmeer*, but I hate houses with no personality and I feel guilty having servants with nothing to do. I had to let the secretary go because every time I passed the library, she was just sitting there buffing her nails. We have a driver who takes the kids to school, but I have to keep thinking of things for him to do.

'Now that Nell is a movie star herself (she plays Joanne as a child in *Rachel, Rachel*) Stephanie wants to be one too. The kids are all marvellous and beautiful and slightly insane—five beautiful blonde ladies and Scott, who is eighteen and looks like a French film star.

'That's what my life is all about. Paul gets most of the fan mail and I read everything that comes to the house. I'm still waiting for one to me that begins, "Gee baby, you were great." The only fan mail I ever get is from twelve-year-old boys. One wrote, "I love you, I love you, you're six months older than my mother."

'We don't have many kooks hanging around. Occasionally, Paul gets the oddballs who want him to take off his sunglasses so they can see his blue eyes, but usually he gets a different breed, which I think is an interesting comment on his dignity as a human being. It must be sad to be an Elizabeth Taylor, who hasn't been to a supermarket for years. I couldn't stand that.

'I remember going to an Actors' Studio première once for Kazan's *East of Eden*. Marilyn Monroe was there and it was one of the most horrible sights I ever witnessed—watching her being grabbed at and mauled. That little white face in a sea of hands. We just don't allow that to happen.

'Oh, there are a couple of things we can't do any more. Paul can't take the kids to Disneyland because he gets mobbed and the kids don't get to see anything. He took them to the World's Fair and had to be slipped into back doors and it was no fun. But it's a small price to pay for everything else.'

Rachel, Rachel came just in time to prevent Joanne from lapsing into a state of non-productive nihilism. In the role of Rachel Cameron, Paul was able to draw from her all the inner radiance, the soft-spoken intelligence and elusive, shadowy sensuality he has always seen in her through the prismatic vision of love.

No wonder she says, 'With due respect to some of the fine directors I've worked with, I just wish Paul could direct every movie I'll ever make.' In an imperfect world we can only be thankful that in *Rachel, Rachel*, despite all the obstacles put in their path by a purblind 'industry' Joanne and Paul managed between them to complement each other's talents in what amounted to an exquisite labour of love.

12

Wheels within wheels

'Don't let's exaggerate this. It's the safest kind of racing driving you can do. It's not that I'm driving Grand Prix formula cars; I'm not quick enough for professional auto-racing.'

'It's still risky,' I persisted. 'So is crossing the road if you're not careful.'

They had a ball making *Winning*. Joanne had for some time been keeping her own counsel on the subject of Paul's addiction to auto-racing. On the surface it seemed non-productive, juvenile and an unnecessary flirtation with danger. Why, when he had so much going for him, should he spend hours racing around tracks in California and on the Eastern circuit where he was a familiar figure in the enclosed, specialized world of auto-racers? What his psychiatrist had to say about it all was a closed book even to Joanne.

So, like many a wise woman before and since who has been faced with such a problem, Joanne quietly resolved that if you can't lick 'em, join 'em.

The decision was made all the more easy when Universal pushed the script of *Winning* their way, a seven-million dollar production packaged as a special vehicle for the Newmans. To make it even more attractive, their very good friend Robert Wagner had been offered a co-starring part in what was to become a little classic of its kind.

Like Steve McQueen, who shares his passion for speed on wheels, Paul is impatient with writers and deep-thinking friends, who try to read something mystical into what they consider a harmless and relaxing hobby. 'Death wish?' McQueen says incredulously. 'Why should I have a death wish?'

Why, indeed.

McQueen could be speaking for Paul when he touches on

the subject of car racing, and in his case, cycle racing as well. 'I enjoy racing in any form,' he says, 'because the guy next to me couldn't care less what my name is. He just wants to beat me. At the start of my racing career I had to prove myself. A lot of people think that actors are a little strange, unmasculine, not like the guys who are riveters at Lockheed and things like that. I had to beat the actors' image.'

He adds that he is past the point where he 'must prove anything—my ego or my masculinity. The only reason I race now is because I enjoy it.'

Paul endorses this fully. Like McQueen, he used to enjoy cycle racing as well, or simply goofing off on two wheels to get away from the wheels within wheels at the studios, where, naturally, his obsession with speed was frowned upon by the biggest wheels of all, the bosses. Partly, he may also have been, metaphorically, thumbing his nose at the brass when hopping on a cycle. But his enjoyment was genuine enough. 'There's nothing,' he would say, 'like racing that old bike along the beach to loosen up.'

When he skidded on an oil slick while speeding along Sunset Boulevard, and was injured sufficiently to be briefly hospitalized, the Newman caution took over. 'I had three bikes and sold them all the next day,' he says tersely. 'I lost shooting time on that one. I may be crazy but I'm not irresponsible.'

He approached the task of working in *Winning* with his usual, Method-instilled thoroughness. The climax of the action is the contest between Frank Capua (Paul) and Luther Erding (Bob Wagner) in the Indianapolis 500-Mile Race, the most famous motor race in the United States. (And because of its great publicity and vast commercial sponsorship, it is also the most financially rewarding motor race in the world. Every year the competitors share well over a million dollars in prize money, the winner taking a quarter of the total. But the drivers have to sweat blood and tears to earn their money. There is danger— and the prospect of a messy death—every mile of the way.)

The 'Indy', as it is called, is the toughest, fastest, longest and most hazardous of all regular motor sport events. Nearly sixty

132

drivers have been killed on the track since the race was first held in 1911. Not to mention the hundreds who have been injured over the years. The story of the 'Indy' is highlighted with a grim record of spectacular multi-car pile-ups. The race of 1964 saw a five-car collision in which two drivers died. There was a sixteen-car pile-up in 1966, and a five-car smash in 1967. (Some of this footage was used in the film.) The going is so tough that many cars simply blow up under the pressure or catch fire.

The contestants must hurtle their specially built racing cars around a speedway for two hundred laps at an average speed of 150 miles per hour, in a race which lasts over three hours. It is held every 30 May on the Indianapolis Motor Speedway, Indiana, and attracts a crowd of some 300,000 spectators.

The track is a gigantic rectangle with a lap length of $2\frac{1}{2}$ miles. Each of the banked corners measures a quarter of a mile in length. The corners are taken at about 150 m.p.h. and 200 m.p.h. can be reached on the straights. It is important for the non-competitive driver to get this scene into focus to understand that filming here is no picnic.

For some years Paul had been working his film commitments to a pattern which gave him a day off every 30 May when he would dash by air to Indianapolis to catch the race and yarn with the drivers, many of whom had become his friends and were regarded by him with some of the awe normally extended to him by his fans. Men like the Unser brothers, Bobby and Al, from New Mexico, whose family have a long tradition at the Indianapolis 500. Their father and uncles raced there, and a third brother was killed on the track in 1959.

Characters like A. J. Foyt, the 'Flying Texan', three times winner of the race, and Jim Clark, Britain's triple world champ grand prix driver known as the 'Flying Scot'. In 1965 the late Jim fought a tremendous duel with the Flying Texan. Foyt was forced to retire on the 116th lap and Clark raced five miles ahead of his nearest rival, Parnelli Jones, to win. The following year Graham Hill, another British grand prix champ, won the race in an American-sponsored British car with Jim Clark second in his Lotus.

To hold his own with his heroes, Paul literally went back to school. Namely, the Bob Bondurant School of High Performance Driving, located near Santa Ana in California, where Bob teaches aficionados how to drive racing cars, transmitting the know-how he has picked up in a couple of decades of motorcycle and auto racing. In 1959, he was named the nation's top Corvette driver. Carroll Shelby offered him a chance to drive on the Ford-Shelby American Racing Team in Europe in 1963. They won the World Manufacturers' Championship in 1965, a first in the history of US automobile manufacturing. Later he drove BRMs, Porsches, American Eagles and Ferraris. With all this valuable experience behind him, he opened his school and began to teach the art of driving high-performance autos.

Two of his first pupils were James Garner and Yves Montand for the picture *Grand Prix*, but that training job was a lot easier because he had a good deal of time available. He had only a few weeks to teach Paul.

'How did we turn Paul Newman into a "winning" driver?' he asks rhetorically. 'Well, we began with lessons in our classroom where Newman and co-star Robert Wagner learned the fundamentals of competitive driving. I tell each driver that he's running two races at once—the first against the other competitors; the second, and most important, against the clock. Everything the student is taught is designed to increase the speeds that he turns around a track. Even something as simple as "heel and toe" helps decrease lap times; the split second wasted each time you take your foot off the throttle and put it on the brake is a wasted second.

'From the classroom we went out to the track, but it was still a little while before Newman and Wagner did any driving. We started by walking the turns, while I explained what action should be taken at each particular moment. Then we studied the approach apex and exit line.

'After this, Newman was allowed into the car to learn the controls, the proper way to hold the steering wheel, and how to find the most comfortable seating position. After completely mastering these fundamentals, Newman began to accompany me in the training car.

'I took him through the turns first, explaining everything I did. Here is where Newman learned that a racing-car engine develops its maximum horsepower in a fairly narrow r.p.m. range and, to get maximum efficiency from it, the r.p.m. must be kept at that point at all times. About the only time a racing engine is allowed to coast, is at the end of a race. Other than that, it must be kept humming all the time.

'. . . In less than a week, Newman advanced to driving our big Lola 270, which is probably as fast as anything he'll drive in actual racing. We finished up at Orange County Raceway, and then spent a day at the famed Riverside track where Newman and I drove a Ford Grand National stock car until he looked so smooth, that you'd think he had been driving for years.

'We then flew to Phoenix where I trained him in a Ford GT40 and Mickey Thompson's Indy car. Here again, I would show him the line and how to handle the car until he could do it on his own. He was coming on strong by then, as evidenced by the 34-second lap he turned. The record for Phoenix at that time was only 28·7 seconds. Newman did this within six days of his first ride in the beginners' car—the Datsun 1600 sedan.

'Three months later, practice resumed at Elkhart Lake, Wisconsin, for another five days. We then flew to Indianapolis where shooting of the movie began. With less than two weeks total high-performance driving time behind him, Paul donned his helmet, strapped himself into an American Eagle, and turned a 143 m.p.h. lap with a speed down the back chute of 160 m.p.h. When it came to choosing the right lane through the turns, cornering smoothly, and using his head, everyone there agreed that Paul Newman would be hard to beat as an actor *and* a racing-car driver. Happily backslapping with the rest, I also hoped my teaching had a little bit to do with this star pupil's driving in *Winning*.'

A far cry from the John Barrymore-and-greasepaint days of acting, when the only speed a performer had to consider was the timing of his entrances and exits. This is what gives such solid contemporaneity to Paul's work; while eschewing the merely trendy he is very much a man of his time, integrated into the realities of each of his working decades. He is keenly aware of the 'feel' of the times and reflects this awareness in his performances. This is also why he wisely keeps clear of costume roles, historical dramas and fantasy stories. Even without the dismal example of Basil the Slave to deter him, he knows it isn't his style to swash and buckle his way through paper castles, cardboard galleons, and a porridge of archaic dialogue. A Paul Newman in coloured plumes and pink tights is no more conceivable than an Errol Flynn in nuns' habits.

As with most things, Paul was a latecomer to sports cars and it was not, in fact, till shortly after his first marriage that he felt he could afford to run a car. 'It was a 1937 Packard. I paid 150 dollars for it which is pretty good, because I was in summer stock at the time and only making 45 bucks a week. We were living—if you can believe it—in a two-bedroom apartment for ten bucks a month, in Woodstock, Illinois. That Packard was a *stock* car . . . it was the only car I could afford.'

Now he confessed to Dick Wells of *Motor Trend* that he gets "stoned" on automobiles . . . for me it's a natural high, which is marvellous. It's the one thing I can be genuinely adolescent about: automobiles. I love 'em! I bought my first Volkswagen in 1953, then in about 1961, I guess, I was complaining to my mechanic about driving the VW back and forth to the theatre in New York and my home in Connecticut. There was a lot of shifting, down-shifting in traffic. He said: "Why don't you dump a Porsche engine in it, and you'll retain your back seat but have the power you need."

'So we dropped in a stock Porsche engine, installed sway bars, Konia, and Dunlop Super Sports. The car handled so well that we put in a Porsche Super 90, and then put Porsche brakes up front. Later we bored out the Super 90 to 1800 c.c. and put a hot cam in it. It was a neat little bomb. I guess that was my first so-called hopped-up street machine.'

Unlike most car enthusiasts he does not spend hours tinkering about. 'I guess I've gotten lazy or spoiled or whatever it is. I've done really minimal work on my cars. I don't tear into 'em or anything like that. Steve McQueen does, and he's very good

136

at that, and he's very good with bikes, too. But I really have not been able to find the time to do it right.

'Of the cars I've owned I've never gotten into anything like a Lamborghini or anything like that, but I gotta tell you, that Corvette is the wildest. I've run it, just taking it up on Tuesdays when they open up my auto club at Lime Rock. It's an extremely forgiving automobile considering that it weighs 3,400 pounds. The steering is slick stuff, it doesn't lag or anything. The car is absolutely neutral. I really couldn't believe it when we really started pushing it. Of course it is set up a little bit; sway bars, heavy duty suspension, and F70 Goodyears on it.

'I guess the most rewarding experience I've had since taking lessons from Bob Bondurant involves a marvellous pilot I had in World War II. He was a great guy. We were in a torpedo bomber which is designed in such a way that you don't see anything out front at all, you can only see out the side ports. You don't see and you don't know what's coming up.

'I made errors in altimeters. When I thought we were at the moment of contact the altimeter read that we were 200 or 300 feet under water, in the sea! And the pilot is sitting up there chortling to himself and having a great time. So he came out to visit us at Elkhart Lake when we were shooting *Winning* out there, and I put him into A. J. Foyt's Group 7 car and took him around about three laps. And they had to *pry* his hand loose from the roll bar. He was in pretty bad shape. That was fun, because it was twenty-five years of rankling until I could finally retaliate.

'The sensation of fast driving on a track is in doing it right, if you can do it right, or at least driving within your own limits with skill. I obviously started much too late . . . I could never be a competitive driver. But look at my type; I'm reminded of Joanne who took up ballet and went *en pointes* when she was thirty-five. So there must be something kinky that she gets out of it. She's not going to be another Margot Fonteyn, but she still gets her kicks from it.

'In *Winning* I actually drove everything that was going. The big stockers, the Indy car, and the Group 7s. We duplicated Bobby Unser's car with an Eagle chassis and a blown Offen-

hauser engine in it. When that blower cuts in, I gotta tell you
. . . that's a sensation. I think I only went off the track once
. . . and not as part of the movie, not in the script. But during
the actual filming of the movie I didn't get into any real
trouble.'

Paul was looking forward to driving in that year's Celebrity
Race. 'It's going to be great fun. I think I'm going to be
driving a new Porsche 914. I think there's going to be some
good driving, but it also could be very funny. There's a lot of
egos—massive egos—involved in that race. Things may not
get better, but they're going to get funnier.

'The cars may get dinged up a little bit, but I think everybody will be careful. We're going to have in the professional
field Jackie Stewart, Graham Hill, Mario Andretti, Unser
Brothers, Roman Polanski, Dick Smothers, Dick Gordon, and
people like Redford, Garner, etc. And who's gonna deliver
the winner's kiss? Raquel Welch, we hope. Can't you hear it
now: "Mr Newman was seen slipping quietly into the crowd
with the race queen . . ."

'Some people play golf, I like cars. It's just kinky, very
natural. It may not offer as much exercise as some sports, but
I love it.'

It bothers him that although he loves to drive cars, he
realizes they are accused of being the biggest contributor to
pollution. He says that if he was part of a mass movement to
cut down on driving he would be willing to make almost any
personal sacrifice.

'The point is that there is no mass movement, there is no
leadership, and until we get that you're going to be driving
your car and I'm going to be driving mine. Because, I suppose,
in the final analysis it's a total hypocrisy.

'There's a dichotomy there that I can't justify. If I drive my
60 horsepower VW through the streets of Los Angeles there's
no way I'm going to feel any pride in that if I know I've got
eighteen Corvettes right in back of me. That's why I feel the
whole situation needs Federal attention. The people aren't
going to do it for themselves, so the government's got to do the
job for them.

'I mean, the government must create the people's conscience; there's got to be a community purpose. The second the individual senses that he is no longer a part of a community purpose, then he loses his own purpose. I just think it's necessary for either leadership by the government, or for the people to make those stands; as I say, to create a conscience for each other.'

With the exception of *Butch Cassidy*, *Winning* was probably the most enjoyable film Paul ever made. An almost holiday atmosphere attended its shooting, and the presence of Joanne was an added bonus. As Paul told Dick Wells, 'She thinks competitive driving is the silliest thing in the world. It is also very scary to her and she doesn't much care for it.' Yet she was there all the time up to her neck in axle grease.

A picture was taken of Joanne looking very grouchy and wearing a racing driver's suit. 'That's my favourite picture,' Paul was to say later. 'She didn't want to get into the car and I made her.' Amateur psycho-analysts are at liberty to read what they like into this remark, but to me it indicates the remarkable way in which Joanne has managed to go along with Paul's whims and wishes without losing an iota of her own strong personality. With Clementine Churchill, she could easily qualify for the wife of the century—in the celebrity category.

When rain washed out shooting of the Victory Lane celebrations for several days, the location unit moved into a small garage and jammed it up with cameras, klieg lights, fans, air conditioners, miles of cable, sound equipment, a racing car, 25 crewmen, and in conditions of oppressive heat cheerfully carried on with Paul doing some voice-off cues out of camera range. A four-minute scene would go on for four or more hours, but nobody was complaining—a situation which always augurs well for the ultimate outcome of a movie production. When this element—this X factor—goes into a film, it invariably infiltrates its way onto the screen afterwards. (This can also happen during theatre rehearsals.)

Between takes Paul never sat still, but would roam about the claustrophobic set, kidding with the crew, twirling someone's

British handlebar moustache, borrowing cigarettes (providing they were to his liking) and all the while chewing gum, taking it from his mouth and rolling it thoughtfully between forefinger and thumb for a few seconds before popping it back. Such is the self-assurance of this man that he can get away with this nauseating habit without giving the slightest offence. When *he* does it, it becomes an act of Olympian grace!

When it's time to roll the camera he at once becomes the complete professional. Even feeding lines to another actor he is acting the while: he gesticulates, screws his face up in a laugh, intones his lines as if on camera. He rarely fluffs the lines he memorized the night before. All the time he is privately resenting 'this lousy weather' and impatient to get out as soon as possible to tool one of the racing cars around the famous track. But he doesn't show his impatience, his self-control is perfect.

During lunch at a nearby Howard Johnson's with Jim Goldstone, the director, John Foreman, and Paul's stalwart stand-in Jim Arnett, a long-term chum, and a few others, Paul holds forth over Michelob beers and hot dogs. He talks easily and constantly, and launches often into a very funny, locker-room story of which there seems to be no end.

Then back to the garage 'studio', sniffing the wind as he goes in the hope of breaking the spell of bad weather. Between takes Paul confides to Australian writer Don Riseborough that he feels himself to be more involved in every aspect of this picture, beyond the calls of acting, since he directed *Rachel, Rachel*.

'It was the most agonizing experience,' he says slowly and carefully, 'because directing is such a delicate business. But I work very well with Joanne—we have our screaming fights off the set. There were moments in it when she was just beautiful to herself. She really had a hold of that character.'

Paul was most emphatic that 'we don't intend to become the second Burtons', filming constantly as a husband-and-wife team. 'Nor would I want to direct a big film with her. With our small project we were able to use some new techniques. I want to stick to the small budget, small film—not necessarily arty films either. But then I wouldn't turn down a film because it would make money at the box office, either.

'No one had any faith in the picture—no one. That is, I always had faith in it. You just have to go into it with your own taste and your own judgment. I hope to go at it again, but at the moment my agent is sitting in the bathroom whimpering about money.' (Both he and Joanne turned down lucrative films to make *Rachel, Rachel.*)

'Yeah, I'd like to do more directing if I can find a script I like. I've always enjoyed the "intellect" of making movies. But scripts don't come along all that easy. I just can't find scripts for the theatre, either. There are too few gutsy plays being written. Besides, the seasons there have been disastrous lately.'

While Newman was on the set, a balding brother Arthur— unit production manager, with the same hard blue eyes, solid jaw and a startling similarity of voice—confesses: 'Every time I talk about Paul the buttons fly off my shirt. Of course, I'm prejudiced.' He doesn't comment too much on his brother's career except to say Paul knows what he's doing. 'You can't be a fool to get to the top—and Paul's no fool. It's like getting to the top in General Motors or Chrysler or any big corporation. You have to have it to get there, and you only hear about those who make it.'

Good, solid stuff, which gives one the feeling that in terms of the Shaker Heights credit-ratings, Paul has made it after all. Briefly, shadow and substance are reconciled; one glimpses the solid rock on which the actor's gossamer talent is so firmly, so unshakably founded.

Shrewdly, John Foreman defines the Newman phenomenon from his particular angle. 'Paul is an intellectual—he gives a thinking performance. Others will give exactly what the directors ask for. Newman will too, but he always asks "Why?" He plays American characters because he thinks they have something to say, like "Hud" or "Cool hand Luke". He is very much concerned with American society today. He doesn't think costume or period films are for him. For example, *Lady L*, with Sophia Loren, was a flop. But he's willing to take the risk and make mistakes. Paul has got to the top with his intelligent acting, his sexual attraction and his physical beauty. If this goes he has other things. He has the ability of a damned good director, but he doesn't give a damn about money.'

Rain or shine, the making of *Winning* remained a 'fun' experience for all concerned. When Paul wasn't scaring the daylights out of his World War II buddies on the racing circuit, or concentrating his burning-glass attention on every detail of the production, he was telling corny jokes, swigging beers and martinis with no noticeable effect upon his equilibrium, or talking shop with the technicians and auto mechanics and race drivers.

Robert Wagner, noticeably glad to be back in a worthwhile feature film after starring in a light-weight but popular television series, *It takes a thief*, had a central role that even Paul jokily envied. 'Joanne gets all the sympathy in this picture,' Paul cracked. 'I marry her in the first reel and in the third reel she goes off with Bob Wagner. I call it *Cool hand Luke loses Rachel to a thief*—the lucky dog.'

Paul need not have worried. In the last reel he wins the Indy, slugs Bob on the chin, and wins back Joanne when he admits he had been neglecting her because of his Faustian need to be in there, winning all the races at the risk of losing her.

Even the reviews were almost unanimously favourable, with the *New York Times*'s Howard Thompson leading off with the opinion that this was, 'Probably the best-rounded and most appealing personalized film of this kind ever made. The Newmans are both splendid, he as the brooding, fiercely delineated "winner" and she in a complex characterization that Miss Woodward shades with wise reserve . . . even with the motors roaring full-blast, in *Winning* it's the people that matter.'

'Newman simply seems incapable of making a false move or sound,' marvelled Stanley Kauffmann; and, while the motor racing background did not exactly grab Judith Crist by the short-antennae, she reluctantly accepted that scene 'since Paul Newman and Joanne Woodward could, for my money, just stand there and read the telephone book—who's to quarrel?'

The public put up no resistance whatsoever, and within a few weeks the movie proved such a money-spinner there were quick returns for all investors. With this picture on the road, *Rachel, Rachel* about to be released, and the figure of Butch Cassidy shaping up in Paul's mind, the Newmans were indeed onto a 'winning' streak.

And doing what they were really interested in, rather than being pressured into dubious ventures because some remote studio boss wanted to make a fast buck out of their talents.

13

A divine discontent

'But as far as Marlon and I were concerned, we were
wasting our time. The community at large—especially the
white members of the various church communities, whatever their denomination—wasn't in the least bit interested,
nobody wanted to listen to anything we said. The mayor
called us rabble rousers and our films were banned from the
local cinemas.'

They were living in an imposing house with sculptured lawns
and the hand-painted sign near the ornamental gates read:
'PLEASE—THEY HAVE MOVED—THE PIERSONS.' Though there
were no Piersons this sad little effort at privacy was at least
more polite than Frank Sinatra's terse injunction further up
the canyon road: 'IF YOU RING THIS BELL YOU BETTER HAVE A
DAMN GOOD REASON.'

Paul and Joanne did their best to discourage the droves of
tourists swanning around their Beverly Hills home trampling
the lawns and clutching movie-star maps and autograph albums
and taking snapshots with their Brownie cameras. Environ-
mentally, the place was sheer heaven; as a home to live in, it
was hell.

If only they were lucky enough to get inside the house, muses
Rex Reed, there on a professional visit, they would catch
America's jet-age Doug and Mary in brief repose. In the
kitchen a chauffeur sits reading the afternoon paper while
little Lissie wanders restlessly from room to room fake-smoking
an unlit True cigarette. Joanne sprawls on a huge sofa in the
library, keeping an eye on Lissie's comings and goings and an
ear open for the next importunate ringing of the doorbell. She
is eating chocolate chip cookies and drinking iced coffee.

'The female half of the Newman team.' says Reed, 'she is
the star without an image, the girl with many faces, none of
which ever get recognized by the dimestore clerks who riot

when her husband walks in. She has glorious white skin, twinkling naughty eyes which always clue you to the fact that encyclopedias are being written behind them, and her hair is
long and golden and soaking wet because she has just come from
a ballet class she takes with the UCLA football team. (Ballet is
Joanne's favourite thing in the world—for Christmas Paul
gave her a complete print of the Nureyev-Fonteyn *Romeo and
Juliet* and she will do all the leaps if you will ask her.)'

Lissie is still faking it with the True and explaining in great
detail that her sister, 9-year-old Nell, has taken Baron, the
family sparrow hawk, to the bird doctor, when Paul bursts
into the room in tennis shorts and a rumpled white T-shirt with
a sheaf of papers in his hands and a defeated look on his face.
'I'm writing a speech for Eugene McCarthy and it has to be
ready in three hours. You don't want to write a speech for me,
do you?'

'Out!' says Joanne, with a delicate Southern accent that is
more magnolia blossom than hominy grits, to Lissie, who is
now standing on her head in the middle of the room. 'I won't
talk; I'll just stand on my head,' 'Go help Daddy write his
McCarthy speech.' Paul scoops up Lissie, still upside down,
and carries her out to the pool.

'I'm the only movie star who still rides the Super Chief,'
Joanne says. 'I'm taking the train back to Connecticut next
week, then Paul starts a new western in Mexico and I'll come
back so he can come home on weekends.'

While other Hollywood stars are dining out at Chasens or
taking yachts down to Acapulco, the Newmans dodge the star
circuit and spend all their free time in their converted coaching
house in Westport, Connecticut, designed by Broadway set
designer Ralph Alswang and set in three acres of apple trees
cut through by a swift running trout stream.

Some time later Joanne told me, 'This sort of goldfish bowl
existence that is mandatory in film circles is one of the reasons
I'm insisting on selling our Beverly Hills home. Hollywood is
too much of a village, it refuses to look at the outside world. In
Connecticut we're within easy reach of New York, and we can
always rent a place in Hollywood when we come here to make

a picture. You know, Paul said that living in Hollywood all the time is like watching an old lady dying slowly of cancer.'

Here were two of the biggest movie stars in the world, with so much going for them, yet they were as if consumed by a Shelleyan 'divine discontent' which had nothing to do with their material success.

The trouble with Paul was his compulsive need always to ask why, not only as an actor but as a thinking American. Here he was, a famous man in what was then accepted as the wealthiest and most powerful country in the world, more concerned with the state of the nation than tomorrow's script. He was, after all, a patriotic ex-serviceman from the Middle-West with a conservative upbringing and a deep love of his country. Why, then, wasn't he a hard-nosed, hard-hatted patriot in the style of John Wayne? A law-and-order guy like Ronald Reagan?

The reason partly lies inside his mind, for he shares with Joanne a high IQ and a flair for asking awkward questions that would have been vastly appreciated in the Athens of Socrates, in the Greek market place where the citizens shouted *baa-baa* at Hunnish visitors and incidentally invented the word 'barbarian'. He is too fastidious to be a rabble-rouser, he abhors the vulgarities of whistle-stop campaigning and despises the ward heeling and wheeler-dealing of party machines. As he was later to tell me, 'I am not against the Establishment, I'm against stupidity.'

In the forefront of his mind he carries a vision of America not dissimilar to that shared by the Second Continental Congress when they passed out the Declaration of Independence. Had John F. Kennedy lived to run for a second term, the Newmans would probably have made an effective contribution to the glory of Camelot-on-the-Potomac. All the key figures of the Kennedy presidency seemed to come closer to his ideal of the philosopher prince in politics: Bob Kennedy, Larry O'Brien, Ken O'Donnell, Ted Sorensen, John Bailey, Steve Smith, Dick Scammon and Arthur Schlesinger, Jr, despite their flaws, were comparatively open-minded and the type of political animal he could understand.

146

It was all very well for a Barry Goldwater, speaking to the converted, to tell a Better Business Bureau banquet in Chicago that the New Frontier had produced '1026 days of wasted spending, wishful thinking, unwarranted intervention, wishful theories, and waning confidence', but this kind of gusty rhetoric blowing from Mayor Daly's windy city could not obscure the fact that, with or without the help of Kennedy, America was changing.

The Newmans recognized that the change did not come from the political top, it was a change in the American consciousness that went much deeper than mere reaction to the bland complacency of the Eisenhower years. A new America was emerging from the consciousness of the young, aided and abetted by the restless iconoclasm of the Brando-Dean cults, the San Francisco Beats, the collective restlessness of 'campus bums' scattered throughout the country.

America was changing, like it or not. By the middle 'sixties square America was surprised and puzzled by a series of increasingly violent happenings in the nation's universities. To the American student the average campus—not only the radical hotbeds of Berkeley or Columbia—symbolized the unacceptable bastions of a system committed to war in Vietnam and racism at home, and this led to a 'them' and 'us' polarization of students and faculty.

The cries of burn, baby, burn, rang through Harlem, Detroit, Watts, New Haven, as Negro Americans came to the end of their tether and vented their frustrations in street violence. For a while it seemed that America would be faced with its second Civil War, and the credibility of post-Kennedy presidents diminished with the incapability of the universities and civic authorities to deal with student romanticism and widespread social unrest.

Yes, America was changing. It was the time of the Movement, of mind-bending experimentations with drugs, with the foundations shaking from Herbert Marcuse's new sensibility. This, according to its most vociferous founder-publicist 'expresses the ascent of the life instincts over aggressiveness and guilt, and would foster, on a social scale, the vital need for the

147

abolition of injustice and misery and would shape the further evolution of "the standard of living".'

The new sensibility was hailed as a turning point in the evolution of contemporary societies. Square Americans were appalled. Whatever was happening to the all-American way of life? Forgetting the greed, brutality and hypocrisy of the past, many traditionalists entered into a dream world of nostalgia for the 'good old days'.

Paul and Joanne foreswore nostalgia as anyone with their intelligence ratio would do. On the other hand, they did not slip into the permissive postures of some of their contemporaries. The nearest they came to relaxing their own exacting standards presumably was in allowing themselves to be drafted into the inanities of *A new kind of love*, the flippancies of *Harry Frigg*, but since Paul also got involved in *Lady L* and *What a way to go*, this might be charitably attributed to a dearth of good scripts rather than the general deterioration of values in the post-Kennedy era when it seemed that 'mere anarchy' was loosed upon the (Western) world.

While the old world was collapsing all around him Paul commendably concentrated on finding stories that worked for him even if they were not in tune with the times. This frequently meant burning the midnight oil investigating the filmworthy possibilities of the most esoteric scripts, but no matter how arcane the field of investigation sometimes proved to be, his patience was occasionally rewarded by striking purest gold.

Among the best of these was an original screenplay by William Goldman, *Butch Cassidy and the Sundance kid*. This property had been floating around Hollywood for some time, but it was only when news reached 20th Century-Fox that both Paul Newman and Steve McQueen were interested in it that the backroom boys there sat up and took notice. As it happened, the Newman-Foreman team managed to snap it up just in time before the elaborate packaging machinery creaked into gear.

At one time it was hoped that Newman and Brando would be co-starred in this film, and it is interesting to speculate on what kind of picture it would have become with Marlon in the role of Butch. But Brando was on a civil liberties kick and going through one of his periodic revulsions against the movie scene, so Paul took the role of Butch, leader of a Wyoming gang known as the Wild Bunch or the Hole in the Wall Gang.

The role of the Sundance Kid was assigned to Robert Redford. With the fluke success of the Bacharach–Hal David song, *Raindrops keep falling on my head*, the end product became one of the biggest money-makers of the 'sixties.

'Ah, those were marvellous days,' Paul told me as he warmly recalled the carefree locations in the Utah desert. 'A glorious, affectionate game one critic called it, and that's what it was all through the shooting stages. I respect Robert Redford as an actor and value him as a friend. It was a perfect example of film-making as a community experience. Nobody had to defend their position and everybody was geared to invent and create.

'Redford and I would fool around during rehearsals, needling George Roy Hill, the director, till he'd say, very anxious, "Hey, you guys aren't really going to play the scene that way?" We'd look kinda dumb until he'd roll the camera, then play the scene for all it was worth. Laughs all the way.'

Paul looked thoughtful for a moment before he went on. 'You know, I don't think people realize what that picture was all about. It's a love affair between two men. The girl is incidental.'

Rona Jaffe visited him during location work in the little desert town of St George, miles from anywhere without even a main street bar. She tracked him down in the manager's apartment of the one and only motel and reacted in a very feminine way to her encounter with the idol.

Paul opens the door. He is dressed in jeans, white T-shirt, white socks. A beer can opener hangs on a chain round his neck. He gives her a big bear hug and says, 'You are the best thing I've seen all day.'

She quickly notices that there are two huge photos of Joanne conspicuously on display, one looking glamorous and the other of Joanne in the racing driver's suit she wore during the filming of *Winning* along with that grouchy expression which had so perversely pleased her husband.

149

Paul mixes her a pale pink Bloody Mary and tells her, 'I'm knocked out over the two records I recently bought, one Bach, one Beethoven. I play the Bach every morning at 5.30 a.m. when I have to get up. It keeps me from getting depressed.'

He spends an hour in the sauna and swimming pool every morning before his 7 a.m. set call. Miss Jaffe notes appreciatively that at forty-four he still has the body of a man in his twenties.

'A thing about the famous Newman blue eyes,' she records. 'After the first few minutes you don't notice them because his personality takes over. You notice his whole face and what he's saying. He never pushes, never plays the star. Just a super-nice, intelligent guy with charisma. Always refers to women as ladies, never women, girls, broads or chicks. A gentleman but humorous with it.'

'Joanne is in London getting a citation from the Royal Academy of Dramatic Art for *Rachel, Rachel*,' Paul says proudly. 'That's like the Pulitzer Prize for acting, better check that though before you write it.' He 'phones Joanne in London about three times a day. 'Well, it's so hard to know when to get her with the time difference.'

Snooping, Miss Jaffe sees a 'loving' telegram on the bar. Paul sent Joanne flowers and sherry, her favourite drink, to London. Married nearly eleven years, the reporter marvels, and still acting this way! Put that in your hubble-bubble, Hedda, and choke on the smoke.

Dinner in the restaurant with Paul, John Foreman, stand-in stuntman Jim Arnett, director George Roy Hill. Paul has a Pyrex coffee maker full of Scotch and ice. He makes a big salad as a nightly ritual, sends what's left to other tables. Though Paul is automatically seated at the head of the table, he doesn't show off, carry on, or dominate the conversation as other stars frequently do. He makes jokes, but also listens attentively to the others around the dining table. As the producer and director turn the conversation to the subject of shop, Paul offers occasional opinions, suggestions, showing great knowledge of film-making.

Later they go down the road to watch rushes of the day's

filming. Afterwards Paul holds out his hands for Rona to see. His palms are glistening with sweat. 'It always happens when I watch rushes,' he says. She remarks that she has the impression that he still manages to get a lot of fun out of life.

Paul ponders this, then says, 'I do but my life isn't all fun, there's also the terror . . . and the pseudo-intellectual. And my private life which *has* to be intellectual. Every piece about me makes me look like a stick. They make me talk about politics all the time which gets so boring. None of them show the humour. Listen, you've known me a long time. You think I'm funny, don't you?'

It's a recurring obsession. Time and again in interviews he raises the subject, tries to steer people away from the portentous or pretentious. Look, he seems to be crying out, I'm a very ordinary Joe with the standard quota of normal instincts and I'm not in a constant state of turmoil over the world situation. I get lonely when my wife's away too long, I miss my kids when I don't see them for a while, and I like corny jokes and enjoy a good belly laugh now and then. All that stuff I project on a screen, forget it for a moment, will you pal?

For this reason Paul enjoys the company of auto mechanics, fly fishermen, farmers, surgeons, electronics buffs, astronomers, jockeys, footballers. They don't talk Hollywood shop, don't theorize, or intellectualize by way of their latest browsings through *Readers Digest*.

On the set the next day in a beautiful desert location spot Paul has recovered from his after-sundown introspectiveness. The sun is already hot, the sand shimmers on a foreshortened horizon. There is the usual interminable waiting between takes which makes it such a drag hanging around a film set when you're not involved in the technicalities. A prop man brings Paul an endless relay of cold beers in cans which he attacks with the can-opener he still wears around his neck under his Western gear. He is wearing his wedding ring on his right hand because he smashed up his left hand in a recent motor-cycle accident.

Showing nice feminine perception Rona writes down: 'The man hasn't even got a wrinkle. Face looks gorgeous, sexy, masculine, lived in. The blue eyes fade out to ice blue in the sunlight.'

Paul perks up when Robert Redford arrives on the scene. They start to act out skits, watched from the corner of his eye by an apprehensive director. They improvise little scenes, nothing to do with their parts in the film, and play them privately for one or two bystanders at a time, never to the full audience. Paul's sense of fun becomes apparent immediately he finds himself in compatible company. Newman and Redford obviously have a great rapport going, jokey, unstated, relaxed as only men can be when they really trust each other and have nothing to gain from exploiting each other. Buddies on a fishing trip, hunters above the forest line of a rugged peak.

Back in the restaurant he's swigging down Scotch from the coffee mixer, chomping on a hamburger, and like so many others his visitor marvels at his capacity for taking strong drink without showing any signs of tipsiness. Paul speaks of the virtues of drinking over the ever-widening influence of the drugs scene.

'The reason why I'm against drugs for kids,' he says, 'is that a forty-year-old man has learnt discipline, or should have done by this time. He can have a few snouts at night, and get to the office the next morning shaved and on time. But kids haven't learnt discipline. So if they smoke pot or take drugs they can't handle it.'

Paul doesn't use pot or pills, he hasn't even been seen taking an aspirin. He eats sparingly, and knows when to taper off. Early morning saunas, swims, and push-ups keep his body in good shape. There was a time when it seemed possible that John Barleycorn would take him over completely but since his marriage to Joanne he has learnt to observe the Churchillian dictum—use drink by all means but never let it use you.

After lunch (during which he switched from Scotch to Bourbon) he was called on to do some hard riding with Redford over fairly rough country. He always says he can't ride, though he rides well, claiming, 'I'm a city boy.' But he stuck in the saddle for several hours under a broiling sun with hardly a break. Afterwards the talk turned to his failure to win an Oscar despite four nominations.

'I'd like to get it when I'm eighty and arthritic and have to hobble up to the stage to accept it,' he said with a self-mocking grin. 'Joanne and I were having a fight once and Joanne said, "I don't have to take this crap." I said, "It's not crap it's logic." She said, "Logic from a four-time loser?" ' He laughs fondly.

His thoughts constantly revert to his children. 'We don't want them to have unreasonable burdens because of us,' he says. 'Or unreasonable benefits either. If they're to be singled out it should be for something they have done. Whether its luck, love, or psychoanalysis or just endurance, it all seems to be working out.' Knock-knock on wood for luck.

The sundance in the desert worked out just fine, too. 'Newman's screen portrayals henceforth, in what promises to be his Golden Era, may some day be seen to date from this picture,' Lawrence J. Quirk observed with remarkable foresight, adding that in his portrayal of Butch, artistic humility and professional sureness produce a Newman on-screen essence that exemplifies a great talent at last commencing to strike exactly the right balance.

'We can only hope that now that his acting style appears to be keeping pace with the sensitivity, compassion and wise balance that his superb direction last year of Joanne Woodward's film, *Rachel, Rachel* displayed, he will not altogether abandon acting for directing.

'He has waited some fifteen years now for the Academy Award that Hollywood has perversely and unfairly denied him for picture after picture—while lesser talents with a greater bent for politics-playing and publicity-saturation have sneaked away with the prize. We need both director Newman and actor Newman—and we hope he will not sacrifice one for the other. A one-time intense but narrow-ranged talent seems unmistakably to be broadening, and the Paul Newman of the 'seventies should have rich characterizations to offer his admirers.'

But it was not all fun and games on schoolboy-vacation outdoor locations during the 'sixties of campus revolutions and ghetto riots.

Having been branded as nonconformists in the formal 'fifties the Newmans continued throughout the 'sixties as scourges of the establishment. In the higher reaches of Hollywood they made new enemies daily by refusing to conform—even though the system from which various reactionary bigots had made vast fortunes was now collapsing around them like so many playing-card houses.

'This may come as a surprise to some people,' Paul told me, 'but I'm not really anti-establishment. I'm absolutely square. I'm anti-idiocy, anti-dishonesty—and the motion picture industry as a whole has its roots in dishonesty. That is from the business point of view.

'From the acting point of view we have mixed feelings about the business. One day you think it's terribly important and difficult and that it *does* take a measure of talent to become what you are. The next day you wake up and say: "This is the most childish activity or vocation that anybody could pick." I don't know which is the correct attitude—probably the latter. It's not a nice thing to admit but I don't know many adult actors—and that includes myself.'

Paul's insistence on gaining his independence was not the only reason why he seems to have antagonized many of the studio bosses. What these dealers in intrigue and compromise found so galling was the refusal of Paul or Joanne ever to compromise themselves or cheapen their reputations by meeting them half way. The deals they made were always above board, and they would never say anything behind a person's back which they were not prepared to say outright to them in person. Such honesty was an embarrassment in a business which flourished on autocratic patronage, hidden assets, and threats of blackmail or even worse.

In contemporary Los Angeles there is still a hard core of thugs and agents-provocateur on hire to trap the unwary into compromising situations, specialists in miniaturized bugging devices, mayhem and murder. There are places in Los Angeles where, if you know the right recognition signals, you can have an 'accident' set up for as little as a thousand dollars. It is a city of desperate people, way out characters, and the first thing a serious actor learns is not to talk to strangers.

The Newmans, man and wife, were also a thorn in the flesh of the moguls because of their determination to make themselves heard on social issues. Paul, for instance, campaigned for Negro rights, and denounced the American intervention in Vietnam, long before it became fashionable or expedient to do so. With his friend, Brando, he would take to the streets in public protest. When I discussed this side of his public activity he became rather bitter about the apparent ineffectuality of making such a stand, and he gave an example.

'One day Marlon called me on the 'phone and said: "Hey, Martin Luther King has been trying to get in touch with you. He'd like us both to get down to Alabama and try and reason with some of the big wheels down there to give jobs to Negroes and other minority groups." Tony Franciosa and another actor, Virgil Fry, joined us in a place called Gadsden, Alabama, and we received a great welcome—from a handful of Negroes.

'So far as the white community was concerned we achieved nothing. Not . . . a . . . thing. According to King, the situation was about to explode. Tear gas, street shuffles, beatings . . . people being tossed into jail for so-called disturbances of the peace . . . it sure looked as if something should be done to stop the rot.

'But so far as Marlon and I, and the other actors and writers were concerned, we were wasting our time. The community at large—especially the white members of the various church communities, whatever their denomination—wasn't in the least bit interested, nobody wanted to listen to anything we said. The mayor called us rabble rousers and our films were banned from the local cinemas. There was absolutely no liaison between the black and white communities. If Marlon and I thought we could pressure people into finding employment for anyone they didn't choose to employ—we were soon disillusioned.'

When Martin Luther King was assassinated, Newman and Brando again took to the streets. 'But there's a lot of apathy,' Paul says bleakly. 'The under twenty-fives are a damn sight more concerned.'

Even spokesmen of the extreme right were admitting that

155

the country was in a mess, but how to put things right? The least sensitive organization man and most vociferous Daughter of the Revolution was silently aware of the Indian reproach, the Negro desperation, the hungry whites queuing up outside the skid row blood banks to trade a pint or two of their under-nourished corpuscles for the price of a shot of hooch.

Visitors from Germany, Japan, Britain, Africa, invariably are shocked when they first see so many sick and demented American citizens walking aimlessly up and down world famous thoroughfares in the big cities from coast to coast. Is this the American dream?

To many honest, decent, hardworking, hardhatted, blue-collared Americans this deterioration of the railways, public services, social amenities, hotels, fleapits, pool-rooms, processed foods, beer quality, bus schedules, with its resultant hordes of have-nots slinking past the chipped portals of a chimeric plenty, was a regrettable but accepted commonplace of modern life. Most of them were too busy keeping *themselves* off the welfare treadmills or just a hop, skip and a jump ahead of the bailiffs, to concern themselves unduly with the state of the nation at large.

But a gradual change was coming over America. Something Raymond Williams has called the long revolution, a pheno-menon 'which our best descriptions only in part interpret. It is a genuine revolution, transforming men and institutions; con-tinually extended and deepened by the actions of millions, continually and variously opposed by explicit reaction and by the pressures of habitual forms and ideas.'

In this crisis the Newmans held their own ground. They were considered amenable to change. Though he was born too early to be part of the youthful counter-culture, giant posters of Paul Newman did not seem incongruous beside those of Ché Guevera, John and Yoko, Bob Dylan, or the cans of Campbell's soup canonized by Andy Warhol.

Instinctively, the kids (as they were with jocular contempt called by the promoters and publishers of pop music, art and haberdashery) allocated a place for the Newmans among the ranks of those artistes who seek behind authority for a personal law that should serve them as a home.

156

One way in which Paul could make a pragmatic contribution at the academic level was in his support through the 'No Such Foundation' of the Center for the Study of Democratic Institutions at Santa Barbara. Among its early patrons, who were automatically granted the right to turn up at any seminar or think-in that interested them, were Paul and Joanne, Kirk Douglas, Steve Allen, Dinah Shore and Jack Lemmon. Some of these patrons have back-tracked for various reasons but at the time of writing Paul has not withdrawn his patronage.

'It's a completely varied group of people up there,' Paul says. 'They've got educators, sociologists, behavioural scientists, physicists, mathematicians, gerontologists. Instead of living a cloistered existence where they would only examine problems related to their own subject, they get together and examine the whole intellectual field.

'For example, they look at this country in the light of possible changes we should anticipate. Very little anticipating is done— it's all diplomacy by crisis, urban renewal by crisis, poverty programmes by crisis. Jeeze!—I've just read about this man— he was receiving some award—who anticipated all the problems we're having now, in terms of radical disturbance, years ago.

'Here's another thing they're beginning to think about at the Center—the possibility of 100 per cent of the goods and services in this country being delivered by 10 per cent of the population. What happens to a human being who is always measuring his sense of achievement by what he produces? What if he produces nothing? What new values must creep into his life?

'I feel like an ass going up to those seminars, but I tell you it is so refreshing to focus my mind on something. Pierre Mendés-France came once, and Bishop Pike, and this guy who was in Roosevelt's brains trust. He was up there speaking on Constitutional Change, and so forth, and it was as exciting as hell.'

In his home state, Paul was appointed co-chairman of the Connecticut Citizens for Duffey in the fall of 1969. Joseph Duffey of Hartford, national chairman of Americans for

Democratic Action, had just announced his candidacy for the Democratic Senate nomination. Paul said he would campaign frequently in Connecticut on behalf of Mr Duffey. He said his main interest was that a Senate nominee should 'not be chosen behind closed doors. Our responsibility is a state-wide primary so the people can make their presence felt. Joe Duffey is a man responsible to the people'. This move was very much in keeping with his abhorrence of backroom politics and a step towards the establishment of a more open society on his home ground at least.

Earlier he had stumped the country on behalf of Senator Eugene McCarthy, whom he admired for his guts—a quality which commends his admiration in whatever walk of life he finds it. Shortly after Paul's support of his local man Duffey, Joanne said, 'We've always been politically active—Paul more so than I, although I did work on the first Stevenson campaign. He just felt so strongly about Senator McCarthy that he wanted to take an active part. And I think he's very good at that kind of thing.' In 1969 Paul and Joanne also received the William J. German Human Relations Award of the American Jewish Committee.

Then in 1970 Paul started work on a film which, on the drawing board at least, in script form, seemed to contain most of the elements of his current thought and feeling about the polarization of America. On the one hand there were the big battalions of corporate banking and financing headed by a handful of powerful tycoons and political wheels and captains of industry, and served by an army of image-builders, influence pedlars, manipulators, bent lawmen and bribable judges, with their field corps of little Hitlers and a tight-fisted, tight-minded beaurocracy. At the other extreme were the revolutionary activists, Black Panthers, heads, freaks, dropouts, Stokely Carmichaels, brothers Huey P. Newton and Malcolm X, brown people, red people, poor people, and the psychedelic threnodies of the Grateful Dead.

In *W.U.S.A.*, Paul plays the part of Rheinhardt, an itinerant radio newscaster who drifts into New Orleans and gets a job with a local radio station which gives the film its somewhat difficult title. The station is run by a wealthy neo-fascist local big shot who also gives a naïve young social worker, Morgan Rainey (Anthony Perkins), the task of organizing a spurious social welfare survey.

Paul gives great conviction to the part of a would-be decent citizen determined not to stick his neck out for anyone and generally keep his nose clean in the old Bogart sense of non-commitment, but nearly quarter of a century had passed since *Casablanca* and Paul indirectly makes it clear that such a position is untenable today.

There are no more sullied knights in rusty armour, no more Philip Marlowes; innocence has disappeared and everyone now knows exactly what the score is. Welcome aboard, bud. Glad to be aboard, boss. Nice to have you aboard, pal. Now go out and cut that guy's throat, and when you've done that chop down that uppity buck and evict them no-good spivs and put that junkhead beatnik gal in the hippy commune to work in Mother Mable's stable on Bourbon Street.

The end product of being a nice guy and collecting your wages, the Rheinhardt role implied, was to make yourself a party to repression and genocide, to collaborate in the final degradation of the 'have nots' and support a paranoid police state. When Rheinhardt's pal, Rainey, realizes this he goes berserk at a political mass rally to promote the fascist boss's special line in 'big, clean, sound' Americanism, and muffs an attempt to assassinate the boss, kills an assistant instead, and is then brutally stomped to death by the crowd.

Newman-Rheinhardt's girl is also at the rally. This is Geral-dine, a hooker whose homespun ethics were perverted by Life, the quintessential whore with a heart of gold, touchingly played by Miss Woodward. She has drugs planted on her and is dragged off to jail, where she hangs herself. Comes the dawn, and we see Rheinhardt leaving Geraldine's grave in the local potters-field and heading out of town towards a future as existentially bleak as his past.

Baldly stated, it is difficult to convey the sense of shock the film generates, especially in a non-American audience. In America most of the critics seem too inured against shock to understand the real horror the film obliquely conveys. Shortly after *W.U.S.A.* was shown in Britain people were reading about the assassination attempt on Governor Wallace and were shortly to be treated to the appalling saga of mayhem in high places as revealed at the hearings of the Senate Watergate Committee.

Even Judith Crist, who should know better, was reduced to complaining about 'fiddling around with lame-brained cynicisms and stereotyped philosophizing, deluding oneself and be-clouding the screen with pseudo-sophistications and pretended subleties will not even convert the converted; it serves only to placate the know-nothings and convince them that they're far from alone. Of course Newman can be a charming alcoholic, cynical as all get-out; Miss Woodward an appealing lost lady . . . and Perkins is still the sweet psycho. But what they're all about in the frenetic context of N'Awlins and White Power in our time is beyond the ken of the unblown mind.'

If Miss Crist had taken her unblown mind to a second screening of the film (even if she'd had to pay for her seat) she might have found subtleties which she missed first time around. But in some perverse way, most critics adopted a hostile stance towards *W.U.S.A.* which virtually amounted to an infantile collective *wish* to denigrate the real meaning of the film. In the same breath they were castigating Newman and his fellow-producers for seemingly not having the courage of their convictions, and complaining that they were promulgating a false premise and had no call to hint at the dangers of a drift towards totalitarianism in the USA.

Typical of the common critical reaction was Kathleen Carroll's sniffy comment in the *New York Daily News*. '*W.U.S.A.* was a complete turnoff for this reviewer. They, I suppose Newman and his co-producers, are trying to bury us with the message that this country's current trend toward neo-fascism is a dangerous thing. Their message is only loud, not clear; and the movie itself amounts to nothing more than a lot of sounding off.'

Pontificated Roger Greenspun in the *New York Times*: 'If it were an ordinary bad movie (and it is a very bad movie),

W.U.S.A. might, in spite of the distinguished names, and less distinguished presence, of its leading actor, be dismissed with no more than a nod to the tension between Stuart Rosenberg's ponderously emphatic direction and Robert Stone's ponderously allusive screenplay. I suspect Stone wins out, for *W.U.S.A.* feels more like poor theater than poor movie-making—so that it continually suggests a failed version of *The balcony* even though it strives to fall short of *The Manchurian candidate*.'

But Mr Greenspun felt compelled to admit that 'at least in its ambitions, *W.U.S.A.* is not an ordinary bad movie. For in its climax, a huge white-power rally sponsored by WUSA (the patriotic hate station based in a Southern state), it means to hold up a mirror to middle America, to show the hate behind the innocence, the chaos implicit in the call to law and order. . . . In this sequence, during which Newman explains Vietnam to a panic-ridden, rioting mass of thin-lipped, pinch-faced silent majority, *W.U.S.A.* has its crucial image, and, presumably, its rational.'

And Frances Herridge in the *New York Post* came up with the following: 'In spite of its flaws, *W.U.S.A.* is one of the most provocative and relevant films this year. . . . It is another joint effort of Paul Newman and his wife Joanne Woodward, and they are both superb. So is the direction by Stuart Rosenberg . . . Pat Hingle creates an impressive atmosphere of evil power as the superpatriot, but his corrupt activities are too vaguely defined. The machinery of dictatorship is there, but its uses are minor.

'Laurence Harvey is amusing. But it is the Newmans who carry the picture and keep it absorbing throughout. Never for a moment do they drop out of character. Their gestures, their expressions, their mannerisms—particularly Miss Woodward's —are original and honest. The dialogue—intelligently written —is always fresh. A fascinating pair, and well worth a visit.'

Yet despite the few pros and many cons of the critics, the picture in any case never stood a chance of obtaining more than a limited circuit screening. The big guns of the studio responsible for distribution, Paramount, simply were not interested. Interested? Most of them were downright hostile when they discovered what the Newmans and their team had done with what they'd considered an innocuous screenplay based on Robert Stone's novel, *A hall of mirrors.*

They were, in any case, in the throes of getting *The Godfather* together, and there were enough fainthearts shaking their heads over the prospect of the Mafia saga making a penny profit. Then when *The Godfather* showed promise of reaping a record box-office harvest (and with the profits of *Love story* rolling in) the power boys at Paramount felt they could ditch *W.U.S.A.* without feeling any pain.

When it is remembered that at this time Paul Newman was secretly on the Presidential list of 'unfriendly ones' who could be liable for harrassment by the Department of Internal Revenue (which was subsequently let loose on the President's own tax returns!) and that official Hollywood had little time for 'the Newmans of Connecticut', anyway, it is not surprising that Paramount found it easier to 'do a Pontius Pilate' and wash their hands of this particular movie

Like *City lights* before it, *W.U.S.A.* was so much of its time that it seemed ahead of it. 'I know it had its faults,' Paul says, 'but I still can't understand the big hate campaign that went on against it.' Interviewed by David Frost, Paul doggedly insisted that the picture 'should be in a time capsule to be seen one hundred years from now' and that all he wanted from it was 'to get people to ask themselves a lot of questions', adding, 'if it does that it will have served its purpose'.

In the course of time, *W.U.S.A.* will be revived in many countries, not least the USA, and the post-Watergate world will ask itself what all the fuss was about, and what was so hard to understand about its 'message'. But what chance did it have in the same year that Spiro Agnew was lambasting the communicators of the Press and TV and talking hopefully of '*a tiny, enclosed fraternity of privileged men elected by no one*'.

The times were indeed out of joint, and anyone in pre-Watergate America who spoke out against them could expect to be thumped, and thumped hard. Alas, poor *W.U.S.A.*, which stood for more than just the call signal of an imaginary (*imaginary?*) Southern radio station.

14

The meaning of marigolds

'I bought it because I thought it was an impossible part for my wife to play.'

When I first walked on to the set where Paul was directing Joanne in *The effect of gamma rays on man-in-the-moon marigolds,* I was lifting my feet up and down like a cat on hot bricks. Dressed in a rust-brown auto-racer's overalls and wearing a big smile, the star quickly put me at ease.

'It's okay,' he assured me. 'You don't have to walk on tiptoe around here except when the red light is flashing to indicate we're shooting a scene on the set in the house next door to this church. Don't worry, they deconsecrated it after the parson hanged himself in his bedroom.'

The church was due for demolition, anyway, and Paul was lucky to have found it, during his preliminary locations search, before the city fathers of Bridgeport razed it for redevelopment. The rundown slums of this manufacturing town in Connecticut, some hundred miles north of New York, was a far cry from the big Hollywood studios where the Newmans had toiled and suffered over the years. There are some wonderful people living in Bridgeport, but the slums there don't come any slummier anywhere in the world.

When Joanne emerged from her makeshift clapboard dressing-room, looking as if it had been slung together in a corner of the church by a demented child, I found it difficult, for a moment, to recognize the attractive, sophisticated star I'd last seen in London six months earlier. Her hair was twisted in knots, there were dark patches under her eyes. In grubby night-shift and torn dressing-gown she looked as if she'd escaped from a prison hospital.

Noticing my confusion, Paul laughed. 'I know,' he said.

'They'll be saying I can't afford to buy my wife any decent clothes any more.'

Sun-tanned and bursting with energy, Paul continued to affectionately tease Joanne about her sorry appearance. When I asked him why he had chosen such a drab character for Joanne to portray, he said: 'I bought it because I thought it was an impossible part for my wife to play.' As Joanne seemed about to heave a coffee urn at him, he quickly added: 'But whenever I place her in front of a camera she disproves me entirely.'

'Man what a woman,' Paul said to nobody in particular as Joanne sauntered away with a wiggle of the bottom that even the prison-shift could not entirely conceal. He gave an appreciative growl, and added: 'Wow.'

The Newmans are amazingly outspoken with each other, but also demonstrably affectionate. Whenever Joanne passed by Paul would absent-mindedly pat her bottom, or, less absent-mindedly, grab her in his arms and whirl her around in the air. Yet whenever he went on to the set and took up his position behind the cameraman he ceased clowning and Paul Newman, director and bossman, took over.

Paul has a natural authority and as a director, the many facets of Paul Newman flow smoothly together into a highly efficient whole: everything gels simultaneously.

Adapted from Paul Zindel's 1971 Pulitzer-prizewinning play, this portrait of Beatrice Hunsdorfer, a forty-year-old housewife abandoned by her husband and bringing up two teenaged daughters in a slummy house contained allegorical overtones about social change in the atomic age which appealed strongly to Paul. He had in fact been looking for this kind of dramatic statement for years and since the actual message was briefly and beautifully conveyed in a single, extremely moving speech by one of the daughters just a few moments before the last fade-out, it had the additional merit of fitting in with Paul's aesthetic notion that a movie should embody the message obliquely rather than allow the message to dominate the movie.

As soon as the Newman-Foreman Company bought the

screen rights, Paul made plans to shoot the film in a location as close as possible to his home in Connecticut, and the slum areas of busy Bridgeport fifteen miles away fitted perfectly into his production requirements. It also helped Joanne to keep her home life flowing smoothly at a time when the younger children were approaching crucial school exams and entering into local sports events.

Shortly before the cameras began to roll on *Marigolds* she said: 'I read Dr Spock to keep up with those modern child-rearing ideas, but use my own commonsense basically. The ones in the middle group have the usual sibling-rivalry problems. We have to advise them on anything and everything, and at times the interplay is stimulating. When we move from one place to another it's like a menagerie—the six kids, and all kinds of pets. It keeps us on the jump, but we love it.'

Paul was able to keep up his driving at weekends in his local auto club, and in April 1971 he had honoured the sport by appearing in *Once upon a wheel*, an ABC-TV network special that explored the excitement and background of auto-racing, serving also as narrator. The special was filmed at various tracks in California and North Carolina, the Indianapolis Speedway and the Soap Box Derby in Ohio, and on several European circuits. Several racing champions appeared on the special, and Kirk Douglas, Glenn Ford and James Garner did cameo-spots as participants in a Pro-Am event at the Ontario Motor Speedway in California.

Joanne was also taking courses at university and visiting the ballet in New York whenever she could. I recall her once asking me questions about the ballet in London and I tried to explain my lack of knowledge of the art by pointing out that I'd been brought up as a country boy and didn't see my first ballet till I was nearly thirty years old.

On hearing the words 'country boy' Joanne misinterpreted my ignorance as bias, and gave me a sharp lecture on what a hell of a man you have to be if you take up ballet dancing. Later she realized I was not being snide, and was really nice about it. The little contretemps gave me an inkling into what it would be like to be really at the receiving end of Joanne's wrath, and I realized that Paul would never find it easy going on those occasions when Joanne decided to get out that pool stick and wave it near his head.

But as Paul told one reporter: 'It's not always fine and dandy —it involves two people with very different approaches and attitudes to things—but I think it has a certain thickness to it. We go through periods where we think we're bad parents and periods where we think we see each other only as reflections of ourselves—all the usual jazz. But there's affection and respect and a good deal of humour. We've also been fortunate in that we haven't had to be separated all that much.'

Most of the time she calls him with only mild irony 'my beautiful husband' and he sometimes calls her 'Charley', but don't ask me why. She is always defensive if, for example, snide references are made to that fact that she has an 'Oscar' while Paul has been denied his so often. (She knows too much about Hollywood politics to crow over this anomaly.) When they did a play together, *Baby want a kiss*, as a labour of love for the Actors' Studio as much as anything, and her notices were better than Paul's, she said, 'The critics were just not bright enough to understand his performance.'

Though she is afraid of water, when he wants to go sailing, it's reported, she will still accompany him, even though on one occasion she left the dock in hysterics.

'Ours is not a two-career marriage,' she allegedly told one interviewer. 'My task is to be ready for him, always, whenever he needs me, no matter what his needs might be. I belong to Paul, I'm no good without him. When he's gone, I just want to hide in a hole somewhere. Acting is a career for Paul, but not for me. Being Paul's wife is my career. I don't forget that for an instant. And I never do anything which would let him think I won't be there when he turns to me. He is basically a Victorian husband, but I like that in him.'

According to Paul, Joanne is not only 'the last of the great broads', as he enthusiastically told David Frost, she is, more elegantly, 'the last of a kind of woman who, unfortunately for men, may soon be extinct. She is the woman who keeps me. She makes me happy. But she makes me a little sad at the same time—sad because I don't feel I'll ever be able to give her quite so much happiness as she has given me.'

Filming *Marigolds* tended to be a family affair. With Eli Wallach's talented daughter playing one daughter, Ruth, the other daughter, Matilda, was played by that veteran of *Rachel, Rachel*, Nell Newman under her working name of Nell Potts. (Nellpots was her nickname as a baby.)

Joanne and Paul love working with their children. Lissie had a part in *Sometimes a great notion* and Paul says: 'You have a whole relationship already, you don't have to start building one from scratch. If she hadn't been right for the film we obviously would have used someone else, but she was. Her quality, not as a performer but as a person, carries her through. Put her face on camera and let her twitch away and you've got a scene.'

According to Paul, Nell only accepted the part to make money to subsidize the feeding of her pigeons, rabbits, horse, skunk and five dogs. She is a splendid little horsewoman, as distinctive a figure on the Connecticut show jumping scene as Paul is on the auto circuits.

In Bridgeport, Paul enjoyed the comparative anonymity of working on a closed set in the deconsecrated chapel. Yet when a huge Negro matron in her fifties stepped out of the crowd as we were leaving for downtown Bridgeport to catch the rushes, and greeted Paul with a wide grin, the star picked her up in a bear hug and whirled her round 'Keep the faith, honey,' he said, putting her down and going over to his car. It was like a benediction, and the rapt look in that lady's eyes was worth his friendly gesture. Paul responds to warmth like a huge puppy, and is only constrained when he is in an artificial situation with self-conscious people.

Asked whether he thought it tough to direct his own wife, he said: 'No, I think it's really very easy to direct her. You know the property! I think you know a little better what her outer limits are'. But he added: 'I've never seen her this difficult on the set. Everything conspired against her as a person. I mean she had to wear the drabbest looking clothes. The set was oppressive and tight. There was no room for her to move

167

around and it was hard for her to be alone. She occasionally felt she was out of control and wasn't doing a good job. But I knew that I was getting the right things out of her.

'But then there were also times when I felt I wasn't cutting the mustard and she was. In the end, your training forces you to get up in the morning and put in your ten hours or whatever it takes. Other people would have walked away from it.

'In many cases I wasn't able to help her. But in a way this was good. She wasn't just a simpering old woman. She gave the part a different kind of humanity, her own natural humanity. The interesting thing is this: Joanne, as you know, is a very pretty lady, and she can create an inner atmosphere that is reflected in her movements and in her appearance.

'You know we're making a documentary about this. Some kids at the Yale Cinema School were on the set all the time. Later, after we got through filming, they did an interview with her out in back of our house by the river. To see shots in the movie of her face filled with jowls (she used no make-up in the film), and then months later see such serenity in her face is incredible. That she is able to do that I think is her discipline. She never backs down.

'Well, there was so much venom and a good deal of monster in the character she portrayed—and she brought that home with her at night. That was a pain.'

Here Paul seemed to be explaining the real meaning in the filming of *Marigolds*; as with *Rachel, Rachel* it was Paul's way of paying tribute to his wife in this special way, a laying at her feet the utmost measure of his talent as a stockbroker might press emeralds on his wife as an anniversary gift. It is the extra privilege of artistes to pay tribute to each other, whether or not they're married, as, for example, Nureyev had paid his tribute to Fonteyn. And Paul's devoted direction, and Joanne's responsive skills paid off when the picture was shown to the critics.

'"MARIGOLDS" IS TRIUMPH FOR JOANNE', headlined the New York *Daily News*. The newspaper's critic, Kathleen Carroll, wrote: 'Newman proves that *Rachel, Rachel* was no fluke and that he is a remarkably sensitive film-maker with a deep understanding of human nature. As for Miss Woodward she displays the full force of her acting ability. The film belongs to Miss Woodward. It is her triumph as she delivers abrasively funny lines with deadly precision. Her natural warmth takes some of the curse of Beatrice. She makes her capable of arousing our compassion. And in the end we bleed for not only what she has inflicted on her children but for what life has inflicted on her.'

And Judith Crist redeemed her blind spot for *W.U.S.A.* when in *New York* she wrote: 'Paul Newman not only confirms his abilities as a director but, with a screenplay by Alvin Sargent, transcends the original, enlarging its scope and significance without any conscious 'opening up' of literalizing. . . . The film—as the play never quite succeeded in doing—underlines the contrasts between life and the realities we create for ourselves; it is the chance encounters, the words overheard, the distortion of memory and the stimulation of a young mind and open imagination that are revealed as the moulders of our lives, the forces of our destiny.

'The values have shifted in the filming and in the performances: Joanne Woodward's mother has a shabby beauty, a Stella Dallas vulgarity that gives her past a validity and her present a compassionate appeal. Roberta Wallach, Anne Jackson and Eli's seventeen-year-old daughter, brings a new air of sisterly caring to her discerning portrait of the elder child, and the Newman's thirteen-year-old, with the stage name of Nell Potts, provides stunning silent strength to the role of the younger girl who has found the path to survival. All provide new power and passion to make a "small" play a moving and significant drama.'

'No, Mamma, I don't hate the world,' says Matilda at the end of this searing and brilliant film. And it was in tribute to this work of art that the judges of the following year's Cannes Film Festival awarded Joanne the 'best actress' prize which a degraded Hollywood could not see through all the hysteria surrounding *The Godfather*, plus the other mandatory ritual in-fighting and publicity campaigns.

As Paul put it to me after a private screening, 'Well, everyone worked hard on that one. I think it works its own passage, too, don't you think?'

For me, it had been a rare privilege to watch this delicate work of film art come alive in the ice-cold midnight backwaters of Barnum's Bridgeport.

15

'I'll settle for what I've got'

'Speaking for myself, I can't imagine my life without Joanne and the kids. Everywhere you look you see signs of rapid change, built-in obsolescence, a sense of impermanence. There's too much fragmentation of ideas, ideals, family . . . I'll settle for what I've got.'

Whenever possible, the Newmans like to retreat *en famille* to their home in the converted coaching house near Westport, Connecticut, to recharge their emotional batteries and take professional stock. They love to create the kind of homely domestic atmosphere they would have enjoyed had Paul elected to be a prosperous Midwestern businessman. In other words, to pretend that Hollywood, 'the business', and all the ghastly, negative trappings of stardom didn't exist.

'It's our only real home,' Paul told me towards the end of shooting *Marigolds*. 'It's really very simple,' he said when I asked him how he and Joanne had found the place. 'We're both very impetuous people. When we finally decided to give up our apartment in New York, since the place had become impossible to live in, we thought we'd find somewhere in this part of Connecticut. I don't think we looked at more than four houses. We drove up to this one in the middle of a cold, wintry afternoon and saw a tree house sticking up in the dusk from behind a thick hedgerow that hid the place from the road. It was the tree house that caught our attention.

'We walked into the kitchen and looked at the living-room, and I asked the guy from the real estate office: "How many bedrooms does it have?" We were told, three. We looked at each other and both said: "We'll take it." It was that quick, and it's one of the best decisions we ever made. A family must plant its roots *somewhere* in order to survive. We've planted ours in this house. It's not a Hollywood showplace—it's *home.*'

He added casually, 'Why don't you come on over for lunch on Sunday. We're having a few neighbours coming in, local people, it should be fun.'

Tom Miller, unit publicist for *Marigolds*, had been listening nearby. When Paul went to take up his directorial chores beside the camera, Tom said: 'You're privileged. The *New York Times* has been on to me for months, trying to set up a home interview. That guy guards his home life better'n a watchdog protecting a chain gang.'

Paul Newman slid his legs under the steering wheel of his incongruously small Volkswagen, thumbed the starting button, and as we roared down the driveway of his home and flattened out on the main road into Westport, the rural Connecticut landscape began to slip by like a back projection in a movie, say Ironjaw Kelly on the lam from the baddies in the classic pattern of the chase.

There's an hour to go before the luncheon guests arrive and Joanne has sent her dutiful husband on a shopping mission to collect some fertilizer for the vegetable garden and more fruit for the table. The morning country air was fresh and the sun lay heavy on the meadows, shimmered on stretches of river that flashed in the middle distance.

'Boy,' I said, my eyes on the landscape. 'Now I can understand why you and Joanne chose to settle here rather than stay in a Hollywood mansion. It all adds up.'

Paul chuckled. 'Yeah, it's marvellous out here all the year round. Here you get the seasons, while all you get in Hollywood is smog.' Another chuckle. 'In any case they tell me Hollywood is slowly slipping into the Pacific.'

He was obviously in his element, relaxed and talkative, the weekend family man after the rush and pressures of filming at all hours of day and night in the streets, slums, and the claustrophobic makeshift set in nearby Bridgeport. Joanne had told me of his ability to 'cut off' and concentrate fully, with deep involvement on whatever he was doing at the moment.

The countryside was widening out, almost a parody of a picture postcard of traditional New England, an admixture of

Puritan America and Peyton Place with its Dutch barns, white wooden churches, clapboard houses, farmyards, stables providing an historical background to the highly contemporary humans dotted on the scene: weekend drivers, family picnics, barefoot college kids from nearby Yale in hot-pants or cut-short Levis. Occasionally, some old-fashioned farming types straight out of Eugene O'Neill.

Paul Newman handles fast cars with the exact skill of Lester Piggott steering a thoroughbred towards the finishing post at Newmarket, and I couldn't resist reintroducing the subject of his enthusiasm for racing autos all over the American circuits.

'I don't want to sound sort of mystical about this, Paul,' I ventured as we carommed around a bend, 'but I can't help wondering why you insist on hurtling around the tracks at a hundred and fifty miles an hour, or more when you've got it made as an actor, when everything is going so good for you as a director, a tycoon, a power in the movie business, and with just about the most successful marriage and home life in Hollywood history.'

The actor covered a quarter of a mile in a few seconds before answering.

'Aw, don't let's exaggerate this,' he said good-naturedly. 'It's the safest kind of racing driving you can do. It's not that I'm driving Grand Prix formula cars; I'm not quick enough for professional auto-racing.'

His face now wore that stern, unbudgeable expression that has made many a movie tycoon bite the dust. 'You see, I really enjoy it. The thing is to find your level and try not to go in over your head. I've just had my own racing car built and I'm in my first year of racing over the north-eastern amateur circuit. I'm a little long in the tooth to start that, but it's the most relaxing thing I've ever experienced.'

'*Relaxing?*'

Paul nodded, popped some chewing gum in his mouth. 'Look at it this way. Joanne goes to the ballet, I go to the auto track.' After a pause, humorously: 'That's one way to make marriage work.'

173

We covered a mile or so in silence, then he said something that would have sent a few Hollywood money guys bananas. 'If I get good enough by the end of this year, I'll race something harder next year. It has its hazards, I know, but if I could drive competitively with the big time professionals I would dump this movie business so fast it would make your head spin. *Just out . . . but quick.*'

The movie business can relax. They are both too firmly hooked to what Paul calls 'the community experience' of making films they believe to be worth while—the creative rather than the tacky business aspects—ever to give up their work. But they aim high, are serious artistes, even if there are times when the wheelers and dealers, petty crooks, musclemen, union hustlers, dishearten them and make them want 'out'.

But nobody—not even Joanne, who at first hated the idea of his driving at speed—can stop Paul from taking off for his auto racing club, a short drive from his home, whenever he can find the time. This man with millions of fans is himself a fan of British racing ace Graham Hill.

'I met him when we were filming *Winning*,' Paul told me, 'and I sent him a note. We started corresponding regularly. I'd trade my job with his any day, if I were good enough. Some fellows dream of going on an African safari. I've always wanted to be a racing driver. Being an amateur is the next best thing.'

Summer was forcing its way into the fresh New England day; the sun was pushing the temperature towards the eighties as we pulled up beside a rustic supermarket specializing in the sale of fruit and vegetables and gardening equipment.

The Volkswagen with the registration plate marked 'Connecticut WC 953' is widely recognized within a twenty-mile radius of the Newman residence, but the reserved locals tend on the whole to leave him alone, respecting his privacy as they cherish their own. Sometimes they shake their heads in puzzlement as the tiny car streaks by at phantom speeds, not realizing that its owner has installed a souped-up Porsche racing engine under its superstructure.

It's still not the usual movie star's car, but then Paul has consistently bucked his 'star image' for many years, and his genuine diffidence is protected all around his home town. Now as we entered the market, with its aroma of fresh apples and stacks of giant pumpkins, the staff carefully played down the occasion.

Mostly the talk was of country matters. 'Howdy, Mist' Newman, how are your tomatoes coming along?' 'Say, was that last batch of fertilizer okay?' Inevitably, the movie he's currently shooting is mentioned, but it is in a family context. 'Hey, how's the picture coming along, Mist' Newman? A niece of mine in Bridgeport was tellin' me th' other day how her front porch was used in one of the scenes. She sure was thrilled to pieces.'

Sacks of fertilizer are dumped at his feet. Paul prowls among the rows of fruit stalls, prodding here, sniffing there.

'What do you think of these?' Paul asks, handing me for inspection an apple the size of a baby's head. 'I'll bet you don't get them this size back in England,' he adds, with a touch of Yankee chauvinism, and, of course, he's right. But then they don't grow crisp red Worcesters or Cox's pippins that rattle like castanets in Connecticut. The girl at the cash register rings up his money and hands him a few cents change. It's all so casually done, so friendly . . . there's not an autograph hound in sight. 'Thank you, Mister Newman.' The smile is pleasant, yet formal. 'Come again.'

I pick up a couple of heavy bags of fertilizer, Paul gathers up the rest of his purchases. Nobody rushes to open doors, help carry things to the car. This is New England, not Hollywood. Great.

Back at the wheel, Paul pops another stick of gum into his mouth and heads for home. Once again the incredibly lovely New England scenery unfurls and I venture on to the subject of marriage. I say that Paul and Joanne are an example to all couples, their marriage a Rock of Gibraltar in the prevailing matrimonial wasteland.

'Oh, I don't know,' Paul drawls cautiously, his eyes on the ribboning road. 'It's impossible to make blanket statements about a thing as personal as a marriage. I would say this though. If you've got a good one going it's worth working at it.'

What, I ask, is the most important factor in the preservation of a marriage?

'Again it's hard to generalize,' Paul replies. 'I've repeatedly said that for people with as little in common as Joanne and myself, we have an uncommonly good marriage. We are actors, we make pictures—and that's about *all* we have in common. Maybe that's enough. Wives *shouldn't* feel obligated to accompany their husbands to a ball game, husbands *do* look a bit silly attending morning coffee breaks with the neighbourhood wives when most men are out at work. Husbands and wives *should* have separate interests, cultivate different sets of friends —and not impose one upon the other.'

'What about a sense of humour?'

'Sure, that's obviously an asset. But then so is a sense of recognition of each other's individuality, a respect for the other's occasional need for privacy. You can't spend a lifetime breathing down each other's necks.' Pause for thought.

'It can never be one long endless honeymoon. You *have* to test each other's individuality.' Paul gave another of his characteristic chuckles, as a thought struck him. 'There's nothing like a good fight from time to time—it's Nature's broom. Joanne and I have had some pretty spectacular hassles at times. It's necessary for two individuals to be able to stand up to each other in argument and debate, in agreeing to be different.

'Everything is changing so fast. The institute of marriage— like most things these days—is under attack. I don't think one can make long-term plans any more. Or make judgments about things being good, or being bad, any more. Once people develop a throwaway mentality it affects personal relationships, too. Joanne and I were born just before everything became fragmented, before the big scientific acceleration became obvious.

'If impermanence works for some people, fine. But speaking for myself, I can't imagine my life without Joanne and the kids. Everywhere you look you see signs of rapid change, built-in obsolescence, a sense of impermanence. There's too much fragmentation of ideas, ideals, family . . . I'll settle for what I've got.'

Joanne is standing at the front door, a tiny apron tied around her slim waist. Tight sweater, hair tousled, halo'd by sunlight . . . the perfect picture of the kind of wife men happily hurry home to. Looking at her it's easy to understand what Paul meant when he once said: 'I know this is going to sound corny, but there's no reason to roam. I have steak at home, why should I go out for a hamburger?'

As it happens, Joanne is in the middle of cooking hamburgers on the stove in her roomy kitchen. When I tell her that I woke up late and haven't eaten she quickly scrambles up some eggs. Paul hands me a tankard of beer as cold as the bottom of Loch Ness. As usual, his refrigerator is packed with bottles of beer. In fact there are two refrigerators, side by side, in the kitchen. The other is filled with large glass tankards with thick handles, their sides and tops rimed with powdered frost.

Informality is the keynote of Newman hospitality. Honest and outspoken themselves to a unique degree, they assume that anyone admitted to their household will be equally direct. In fact, it would be difficult to be otherwise. The Newmans can detect a false note, a phony move, with the precision of a geiger counter passing over uranium.

I take my beer and scrambled eggs over to the back porch where I'm introduced to Joanne's mother and step-father. They're up on a visit from the south, a friendly, unstuffy couple remarkably young in spirit. Looking at Joanne's mother, it is easy to see from where the star inherited her own outgoing warmth, her unforced interest in others. I remembered that party in Hollywood when Joanne had told me how, as a child, her mother had taken her to the première of *Gone with the wind*, in Atlanta, Georgia, setting of the big battle scene in the old movie.

'Oh, yes, will I ever forget taking her!' Joanne's mother exclaimed. 'She was so excited, she kept jumping up and down in her seat. Whenever Vivien Leigh, as Scarlett O'Hara, came

177

on the screen, Joanne would point her finger at her and tell me in a stage whisper: "I shall be a great actress one day." You know something? She was so convincing I was ready to believe her even then, though she wasn't anywhere near ten years old. She was always gifted with a vivid imagination, but highly intelligent with it. Oh, here she is. I hope you don't mind my reminiscing about your childhood, Joanne.'

Joanne did not mind. Considering the way the house was filling up, Joanne struck me as a remarkably unflappable hostess. Hovering close by, of course, was the Newman's equally jolly, unflappable English house-keeper, Duffy. This paragon, who does all her shopping on a motor-cycle, is an expert at moving the entire Newman family at short notice from California to Connecticut, from Spain to Ireland, wherever their film commitments—or holidays, or both—take them.

I never did discover how many of the Newman children were in the house at any particular time. Once a guest has been made to feel at home he is expected to roam about at will. Paul's son Scott, then twenty, was away for the weekend, I knew, but a charming teenager could have been Susie or Stephie, children from the marriage to Jackie Witte, but everyone—including neighbours—mingled so informally it would have been a drag to sort out who was who—unlike most Hollywood gatherings this was a real family gathering.

Nell, Joanne's eldest daughter, was of course easy to spot as she wandered in from the riding stables, her blonde hair streaming from her black velvet jockey cap. Her feats of horsewomanship are legendary on the show jumping circuit in New England, and her remarkably sensitive performance in *Marigolds* belonged to another world.

It is almost as if Nell has inherited her father's gift to departmentalize, to live out each separate aspect of existence without reference to any other. In the studio with the camera on, she was a superb actress. Now, in riding togs, she was every inch the young horsewoman. Even without the Newmans as her parents, Nell would be going places. With them, she's earmarked for an enchanted life. Nothing can spoil her now, she is too well insulated against bad vibes.

'Yes, she's an attractive girl,' Joanne admitted to me without a trace of maternal gush, 'but she has a long way to go before she becomes an actress. Still, she has the right instincts. She doesn't let the camera frighten her, put her off, she's not excessively self-conscious when being filmed. Some actresses take years to achieve camera compatibility. Nell, I'm glad to say, takes it all in her stride. But if you want to get along with her, talk about show jumping and martingales; steer clear of *cinema verité* and zoom lenses.'

The house is open plan, rooms leading into one another with a minimum of closed doors. I found Clea, Joanne's youngest daughter, in a playroom surrounded by toys and books while Paul was leaning in the open doorway, a glass of beer in his hand, talking about the upcoming Indianapolis 500-Mile Race with a young married couple, local people unconnected with showbiz, who had dropped in as casually as the rest of the people in the house.

But if the house is largely on open plan to guests, there is one hideaway to which only a few people have ever been admitted. Taking a key from a rack in the kitchen, Paul took me by the arm and, with a conspiratorial look, said: 'Follow me, and I'll show you my real retreat.' I followed him out through the front door and along a winding path which led to a separate building massively perched on the steep banks of the fast-flowing trout stream.

'Nobody comes in here without my say-so,' he told me mysteriously as he turned the lock and pushed the door open. 'After you,' he grinned, and I stepped into a vast, high-vaulted split-level room, the two floors linked by wide steps, a quiet hideaway designed for solitary thought or concentrated reading or creative work.

This is the inner sanctum to which Paul Newman retreats whenever he wishes to read important scripts, try out passages of dialogue, or simply catch up with the current newspapers. A slow, thoughtful reader, Paul has always needed absolute quiet when he is trying to assimilate words.

Books, magazines, scripts, were piled in neat stacks on massive shelves. Correspondence was carefully filed away, with letters from President Kennedy, Martin Luther King, and some of the most important figures of our time nestling alongside letters from unknown social workers, civil rights organizers, obscure teachers and professors, struggling writers and actors, and the more literate fans who have made points in their letters which Paul thought worth keeping.

There is absolute quiet in this room apart from the babbling of the stream as it rushes, out of sight, below the big window. From this window you have a view of tangled greenery on the opposite bank, a tree or two, but nothing dramatic to disturb the flow of one's thinking or distract the eye.

Typical of Paul's rather sardonic sense of humour, I thought, was a framed letter on one of the walls—the only one, among so many collector's items, thus honoured. It was from the chairman of the Jack Daniels whisky distillery, apologizing profusely for the fact that Paul had complained about the quality of the contents of a bottle of this honoured tipple sold to him in a bar.

'You wait,' I said. 'One day there'll be your own, personal Oscar standing in this room.'

Paul shrugged. 'Does it really matter all that much? I'm not counting on it, one way or the other.'

I liked his matter-of-fact reaction to my rather brash observation. Hollywood remains incorrigibly vindictive to its unrepentant iconoclasts, no matter how much they are admired by the rest of the world. But Newman is in good company. Griffiths, Chaplin, Welles, Brando, George C. Scott. It's virtually an honourable tradition—there are plenty of yes-men who aren't eating, anyway.

Reluctantly, I followed Paul back into the garden; as he turned the key on his 'sanctuary' he asked: 'Well, what do you think of my hideout?'

'Wow,' I said. 'A man could write *War and peace* in there and feel no pain at all.'

Paul smiled as he pocketed the key. 'Come on, we better get back. I've promised some people a game of tennis. Care to watch?'

Leaving the tennis players, I wandered to the back of the

house and, clambering down the slippery banks of the stream, sat down on a cluster of rocks. The sunlight shone crystal bright on the rushing water as I tried to sort out my impressions of Paul Newman, seeking to define the man behind the giant image.

What had I learned from my weeks of close observation of this man? He seemed to operate on so many different levels of being. Which most closely approximated the 'real' Paul Newman? Where did personality end and performance take over? How, above all, had the cheerfully extrovert campus hero from Cleveland achieved the metamorphic dimensions of *tragic* hero? How had a 'square' become one of the dominant figures of the contemporary American screen?

Actor, skilled director, household name, whose life-sized posters sold briskly in suburban supermarkets as well as trendy boutiques, he is an idol who commands critical respect.

'He works hard at whatever he does,' I remember technician Bob Ruscoe, telling me over a beer between location shots in the Bridgeport ghetto. Bob had worked for Newman on *Rachel, Rachel,* and 'on the first day, Paul called the crew together and laid it on the line. "Look, fellers," he told us, "I'm a new boy at directing. There's a lot of you who have been on this side of the camera for a great number of years. I'm not aiming to tell anyone their business. You're all professionals and I'm aiming to do a professional job. Making movies is a co-operative effort, and I shall truly value the co-operation of each one of you working on this picture. So let's go, shall we, ladies and gentlemen? Let's *all* try and make this as good a goddam movie as we possibly can." '

Paul never throws his weight around. He doesn't bully people or 'pull rank' on them, preferring to get the best out of them by assuming they *are* the best at whatever their jobs happen to be.

Watching him direct Joanne can be an embarrassing experience. There are moments of such great intensity generated between them that the onlooker comes close to feeling like a Peeping Tom.

This was most noticeable on the tiny bedroom set designed

for *Marigolds*, in a tottering slummy house in Bridgeport. This room was so cramped that even the camera crew could barely squeeze in. Paul allowed me to watch, however, while he coaxed Joanne through highly emotional scenes.

He must have infinite patience, and powers of concentration, for I know of few directors who could have worked under such claustrophobic conditions without losing their cool and clearing all visitors from the set.

In the end it was I who,tiptoed silently away. Paul had created such an intimate atmosphere I felt I was peering into a private bedroom. No wonder Joanne says she prefers Paul to any other director. If another director had played so closely, so intimately, on her emotions, Paul might have been tempted to punch him on the nose.

And yet . . . Paul, though unquestionably the dominant partner in this unique relationship, happily accepts the fact that if she chose to do so, Joanne could twist him round one finger. Instead, she supplies the feminine 'mirror' that reflects and enhances his stolid, sure masculinity. As one of the girl assistant directors whispered after one of these emotional scenes: 'They're made for each other. Separate them, and they'd be like fish without water.'

'Paul *likes* women,' Joanne told me. 'And I like men. I like their company and conversation. I like to listen to their ideas. Yes, I'm a good listener. Men are the real dreamers of this world, to them dreams *are* real. Oh, women also dream, but they're practical dreams. Yes, I like men. Creative men, men with ideas.'

She frequently enthuses about Gore Vidal, not everybody's cup of java. She's extremely loyal. When Vidal was being criticized for his bitchiness to Jacqueline Onassis, shortly after the widow Kennedy married the Greek tycoon, Joanne was noticeably at pains to be seen in his company and raved about his writings. On this particular Sunday afternoon, she told me how much she was looking forward to seeing him in Italy during her vacation.

Unkind people have remarked of the Newmans that you only have to belong to a minority group—as a Negro, Indian, activist, homosexual—to immediately win their interest. Actually, they are too shrewd to be taken in by the surface label tagged onto anyone, but it is true that they have an immediate and instinctive compassion for the underdog, and woe betide anyone rash enough to play the reactionary in their presence.

Yet, generally, the joint Newman charisma carries them through the most awkward situations, and they seem to appeal to most types and sexes. Men feel they will get at least a sympathetic hearing of their problems from the intelligent, articulate Joanne, while women see in Paul the strong yet sensitive man who can instinctively sympathize with them, and even offer a chunky shoulder on which to cry.

Once Joanne was telling me about a portable reading lamp which Paul had given her. 'It means I can sit in the back of a car at night and catch up with my mail and even write letters,' she said, adding with childlike delight, 'it's one of the nicest presents Paul has ever given me.' A far cry, this, from the yachts and jewels Richard Burton used to shower upon Elizabeth Taylor during their starcrossed marriage.

The compatibility of the Newmans is a joy to watch. When I commented that Joanne struck me most favourably as the kind of wife who doesn't immediately squawk when she sees her husband reaching out for a can of beer, Paul grimaced.

'No-o-o,' he admitted cautiously, 'but she does carry this long pointed pool cue around the house and when I reach for one too many she hits me over the head with it.'

Not often, though, I'd imagine. Especially in recent years. There was a time, however, when the pressures of the business placed him in serious danger of becoming like one of those crazy, mixed-up Tennessee Williams characters he and Brando so often played in their early days in Hollywood.

Looking back at that period, Paul ruefully told me: 'In those days there was at times a serious problem of moderation. Sure there was a monkey on my back and its name was booze. If things were going well I would drink to celebrate. If I was in the doldrums I'd drink to get out of them. There was a lot of booze floating around in those days, long before the psychedelic revolution and turning on with pot became a national pastime.

183

There probably still is, if you look hard enough in the right quarter, but that's not my scene any more. But in the 'fifties some of the guys I ran with were real hard drinkers.'

Paul recalled: 'I used to fill our tumblers with ice cubes and then pour gin up to the brim of each glass. The trick was to drink the gin before the ice cubes melted. Then we'd set up another round of the same—what a way to go!'

I asked him if he still subscribed to the philosophy that drinking was good for certain types of creativity, or at certain periods when an artiste was sorting out his talent and finding his style.

He said darkly: 'It would even help some politicians I know. Not the hard stuff, though, they just might go straight back and push the button while at a drinking peak. But beer, yes, beer is fine. Yes, beer is okay. This applies to many artistes, too, and certain actors as well. But to rot your insides away with the hard stuff—the deterioration that goes on as a result of that kind of drinking—no-o-o-o, I don't think so. It can't help a talent, it can only debilitate it.'

The tennis game was over when I left my rocky perch beside the trout stream and strolled back into the house. The younger Newman girls, Melissa and Clea, were watching television, and as Paul, unprompted, handed me another tall glass mug of cold beer his eyes momentarily strayed towards his daughters. Catching my eye, he said with a deprecating smile: 'This is what turns me on—do-mesticity.' He seemed to be sending himself up and at the same time talking seriously.

I asked him what he thought of the future prospects for the young people in this Age of Aquarius.

'Kids,' Paul ruminated, shaking his head slowly. 'It's a fantastic time for the young. In some ways they have less imposed upon them than my generation did—at least, in terms of the American dream of two cars in the garage and keeping up with the Joneses. They are less acquisitive, property no longer has such importance, and they're less inhibited.

'Yet they have other things imposed on them that are far harsher than anything we had to face. Things are no longer clearly defined in black and white, good and bad . . . there's this acceleration of change, things are moving so fast, it's enough to drive them all crazy.

'Change occurs with such rapidity,' he went on. 'That's why people have such a short attention-span. America is a country of fads. It's beginning to happen in Britain too. Civil rights one minute. Politics the next. Flower power . . . remember that? Jesus freaks. Skinheads. Hell's Angels, Hairies. Mods. The institutions rise and fall with such rapidity. Goals are set up and three or four years later they are considered to be unworthy. Ideals become obsolete overnight.

'It's incredible, the rate of acceleration that's going on all over the world today. The kids have got to keep adjusting, keep sorting things out for themselves. Throwaway bottles throwaway relationships . . . it's wild.

'Freaky, as the kids say.'

Yet in the increasing bedlam of American life, Paul and Joanne appear to have achieved a measure of stability, and moderation, which makes them a tower of strength in the eyes of their less fortunate friends. They symbolize certain values which seem to be crumbling in the 'now' world. Pot, LSD, good trips, bad trips . . . that's just jargon to them.

Paul remembers the old-fashioned, boozy world of Bogart and Errol Flynn, but his children are tuned in to the sounds of terminal rock and campus scepticism . . . the symbolic rejection of values, more subdued, less overt, than it was in the 'sixties, but an ever-present atonal humming of something in the wind.

'You know something?' Paul smiles. 'I've discovered that if I don't drink beer before six o'clock I lose three pounds a day. For the first two days, that is. I've kept my weight level at between one hundred and sixty-five and one hundred and sixty-seven pounds—under twelve stone—consistently for the past six or seven years.'

That's quite an achievement for an ageing idol who might easily have gone the boozy Hollywood way of Flynn, Bogart, and all the other hell-raisers. Instead, he married Joanne and grew up.

185

Psychologically the most 'balanced' actor I have ever known, he has not overcompensated in the other direction and become a health food nut, a religious proselyte, a compulsive banner-carrier. His political views are widely known. He campaigned extensively for McCarthy in '68, and for Joe Duffy, who ran unsuccessfully for the senate in '70, and also for Pete McClosky in California. He did fifty-three speeches for McClosky in three days, and campaigned for zero population growth. 'Hah, that's a laugh for a guy who's got six children.'

As he explained, 'What's happened to me in a political sense is that I've gotten tired. Actually, I think, say, Jane Fonda is probably a little more radical than I am, although not all that much. I suppose the main thing she and I have in common is that we are both fighters for certain causes, but at a particular point I got tired, and it'll be interesting to find out if she does, too. It'll be interesting to see how long her fire lasts. Unless, of course, she takes it up as a vocation.

'Jane's committed herself to an action position a lot more than I have, and she's also invested a lot more of her time than me. Trying to have visibility without being visible has always been my impulse. The main distinction between Jane and me, I think, is that she enjoys it—she enjoys that hassle. Me, I never enjoyed the hassle. Making speeches, shaking hands, dealing with the Press—it's all a pain in the ass.

'Which is why I wouldn't ever get into politics. It would drive me *wild*. It would blow my marriage and drive me crazy. If Joanne suddenly found herself in a position where she had to throw one of those fancy Washington bashes, she would—well, that'd be the end of the relationship. She'd say, "Well, you're on your own, kid." '

No, much as he loathes the negative side of 'the business' he is happier fighting for his right to shoot a good script, or play a role that he feels is right for him, than parading through the Washington circus. Congressman Newman? Senator Newman? 'No way, keed. *No way*.'

It was time for me to leave. The sun was lowering, the tree house was casting a shadow several times its size across the cooling lawn. A car was on its way to take Joanne to New York for a gala evening of ballet with Nureyev and Fonteyn. She would not travel in movie-queen style; a local car rental firm was good enough for her.

Paul planned to work alone behind locked doors in his retreat beside the river. The children would mind their own business, supervised by that ever-watchful treasure from England, Duffy. This house of easy hospitality of really *gracious* living, was creaking down for the night.

My own rented car waited at the front door. We shook hands, I told Paul I would be drifting in and out of the Bridgeport location for another day or two, and then return to England and get off his back.

'You're not on my back, Charles,' he said soberly. 'You never were, it was nice having you around.'

My last impression was of seeing them standing closely together on their doorstep, waving as my car rolled slowly down the drive, when Joanne dropped something, a purse or trinket. Paul swiftly bent down and scooped it up, then as he returned the object he kissed Joanne lightly on the cheek. They turned back into the house, Paul's arm resting casually on Joanne's hip.

Even the greatest actors in creation can't fake that kind of body language.

Envoi

Hyped on Hemingway

'That bear was the biggest ham I ever came across in the whole of my acting career. He only liked me for my tootsy rolls. By golly, he stole everything from me, including the film.'

Where does he go from here?

Paul Newman from time to time threatens to chuck everything and become a private citizen. We have heard this before from other actors. Brando is always threatening never to make another movie. Elizabeth Taylor, Steve McQueen, Robert Redford, Kirk Douglas, have all at some time told the present writer what they think of 'the business' and how they will turn their backs on it and live happily ever after.

Sinatra even got so far as official retirement, and I personally was witness to the resulting bottled-up frustration that ensued as he drifted from bar to bar, toy playmate to drinking buddy, distraction after distraction, in the aimless emptiness of Palm Springs, the 'golfing capital of the world'. As Sinatra put it after he recorded his first come-back album, 'I just figured I'd do some work. No fun trying to hit a golf ball at eight at night.'

Paul Newman, family man, reluctant intellectual and concerned democrat has more resources than some to fall back upon, should he ever elect to go into semi-retirement. But this will never happen. He's too involved in the creative process, as well as the technical and business aspects of film-making. With Joanne, he's genuinely interested in writing, acting, and the artistic presentation of a dramatic concept in terms of film.

Though frequently dissatisfied with his own performances, and quickly bored with the ancillary fatuities of production, Paul is too committed to throw it all away and settle for cultivating his garden. There is also enough of the 'ham' in him to keep him in front of the cameras for a long time to come.

Discussing Newman over lunch with a friend, the London critic Tom Hutchinson, I goaded this perceptive afficionado of Film into a personal assessment of Paul Newman as an actor, and later asked permission to quote the following random jotting of this conversation.

'He's a star,' Tom Hutchinson observed, 'in the sense that he illumines the screen whenever he comes into vision, igniting it with his own particular magical fire: the kind that women like but men don't mind. Where he seems to me lacking is in his inability ever to seem to want to reach beyond his own capabilities; to attempt the big gamble in terms of a characterization that will stretch him just that bit further: beyond the dimensions that he—and we—already know.

'The only time I ever felt him move beyond that self-imposed limitation was in *Cool hand Luke*; for the rest he has kept moving, but jogging, in the kind of Tennessee Williams' territory which he inhabits with, strangely, a kind of cosiness which always runs marvellously counter to the inherent perversions of that landscape.

'What I'm really saying is that I want Newman to surprise me, just once. I could never imagine him playing Hamlet, for instance; I could imagine Rod Steiger playing Lear. The impression I have is of a nice guy, too security-minded for his own talent's good. Maybe I'm reaching at the moon; I wish that *he* would some time.'

My own hope, especially in view of the rapport he enjoys with John Huston, is that he might one day tackle a portrayal of Ernest Hemingway in his last years. This would answer the criticism that he is satisfied to remain inside his skin too closely for his own comfort. It would certainly stretch him, but it would also take him into a dimension in which he is perfectly at home.

By this, I mean that dimension of the artiste *in extremis* which he knows only too well from his encounters with Tennessee Williams, and his understanding of such characters as Norman Mailer, James Dean, Brando, Clift, and poets like Harte Crane.

Newman is a writer manqué who could worm his way into

the skin of Hemingway as easily as he has managed to move through the worlds of Faulkner and Williams, and the pool-room hell-holes of Eddie Felson.

When this was recently mooted at a conference in Holly-wood, the proposer of the motion was told, 'Yeah, but you're hyped on Hemingway. Do the kids care any more what happened to that rumdum?' More important, Paul Newman knows and cares. He could fit into a dozen Hemingway moulds. There's Colonel Cantwell, of *Across the river and into the trees*. He is still not too old for flashbacks to the era of *A moveable feast*. He could play the Hemingway of the last years in Cuba or the wartime mariner of *Islands in the stream*. Colonel Cantwell, Huston, Venice . . . what a combination that would be!

Again it is possible to see an older Newman moving into the territory once dominated by Paul Muni, perhaps even starring in a revival of the story of Emil Zola told with contemporary hindsight. He could play Beethoven, Barnum, Buffalo Bill. Who knows what scripts and stage plays and novels are not already in the melting pot as potential vehicles for his mature talent?

With his increasing stature as a director, it will be a problem to find time for all the parts that will be available to Paul, crying out for his uniquely personalized interpretations. Nor is it too late for him and Brando to get together and make a picture on a subject close to their compatible thinking, shot on location, perhaps, on Brando's island retreat off Tahiti?

When Paul and Huston worked together on *The life and times of Judge Roy Bean*, the two rebels had the time of their lives on the desert location in and around Tucson, Arizona. Huston described the picture as 'a romp, a lark' and spent as much time fussing over a temperamental mountain bear and a tame lion as he did over his star. Paul was encouraged for the first time to grow a grizzly beard to blend in with his pal the bear!

Unlike most films where a set is built and used throughout the picture without any major changes, the key set for *Roy Bean* was changed almost daily. The story opens with the future town of Langtry, Texas, consisting of a lone saloon out on the dusty plains. As the story progresses, the saloon is joined by one building after another until a sizeable community has developed, complete with oil-well rigs. Then after all this heroic effort by the construction crew, the entire town goes up in flames as the climax of the picture.

Bruno the bear stole every scene in which he appeared. 'That bear was the biggest ham I ever came across in the whole of my acting career,' Paul told me. 'He only liked me for my tootsy rolls. By golly, he stole everything from me, including the film.'

Though the critics were lukewarm about the overall effect of the film, it marked a breakthrough for Paul, with Huston's direction giving his performance just that extra bite that Huston extracted from Bogart many years before.

Paul certainly was happy enough to work with Huston again in *The mackintosh man*, once more something of a romp with the director in his element organizing a chase through the Irish bogs. In spite of Huston's known eccentricities, he never allows the grotesqueries of his pixie vision to diminish Paul's acting efforts and the two nonconformists make a great team, no matter what their detractors say to the contrary.

Paul also made *Pocket money* with Lee Marvin and himself starred in and directed *Sometimes a great notion*, based on the novel by Ken Kesey. It was during the filming of *Marigolds* in Connecticut that I chanced on a review in the *Observer* by George Melly of *Sometimes a great notion* which, in Britain, was released under the title, *Never give an inch*.

'If John Wayne had acted the Henry Fonda part,' Mr Melly complained, 'and it had been directed by, say, Mark Rydell, it would be easy to deplore its union-busting bias, praise its tight narrative line and excellent acting, and write it off as a well-made, enjoyable if deplorably right-wing film. As it's directed by Paul Newman, however, this becomes more of a problem. Newman after all made *W.U.S.A.*, a flawed but interesting parable about pop-fascism in America. Has he simply miscalculated the presentation of his intentions here? Does he, while deploring fascism, admire conservative individualism and abhor collective action? Has he had an overnight conversion to the right? There is enough in the film to suggest the first explanation, but it would be interesting to hear from him what he was aiming at.'

Since the critic had entirely missed the irony of the story and obviously did not know that American unions are as different from British ones as chalk is from cheese, and that Americans can find it possible to admire individual gutsy action within a rigid social framework, I raised this point with Paul in the expectation of hearing a reasoned defence of what, after all, was merely a busy critic's aberration.

All he said was, 'You can't win 'em all, can you?' placing Mr Melly's fulminations into their proper context.

John Huston has remarked that films of his which were viciously attacked when first shown, have over the years accumulated the dignity of works of art. So who's to worry? You certainly *can't* win 'em all and perhaps that is what makes the performing arts such an exhilarating, if chancey, enterprise. The start of each new film is a Columbus-like venture into unknown territory.

In addition to the films he does for others at a million dollars each plus a percentage of the profits, and those he packages through the Newman-Foreman company, in 1969 with Barbra Streisand, Sidney Poitier, Steve McQueen (and later Dustin Hoffman), Paul formed a company titled First Artists—some fifty years after the Fairbanks and Chaplin got together to form United Artists.

Partly financed with three million dollars of European money from City of London merchant bankers like Keyser Ullmann, Slater Walker and the Crown Agents, the company's shares have had a chequered career and it recently planned to diversify into music publishing to boost the month by month earnings.

It is a gamble which yet has to pay off, despite the enormous success of such ventures as Steve McQueen's *The getaway*, directed by that genius, Sam Peckinpah. As a movie company unlikely to complete more than two films in any financial year, the gambling element is enormous. One flop in twenty can be carried; one flop in two would be a disaster. The appointment of veteran film producer Jay Kanter as president of the company should help to bring in outside projects to keep First Artists flowing.

Whatever his involvement with the business aspects of production and direction may become, there is little question of Paul Newman's personal popularity as he approaches his fiftieth birthday. In one of his more recent films he again teamed up with his old sundance buddy, Robert Redford, and the picture they appeared in, *The sting*, was enormously successful. The sting refers to the underworld description of the payoff of a confidence trick.

Redford plays a naïve young crook who falls foul of a big gangster—Robert Shaw—and runs to Paul, a seasoned conman, to help him work an elaborate con on the big man. Set in the Chicago of the late 'thirties, it has a sharp, Runyonesque period flavour underscored by the musical setting based on the early rags of Scott Joplin.

'Two hours of better entertainment it would be hard to obtain,' enthused the London *Evening Standard*'s highly discriminating Alexander Walker. 'In his button-down cap, waisted jacket and big wide grin, Redford is perfectly paired off against Newman's frayed-at-the-cuff expertise; and the two actors somehow bring each other up to a pitch in ways neither really seems to achieve alone or in other company in other films . . . *everything* is worth paying to see in *The sting*.'

The sting was well received everywhere, and the pairing of Newman and Redford as freewheeling quasi-criminals won the seal of approval from world audiences: the kind of approval necessary for those quick returns needed for reinvestment in other worthwhile projects by independent—and independently minded—actors determined to work out their own artistic salvation free from the 'advice and guidance' of the financial conglomerates. Wherever *The sting* was booked for a week's run (with options on an extended run if the Newman-Redford magic drew record attendance figures, as was the case with *Butch Cassidy and the Sundance kid*), the run was inevitably extended from four weeks to three months. From Birmingham, Alabama, to Birmingham, England, George Roy Hill's masterful direction of this exercise in the lighter side of conman-ship, Chicago-style, thirties vintage, hit a responsive chord on many levels all through 1974.

The idea of a handful of freelance conmen banding together against a big gang boss and his henchmen had an added (un-intended) piquancy at the very moment when the political soap opera of Watergate was moving inexorably toward its banal final fade. Like the shenanigans in Washington, the movie teetered dangerously on the razor's edge of nostalgia for past certainties and concern over present moral ambiguities.

As John Simon, writing in the *New Yorker*, put it, 'This is one of those precarious movies in which murder must look absurd or funny—except in one case, where it must be taken seriously —and it is to Hill's and his scenarist's, David S. Ward's, credit that they just about carry off this colossally queasy task. It must be said right away that certain plot elements in these cinematic rodomontades are bound to be unbelievable; the question is merely to what extent the film makers, con artists in their own right, can carry off the caper without allowing us time to unsuspend our disbelief. The main tools at their dis-posal are surprise, wit, credibility in trappings and details, fast pacing, and good performances. *The sting* possesses them all.'

The background score by Marvin Hamlisch, adapted from Scott Joplin rags, was an extra bonus, contributing to 'the bush telegraph of the ear' (showbiz jargon to parallel musi-cally with 'word-of-mouth') as effectively as *Raindrops keep falling on my head* had helped to promote *Butch Cassidy*, spread-ing the good word with tinkling riffs that lingered in the mind long after the story details became as blurred as mislaid holiday snapshots.

The sting also had a more clearly recognisable target for the anarchical antics of the chief protagonists, something more substantial than the diffused—and toward the end self-de-feating—activities of Butch and the Kid. This target was magnificently enfleshed and slyly rounded out by the sardonic, understated performance of the British actor Robert Shaw. A deep, dark horse, Shaw has a wit as sharp, an intellect as acute, as those of Newman and Redford, though it's subdued, camouflaged in the best deadpan British manner.

Cinematographer Robert Surtees, working with remarkable ease in color, not his favorite medium, helped considerably to flesh out this strong counter-performance of Shaw's by setting him against massive, club smoking-room decor and working close to the grainy structure of this performer's strong-jawed features in a simulation of rotogravure. It was left to the steely glitter of Shaw's eyes, those controled windows of the soul, to semaphore to audiences that this 'mark' wasn't as thick in the skull as the other two would have us believe.

That this dumb ox consistently came over strongly in his scenes, an Americanised Gibralter, even in final defeat, is a triumph of a flint-sharp actor's mind over gritty, hostile material. And without Shaw putting on such a show of force as their formidable patsy, Newman and Redford would have been obliged to work just that bit extra hard to con us into the spurious belief that their crookedness was, somehow, admirable, their intentions really quite honorable.

Baldly outlined, the plot of *The sting* is the stuff of paperback potboilers. There's this big New York bookie, see, Doyle Lonnegan, who, by the remote control of his criminal chain-of-command, is responsible for the death of an elderly black cheat and petty crook, Luther Coleman. Luther, a friend of Hooker (Redford) and Gondorff (Newman), is murdered by Lonnegan's torpedoes for 'doing a switch' on a runner in the numbers racket working for a Chicago house run by Lonnegan from his headquarters in New York.

Gondorff and Hooker decide to avenge Luther's killing. They get together and review Lonnegan's habits and figure to set him up as a mark for a betting swindle in a phony, protected ('past post') bookies parlor. In a Chicago slum neighborhood, they begin work on 'a store,' an off-track betting club with a veneer of class staffed by other conmen. After a whacky poker game on the train between New York and Chicago, where Gondorff cheats Lonnegan into losing a bundle, Hooker takes the bookie-racketeer aside and tells him how he can take Gondorff's 'store' for half a million bucks through Hooker manipulating the wire service in Lonnegan's favor.

From here on the tension has all the lethal menace of an electric cable shredding apart in a high wind. Soon everyone suspects everyone else. Gondorff-Newman is the man in the middle: If his tale or his timing is off by a hair's breadth there will be no 'sting,' no half-million payoff. There will be only death.

It needed the humor of a Damon Runyon and the callous tension of a Hitchcock to make this work effectively through the length of a feature film. In this they were fortunate in the script. However well Hill controled the actors involved in this caper, it was in the long run David S. Ward's perfectly paced screenplay that dictated just how far the director could take audiences out on the limb of credibility before hauling them gently in again. It is as intricately constructed as a Swiss watch, justifying John Gillet's summing-up in the British Film Institute's monthly bulletin: 'This, without doubt, is the most elaborate "heist" film to date, pulling red herrings on top of each other in thick profusion.'

The success of this latest effort by the Newman-Redford team was responsible for a fresh outcrop of pictures with the underlying theme of the affection of two footloose buddies joining forces as genial enemies of society. This theme, which actually started its current cycle in *Midnight Cowboy* and *Scarecrow*, has been extended to the verge of bathos in *Thunderbolt and Lightfoot* with Clint Eastwood as the chief bank robber and Jeff Bridges (briefly in drag) as his accomplice in an elaborate Montana bank robbery.

As Felix Barker pointed out, you don't need to be a psychiatrist to see that a different sort of affection—latent, suppressed, and nonphysical of course—exists between Eastwood, the older man, and Bridges, the pretty boy who looks just peachy in long wig and pantie hose. This is exactly the twilight borderline that Newman and Redford so skillfully manage to avoid, making their teamwork as naturally masculine an enterprise (if not more so) as the ruggedly stoical relationships cinematically projected previously by, say, John Wayne and

Ward Bond, Humphrey Bogart and Walter Brennan, or, somewhat more suspect, James Cagney and Pat O'Brien. But both Newman and Redford have the sexual confidence to skate through the nuances of this 'love affair between two men' without resorting to Flagg and Quirt butch or lapsing into Stratford-upon-Avon camp. To put it bluntly, neither of these graceful men has so much as a single homosexual muscle in his makeup. They're just two guys having a good time, easy and natural, and this is the ultimate clue to the remarkable success of this gifted team. Nobody, nobody at all, least of all the ladies, would deny them their fun. The partnership *works* in every way and strikes a warm response from every quarter, and at every level of perception.

I have recorded how greatly Paul enjoyed working on location with Redford in *Butch Cassidy*. The same spirit of fun, irony, and general horsing around entered into the location work for *The sting*. Grover Lewis in a memorable report for *Rolling Stone* graphically describes the excitement the two stars generated even on a dreary April Monday morning of freezing weather in the high-vaulted waiting room at Chicago's Union Station, 'an imposing marble-appointed structure that falls architecturally somewhere between San Simeon and Lourdes.'

The crowd of about a thousand, assembled behind police rope barriers, is orderly and polite, but 'hums with muted expectancy. All these men, women and children—with the emphasis distinctly on women—are waiting to catch a glimpse of their fantasies fleshed out. . . . Over in the crush of spectators, a fetching young secretary in a *Tango* ensemble of miniskirt, maxicoat, and high, glossy boots nudges her girlfriend excitedly: "Oh, I'm so *thrilled*. Nothing like this ever happens in Chicago. I'd even take Redford's stand-in." Then her eyes go wide and she squeals, "Oh, my God, look, look! Jesus Christ, it's *him*. It's Paul Newman Superstar!"

'The same old implosions of adrenalin for Superstar Newman are blowing the collective mind here in Chicago; the same dark magic, the same frenetic fission of the emotions are stirred up by the phenomenon of Newman's presence. And with Redford for extra measure. This might be in Haifa, London, Paris, Rome, Rimini, Grauman's Chinese, or Bridgeport, Connecticut. Wow! Paul Newman. The name is an incantation, a rubric, a preliminary to a prayer. And the worshippers range from duchesses to dishwashers, emeritus professors of Middle English to floosies in a tank town beer parlor.

'Near the edge of the crowd,' Grover Lewis observes, 'a couple of middle-aged data analysts who work for the Milwaukee Road are still agog over the furor Newman's arrival caused, too. "I used to go see Sinatra at the Paramount in New York when I was a kid," one man tells the other, "and, my God, I never say anything like *that*. I bet the temperature in here went up twenty-two degrees when Newman walked in." "I never saw anything like it, either," the second man says. "Myself, I think we ought to rope off that center aisle and never let anybody use it again." Ringed three-quarters around by avid faces, mostly women's faces whose eyes are rapidly ping-ponging back and forth between Newman and Redford, the scene requires little more than an hour to shoot. From take to take, both Newman and Redford vary their dramatic business, and it's obvious that they're having fun and relishing each other's company.'

George Roy Hill declares the scene a wrap just before noon. When they hear where Newman's going, Redford, Shaw and Hill all decide to tag along, too, and a police escort is assembled. On the way to the nearby commodities exchange, which involves traversing several heavily-travelled corridors and stairwells, Newman picks up a Pied Piper-like entourage of followers, numbering at times around 300 people.

Everybody wants to touch him, as if to reassure themselves that he really exists. Nobody attempts to separate him from his clothes, but the men scramble to shake his hand, and the women jockey for position to pat him on the arm, the shoulder, the back. To those who ask him for his autograph, Newman politely but firmly declines, muttering some variant of 'I'm waging a one-man war against autographs.' The same scene, the same dialogue, could be taking place anywhere in the world except maybe the farther reaches of Outer Mongolia. Newman is global, a symbol as instantly recognisable and as potently magical as the sun rising over Malibu. Star value, box office.

Over a drink in his hotel suite later, Robert Shaw tries to define this quality in Paul: 'Newman is a movie star, I say. I know better actors and I know worse actors, you know what I mean? He absolutely has a quality which is remarkable when it's on the screen. And that seems to be something that hasn't particularly to do with him as a person or anything else. I recognise it—it's very powerful. I've known it in other people. And it's nothing to do with intelligence, although Newman is a pretty intelligent guy. . . .

'Look—what I mean is, you cannot define this kind of magnetism that he has any more than you can define a kind of animal magnetism that Olivier has, or one or two others. But he has it. It's a quality that's so powerful that I don't know where it comes from. A lot of very good actors don't have it at all, yet I'm questioning myself because I don't know if it's been built up in my mind as a bit of a myth by now.

'I mean, I don't know what I would've thought, you know, if he'd come into this room when he was eighteen or something. I certainly don't feel in any way as an actor that he's overawing at all. I tell you candidly that he does always seem to me to be better in the daily rushes than I think he is at the time. That's because of the very quality we're talking about. There's something photogenic—a chemistry. If Newman were a completely unknown actor and had two lines in a potboiler, he would absolutely stand out. . . . I think that Newman and Olivier are, in some ways, very similar people. In that charismatic, in that animal sense. I think all their best effects are instinctive, and they're great technicians.'

Shaw sums up drolly: 'Newman, I must say, is a kind man. Occasionally, he expresses concern about my leg. On the other hand, Redford couldn't give a damn if my leg falls off at the hip. As far as he's concerned, if you drop out of the posse, that's it. You crawl up the mountain trail on your own.'

Shaw had injured his leg in a recent spill on a handball

court and was deadening his pain and humiliation with whisky.

Summing up the hysteria, the adulation which had followed Paul's royal progress through Union Station, Shaw said with just a touch of green in his eyes: 'Everybody came out, and it was Newman that they shouted about, not Redford. Myself'—Shaw grimmaced wryly—'I found myself grappling in the wake. With my broken leg. Well, I felt absurd, you know. I was trying to keep up, and I became separated from the police escort, and when I got to the commodities exchange where coffee was being served for the unit, I had to explain who I *was* in order to get in. But I did notice it was *Newman* everywhere we passed through. I mean, I picked up about two fans on the way, and those two ladies guided me back to the station, and with great joy they introduced me to people along the way . . . and none of these absolute *layers* of girls knew who I was. But they all recognised Newman, to be sure.

'There's no question about it—that was a pretty powerful reaction. I mean, it never happened to me, except years ago when I was in television. But I found it absolutely *amazing* that those businessmen should stop their transaction on the exchange—I presume they dropped thousands of dollars in trade—simply because of Newman's presence.

'What I think is that his image is so constant from picture to picture. As John Wayne's is, also. That really is the "movie star" in the old-fashioned sense of the word. . . . It's the same reaction as if any fairy tale prince came to town. It's like when we were children and we went to see the queen, I mean to say. Obviously, he carries for them enormous glamor.'

And they're gratified to see that one of their fantasy creatures *exists* in flesh and blood, Shaw suggests.

Later, Paul had this to say: 'Oh, sure, it's flattering to your ego to have droves of women flocking after you. At first, anyway. I remember first noticing that beginning to happen to me when we were filming *Hud* down in Texas. I mean, women were literally trying to climb through the transoms at the motel. It was a bad scene, really, 'cause there were all these teenyboppers coming from hundreds of miles around. And there was a junior college right close by—that's where a lot of the problems came from. Some of the guys on the crew were taking these young ladies to their rooms and feeding them beer and booze and . . . somebody finally called the vice squad.

'God, I remember this one broad was banging on my door at three o'clock in the morning for about fifteen minutes. . . . Well, I mean, I try not to have too much of a fat head about myself. Actually, the advantage that Redford and I have had is that it's a very, very slow process making it up the ladder. I first appeared professionally as an actor in 1950, and this is twenty-three years later. And you can't get a fat head from that kind of thing, because it happens very, very slowly. The people I feel sorry for are the instant celebrities, the guys like Mark Spitz. I figure those guys have got a very, very tough time of it.'

With *The sting* clocking up highly satisfactory returns at the international box office, Paul was able to concentrate on more serious matters closer to home. As a good American he was getting no joy out of the increasingly deteriorating situation over Watergate, the degradation of the near-mystical office of the presidency, and the revelations of blatant graft in high public places which he had mordantly depicted in *W.U.S.A.* and in his constant outspoken championship of human rights. As a former navy man who had put his life in hazard for his country, and being conditioned by education and patriotism to salute and respect his national flag, he found cold comfort in seeing that flag trailed in the muddied waters of Washington and seeing democratic values, which remain the keystone of America's hopes for survival, mocked by banana republics and various fascist juntas more venal than the mass of Americans would ever allow their country to become.

His innate good taste abhorred the totalitarian excesses of the radical Left as much as he sturdily attacked the blinkered self-interest of corporate capitalism. In short, Paul and Joanne are primarily interested in examining ways and means of making their country a better place to live: a commonsense updating of the principles of the Constitution as ratified with the blood, sweat, and tears of Congress right through the winter of 1788–89 into the glorious spring 1790 when Rhode Island put the final seal on American democracy. As America becomes more mature, the maturity of the Newmans—the way they handled themselves during the sixties and seventies when so much mud was slung and so many professional Mr. Cleans fell by the wayside—will become apparent to all but the most bigoted. Staying clean, honest, and honorable for as long as the Newmans have is an enviable achievement. They have won the respect of the world, and America has good reason to be proud of their track records as citizens as well as artists.

With Brando, George C. Scott, and several other kindred spirits, they put their heads together to plan a movie or two that would present some of our contemporary problems in documentary form. Giving their services free and investing their own money in the production, they decided that the end product had to be right, beyond mere journalism. If, as Victor Hugo claimed, there is nothing as powerful as an idea whose time has come, there is nothing as dispiritingly dated as a cause which has run out of steam.

Paul did not run out of steam, however, in the preproduction planning of *The Wild Places*, a documentary for television which stresses the importance of the unspoiled lands to the future of America. They were to be seen in the icy peaks of Alaska, the tree-capped range in New Hampshire's White Mountains, desert regions of Utah, the lakes of Minnesota, and the swamplands of South Carolina.

It has always been my belief that if John F. Kennedy had escaped assassination and been able to found a Kennedy dynasty in presidential politics (at least the lesser of evils when you consider what has happened instead in the decade or more since that outrage at Dallas) Joanne and Paul would have moved easily in the ambience of Camelot—as artists in the nonpolitical sense, it must be stressed. It is interesting to note that in the latter part of 1974 the Newman production company received the backing and participatory interest of R.

Sargent Shriver, the Kennedy brother-in-law who became the first head of the Peace Corps. The spirit of J.F.K. must be a heartening stimulant to Paul's future efforts under this civilized aegis.

On the lighter side, whenever possible Paul continued to take off for rallies with his auto team. As a fan, he was the commentator for a TV documentary honoring the British driver Graham Hill, giving grace and intelligent emphasis to the words prepared by the doyen of international auto racing commentators, David Benson. He was involved in a minor spill in the spring of 1974, which he insists was vastly exaggerated in the press reports, but his constant playing down of the dangers of competitive driving at his age does not diminish the unspoken concern of his friends—not to mention Joanne's private reservations—over his chosen form of recreation. He intends to stay with it for some time yet, and it will take more than an occasional brush with the guy with the scythe before he reverts exclusively to less strenouus alternatives such as pool or tennis.

Through the summer of 1974 he managed to cover a dozen track events all over the racing circuit. After clocking 175 miles an hour in his first practice run as a member of a team trying to shatter a world speed record on the savage Utah salt flats, Paul stepped calmly from his red Ferrari and said: 'I think that calls for a round of nice, cold German beer.'

Asked bluntly why he risks his life in these grueling tests which have killed off many star drivers before their thirtieth birthday (Paul was fifty in January, 1975), he said softly, 'I've paid my dues and I'm old enough now to do what the hell I want. I go out for the kick in the behind I get from driving, and for the most part it's a load of laughs.'

His attitude hasn't changed by an iota since I broached the subject with him back in Bridgeport, and nobody close to him will ever budge him from his conviction that it's safer on the circuits than the freeway.

Say what they will in Hollywood, it's outsize characters like Newman, Redford, George C. Scott, Clint Walker and Burt Reynolds who are keeping the former 'motion picture capital of the world' from descending into a celluloid Detroit producing little more than movies-for-television from assembly lines. How many formula movies can even television accept in the long run? Even in this degraded spinoff of picture production it is largely the charm and pulling power of a Telly Savalas, Rock Hudson, or Dennis Weaver that induce viewers to switch on their sets and endure yet another car chase along Highway 101, a manhunt on the waterfront at Long Beach, or a superannuated movie actress being scared to death by unwholesome young punks in that same old haunted house on the Universal lot.

It came as no surprise, therefore, when the corporate accountants, who run what's left of the studios, totted up the returns on *The Poseidon Adventure*, and figured out in their tiny minds that large-scale filmic disasters might postpone the ultimate disaster of a Hollywood exclusively geared to turning out television fodder. So Universal poured eight million dollars into *Earthquake*, in which Charlton Heston and Ava Gardner were merely window dressing to the special effects men, with, for good measure, 'Sensurround' to give audiences the feeling of being in a quake. Heston was also put to work in *Airport '75*, dealing with the awful aftermath of a jumbo jet crash, while Robert Wise, the director of *The sound of music* and *West Side story*, turned his attention to the explosion of the German-made airship *The Hindenburg*. This three-million-dollar picture came complete with a mock-up of the flying coffin and the admirable George C. Scott and Anne Bancroft. As Scott put it: 'In the sixties people were making half-a-million-dollar *Easy rider* pictures. That was marvellous two or three times, but when a score went down the toilet, that was the end of that. Now we've entered the cycle of the disaster movie.'

Disaster followed disaster. The cycle continued with an epic called *The swarm*, showing a bunch of blown-up carnivorous bees devouring New York, and *The day the world ended*, a picture whose focal point of interest was a volcano erupting. So where did Paul Newman fit into the prevailing *sturm und drang* on the West Coast?

Well, Irwin Allen, who had brought millions of lovely

dollars back to Hollywood with his *Poseidon* epic, shrewdly calculated that all the special effects in the world are wasted unless there's a good story, with massive star power to put it across as well. He had every reason to be thankful for the human qualities of Shelley Winters, Ernest Borgnine, and the always effective Carol Lynley, who put the punch into his *Poseidon*. So when he was given a budget of over thirteen million dollars to duplicate his success with the biggest disaster movie of the bunch, *The towering inferno*, he wisely pitched his script to give minimum offense to the intelligence of Newman, Steve McQueen, Jennifer Jones, Robert Wagner, Richard Chamberlain, Fred Astaire, or any other really choosey box-office names he hoped to lure into this story. After all, the real hero is 'the world's tallest skyscraper,' whose blazing end could have barely extended its appeal beyond pre-teen steeplejacks and rain-coated pyromaniacs. With Newman, McQueen, Wagner, ad infinitum, Irwin Allen had every reason to hope for a really successful 'disaster' in this lucrative trend which, for a while at least, allowed Hollywood to find that old Midas touch again.

With Paul picking up a cool million of 'up front' money, plus a percentage on the profits, simply by taking a short walk through the new Hollywood 'disaster area,' his hand is strengthened for the production and direction of motion pictures that really engage his interest—be it a film on ecology or directing Joanne in a script they jointly admire. Then should he ever feel the need for the extra buck, he can always team up with Redford again for another caper in the anar-chical hinterlands of buddy-buddy mayhem. Their joint names on a contract for such a venture would automatically give them enough cash to buy themselves a battleship apiece or a couple of jumbo jets, should they feel the urge for such extravagances. That kind of loot would almost reconcile Paul to an occasional stopover in Hollywood, to take gifts of fruit and flowers to 'the once-lovely woman dying of cancer.'

The Newmans, however, refuse to make polite noises. Paul grows more serious with the passing years, without any diminishing of his sense of fun or his commitment to ideas which he feels worth his support in the interests of the community at large. As for Joanne, she remains adamant in her refusal to come to terms with the Hollywood Cage from which she successfully escaped after becoming Mrs. Newman. Not that marriage affected her uncompromising attitude toward the set-up out there. Quite early in her career she brought to Hollywood from Broadway a fastiduous classiness, an intellectual aloofness, which has always directed her interests towards the literary, the artistic, and the academic.

She has also long been a film favorite of the film-festival crowd. (The artistic organisers, the dedicated movie buffs, *not* the hucksters and publicity hounds who are doing their best to cheapen the whole idea of these gatherings.) After the release of the picture she made with Martin Balsam, *Summer wishes, winter dreams*—in which she again reached into her mysterious emotional treasurehouse to come up with an entirely fresh character-creation as the type of neurotic New York woman she would normally run a mile from—Joanne accepted an invitation to attend the film festival at San Francisco, where this movie was a prize exhibit.

San Francisco is sufficiently far north of Los Angeles to lure Joanne into a visit, and it is, in any case, one of the major urban connurbations in the U.S.A. for which the Newmans have some affection and not a little hope—in spite of what the architectural vandals, with their indiscriminate passion for high-rise building, have done to ruin it visually.

'If the term gracious lady still means anything in this freaked-out world, then it can be used to describe the impact Joanne Woodward made on some of us kids who attended the festival,' I was told by Thea Anderson, a young writer for the underground press on the West Coast. 'We'd heard good things about her, but we still half expected to come up against a toney New York actress with only a token interest in the common herd. A sort of radical-chic Helen Hayes, if you understand, a well-meaning do-gooder with star written large over her despite her good intentions. What we didn't expect was her directness, her outgoing warmth, her ability to connect. She was one of Us, in no way a part of Them. She didn't try to ingratiate herself, she didn't seem to be trying to do *anything* . . . except be herself. And it worked; everyone loved her.'

Not being subject to the pressures of stardom-in-residence as they apply to most actresses who live and work in Hollywood, Joanne manages to live a full, rich life which must be the envy of her more ambitious rivals. She has the chameleon quality of merging into a crowd and enjoying the 'visible invisibility' that Paul hankers after but rarely achieves. She recently spent a semester studying the Industrial Revolution at Sarah Lawrence and has since picked up an honorary degree from the University of Connecticut at Bridgeport. She attends ballet classes regularly between practicing the piano and guitar, does a great deal of needlework and dressmaking, and bones up on languages, especially French and Hebrew.

Then there are her many friends, some in the obscurer backwaters of academe and Upper Bohemia. Says John Foreman: 'Joanne has creative people stashed all over the place, and neither rain, sleet, nor snow stops her from her appointed rounds of all that is beautiful and artistic.'

This somewhat brash portrait of an arty Lady Bountiful handing out bowls of inspirational gruel to the needy does not altogether do justice to Joanne's very real interest in people, be they artistic waifs and strays or 'doers' like Ralph Nader and Benjamin Spock. And despite her full social calendar, she gives a great deal of time to running her home and bringing up her children.

On the subject of her children and her home life, she says: 'I suppose Peter Ustinov was right when he said that in our lives together Paul and I had "shut out the drafts of difference." We have our differences, but the outside world doesn't often get a chance to get inside our house.'

Inside that house Joanne rules by means of the firm-hand-in-a-velvet-glove technique, and though her presence is sorely missed when she is out, she instills independence in all her children. 'It's bad for parents to have children staying around the house too long: It makes the parents too dependent on the children. I give my children love and security and a home

207

until they leave college. Then I tell them they will be on their own and they won't have to worry about their old mother, but they can always come home when they want to. I am impatient when I'm doing nothing. I just can't stand it.

'I am impatient and perhaps overly emotional and throw things, and then I say, "And that's after years of analysis," but I have learned now about living—and that only comes later in life. To this extent, I suppose, the younger children have the benefit of my more mature outlook on things. But in the end it's a wise parent who understands that, deep down, every child has a healthy urge to fly from the family nest—and in the long run they love most the parents who can fully understand this urge rather than the overprotective parent who hangs on, hangs on, hangs on . . . until the instinct is dulled and the sense of adventure is crushed out of them.'

Despite all this domesticity and motherly know-how, she remains an actress to her fingertips—an actress who really cares about her craft, aware of her responsibility toward its precious and precarious mystique. This is why she is capable of suffering such intensities before, during, and after creating a character, especially when she has reason to suspect the quality of the project in which she has involved herself as an actress.

Shortly after *W.U.S.A.* she commited herself to making *They might be giants,* in which she played a whacky lady psychiatrist pretending to be Doctor Watson to George C. Scott's portrayal of a fruitcake believing himself to be Sherlock Holmes. She has always found it hard to say anything kind about this venture, and in her forthright way she had some succinct points to make on acting in her throwaway comments on her involvement in this odd farrago!

'It was the most miserable experience I've ever had, making that film. I hated it. It would be pointless to go into the reasons now, although I must say they had nothing to do with George Scott, who was a perfect gentleman throughout. But there was a time after that when I said I would never make another picture as long as I lived, and I really didn't want to work for a long time.

'Acting should be a matter of fun and games but, even in films, it's not as much fun as it used to be. There's no such thing as a picture that does okay anymore; it's either an enormous hit or an absolute bomb. So nobody will let you take a chance, and you've got too much riding on you. It's exhausting. But when you believe in something—Paul and I both think films can illuminate life, as well as decorate it—and it *really* works on *every* level, then there are times when art becomes life itself. You become part of some miraculous living entity that, somehow, justifies all the tears and doubts and agony. No, I have no regrets about being an actress, because through it I have experienced such moments.'

Since Joanne has played such a large part in the shaping and molding of that phenomenon which over the past quarter century has been lodged, poster sized, in the collective unconscious of the global village, and labeled Paul Newman, it is perhaps fitting that she should have the last word in this preliminary interpretive study of the man, the image and the legend.

'He improves in beauty as he grows older,' Joanne sums up. 'I can fake beauty or be a plain old shoe. I don't mind. I'm lucky to have a husband who thinks I'm a sexpot and that is lovely to live with because his personality radiates to everyone else around.

'Deep down, in spite of what many people think, he's a shy, retiring man. He's getting kind of grizzly now. He's always looked like a Greek statue, but these days he's beginning to look like an older Greek statue. He can't be a sex symbol forever, can he?

'But then, you see, even if he grows old there are all his children coming along. I'm used to people saying to me, "Aren't you Paul Newman's wife?" rather than "Aren't you Joanne Woodward?" That was bad enough. I have *some* ego, for God's sake. But the other day I had the worst moment of my life. Some girl came running up to me and said: "Aren't you Scott Newman's mother?"

'I just said, "Oh, shit!" and walked away.'

Filmography

The silver chalice   1954   Warner Bros.
CREDITS   A Warner Bros. release of a Victor Saville Production. Directed by Victor Saville. Screenplay by Lester Samuels from the novel by Thomas B. Costain. Edited by George White. Music by Franz Waxman. Photographed in CinemaScope and Warnercolor by William V. Skall. Running time, 142 mins.

CAST · Virginia Mayo, Pier Angeli, Jack Palance, Paul Newman, Walter Hampden, Joseph Wiseman, Alexander Scourby, Lorne Greene, E. G. Marshall, Natalie Wood, Peter Reynolds, Mort Marshall, Terence de Marney, Philip Tonge, Albert Dekker, Beryl Machin.

Somebody up there likes me   1956   MGM
CREDITS   Produced by Charles Schnee. Directed by Robert Wise. Assistant Director, Robert Saunders. Associate Producer, James E. Newcom. Screenplay by Ernest Lehman, based on the autobiography of Rocky Graziano, written with Rowland Barber. Film Editor, Albert Akst, A.C.E. Music by Bronislau Kaper. Song, *Somebody up there likes me* sung by Perry Como. Lyrics by Sammy Cahn. Director of Photography, Joseph Ruttenberg, A.S.C. Art Director, Cedric Gibbons and Malcolm Brown. Perspecta Sound. Running time, 112 mins.

CAST   Paul, Newman, Pier Angeli, Everett Sloane, Eileen Heckart, Sal Mineo, Harold J. Stone, Joseph Buloff, Sammy White, Arch Johnson, Robert Lieb, Ray Stricklyn, Judson Pratt, Matt Crowley, Frank Campanella, Ralph Vitti.

The rack   1956   MGM
CREDITS   Produced by Arthur M. Loew, Jr. Directed by Arnold Laven. Assistant Director, Robert Saunders. Screenplay by Stewart Stern. Based on the teleplay by Rod Serling. Director of Photography, Paul C. Vogel, A.S.C. Art Directors,

Cedric Gibbons and Merrill Pye. Set Decorations, Edwin B. Willis, Fred MacLean. Recording Supervisor, Dr Wesley C. Miller. Film Editors, Harold F. Kress, A.C.E. and Marshall Neilan Jr. Music by Adolph Deutsch. Makeup by William Tuttle. Technical Advisor, Col. Charles M. Trammel, Jr. USAR. Running time, 100 minutes.

CAST Paul Newman, Wendell Corey, Walter Pidgeon, Edmond O'Brien, Anne Francis, Lee Marvin, Cloris Leachman, Robert Burton, Robert Simon, Trevor Bardette, Adam Williams, James Best, Fay Roope, Barry Atwater.

Until they sail 1957   MGM
CREDITS Produced by Charles Schnee. Associate Producer, James E. Newcom. Directed by Robert Wise. Screenplay by Robert Anderson. Based upon a story by James A. Michener. Film Editor, Harold F. Kress, A.C.E. Music by David Raksin. Lyric for song *Until they sail* by Sammy Cahn. Sung by Eydie Gormé. Director of Photography, Joseph Ruttenberg, A.S.C. Art Directors, William A. Horning and Paul Groesse. A.C.E. CinemaScope. Perspects Sound. Process lenses by Panavision. Running time, 94 mins.

CAST Jean Simmons, Joan Fontaine, Paul Newman, Piper Laurie, Charles Drake, Sandra Dee, Wally Cassell, Alan Napier, Ralph Votrian, John Wilder, Tige Andrews, Adam Kennedy, Mickey Shaughnessy.

The Helen Morgan story 1957   Warner Bros. (*Both ends of the candle* in Britain)
CREDITS A Warner Bros. release of a Martin Rackin Production. Directed by Michael Curtiz. Screenplay by Oscar Saul, Deal Riesner, Stephen Longstreet and Nelson Gidding. Camera, Ted McCord. Art Director, John Beckman. Editor, Frank Bracht. Musical numbers staged by LeRoy Prinz. Songs sung by Gogi Grant. Running time, 117 mins.

CAST Ann Blyth, Paul Newman, Richard Carlson, Gene Evans, Alan King, Cara Williams, Virginia Vincent, Walter

Woolf King, Dorothy Green, Ed Platt, Warren Douglas, Sammy White, Peggy De Castro, Cheri De Castro, Babette De Castro and Jimmy McHugh, with Rudy Vallee and Walter Winchell.

The long, hot summer 1958   20th Century-Fox
CREDITS   Produced by Jerry Wald. Directed by Martin Ritt. Screenplay by Irving Ravetch and Harriet Frank, Jr. Based on two stories, *Barn burning* and *The spotted horses* and a part of the novel *The hamlet*, all by William Faulkner. Director of photography, Joseph La Shelle, A.S.C. Art Directors, Lyle R. Wheeler and Maurice Ransford. Film Editor, Louis R. Loeffler. Music by Alex North, conducted by Lionel Newman. Song *The long hot summer* by Sammy Cahn and Alex North. CinemaScope. Colour by Deluxe. Colour Consultant, Leonard Doss. Running time, 115 minutes.

CAST   Paul Newman, Joanne Woodward, Anthony Franciosa, Orson Welles, Lee Remick, Angela Lansbury, Richard Anderson, Sarah Marshall, Mabel Albertson, J. Pat O'Malley, William Walker, George Dunn, Jess Kilpatrick, Val Avery, I. Stanford Jolley, Nicholas King, Lee Erickson, Ralph Reed, Terry Range, Steve Widders, Jim Brandt, Helen Wallace, Brian Corcoran, Byron Foulger, Victor Rodman, Eugene Jackson.

The left-handed gun 1958   Warner Bros.
CREDITS   A Warner Bros. release of a Fred Coe production. Directed by Arthur Penn. Assistant Director, Russ Saunders. Screenplay by Leslie Stevens, based on a teleplay, *The death of Billy the kid*, by Gore Vidal. Camera, J. Peverell Marley. Film Editor, Folmar Blangsted. Music by Alexander Courage. Art Director, Art Loel. Sound by Earl Crain, Sr. Running time, 105 mins.

CAST   Paul Newman, Lita Milan, Hurd Hatfield, James Congdon, James Best, Colin Keith-Jonston, John Dierkes, Bob

Anderson, Wally Brown, Ainslie Pryor, Martin Carralaga, Denver Pyle, Paul Smith, Nestor Paiva, Jo Summers, Robert Foulk, Anne Barton.

Cat on a hot tin roof 1958   MGM
CREDITS An Avon Production for MGM. Produced by Lawrence Weingarten. Directed by Richard Brooks. Screenplay by Richard Brooks and James Poe. Based on the play by Tennessee Williams. Photographed by William Daniels. Art Direction, William A. Horning and Urie McCleary. Set Decoration, Henry Grace and Robert Priestley. Special effects, Lee Leblanc. Editor, Ferris Webster. Miss Taylor's Wardrobe, Helen Rose. Hairstyles, Sydney Guilaroff. Makeup, William Tuttle. In Metrocolor. Running time, 108 mins.

CAST Elizabeth Taylor, Paul Newman, Burl Ives, Jack Carson, Judith Anderson, Madeleine Sherwood, Larry Gates, Vaughn Taylor, Deborah Miller, Hugh and Brian Corcoran.

Rally 'round the flag, boys! 1958   20th Century-Fox
CREDITS Produced and directed by Leo McCarey. Assistant Director, Jack Gertsman. Screenplay by Claude Binyon and Leo McCarey. Based on the novel by Max Shulman. Editor, Louis R. Loeffler. Music by Cyril J. Mockridge. Conducted by Lionel Newman. Orchestrations, Edward B. Powell. Photographed by Leon Shamroy. Art Direction, Lyle R. Wheeler and Leland Fuller. Set decoration, Walter M. Scott and Stuart A. Reiss. Special photographic effects, L. B. Abbott. Wardrobe design, Charles Le Maire. Hairstyles by Helen Turpin. Makeup by Ben Nye. Sound, Eugene Grossman and Harry M. Leonard. Colour consultant, Leonard Doss. CinemaScope. Colour by DeLuxe. Running time, 106 mins.

CAST Paul Newman, Joanne Woodward, Joan Collins, Jack Carson, Dwayne Hickman, Tuesday Weld, Gale Gordon, Tom Gilson, O. Z. Whitehead, Ralph Osborn III, Stanley Livingston, Jon Lormer, Joseph Holland, Burt Mustin, Percy Holton, Nora O'Mahoney, Richard Collier, Murvyn Vye.

The young Philadelphians 1959   Warner Bros. (*The city jungle* in Britain)
CREDITS Directed by Vincent Sherman. Assistant director, William Kissel. Screenplay by James Gunn. From the novel *The Philadelphian* by Richard Powell. Director of Photography, Harry Stradling, Sr, A.S.C. Art director, Malcolm Bert, Film Editor, William Ziegler. Music by Ernest Gold. Musical Supervision by Ray Heindorf. Sound by Stanley Jones. Main title designed by Maurice Binder. Costumes designed by Howard Shoup. Set decorations, John P. Austin. Makeup Supervision, Gordon Bau, S.M.A. Running time, 136 mins.

CAST Paul Newman, Barbara Rush, Alexis Smith, Brian Keith, Diane Brewster, Billie Burke, John Williams, Robert Vaughn, Otto Kruger, Paul Picerni, Robert Douglas, Frank Conroy, Adam West, Fred Eisley, Richard Deacon.

From the terrace 1960   20th Century-Fox
CREDITS Produced and directed by Mark Robson. Screenplay by Ernest Lehman. Based on the novel by John O'Hara. Photographed by Leo Tover, A.S.C. Art Directors, Lyle R. Wheeler, Maurice Ransford, Howard Richman. Film Editor, Dorothy Spencer. Music by Elmer Bernstein. Set Decorations by Walter M. Scott and Paul S. Fox. Special Photographic Effects, L. B. Abbott, James B. Gordon. Assistant Director, Hal Herman. Orchestration, Edward B. Powell. Hairstyles by Helen Turpin. Gowns designed by Tavilla. Makeup by Ben Nye. Sound by Harry M. Leonard and Alfred Bruzlin. Colour by DeLuxe. Colour consultant, Leonard Doss. Running time, 144 minutes.

CAST Paul Newman, Joanne Woodward, Myrna Loy, Ina Balin, Leon Ames, Elizabeth Allen, Barbara Eden, George Grizzard, Patrick O'Neal, Felix Aylmer, Raymond Greenleaf, Malcolm Atterbury, Raymond Bailey, Ted De Corsia, Howard Caine, Kathryn Givney, Dorothy Adams, Lauren Gilbert, Blossom Rock, Cecil Elliott.

Exodus 1960   United Artists

CREDITS An Otto Preminger Production released through United Artists. Produced and directed by Otto Preminger. Assistant Director, Gerry O'Hara. Screenplay by Dalton Trumbo, based on the novel by Leon Uris. Photographed by Sam Leavitt. Film Editor, Louis R. Loeffler. Music by Ernest Gold. Art Director, Richard Day. Set Decorations by Dario Simani. Titles designed by Saul Bass. Sound by Paddy Cunningham, Red Law and John Cox. Sound effects by Win Ryder. Special effects by Cliff Richardson. Makeup by George Lane. Wardrobe by Joe King, Marge Slater and May Walding. Hairstyles by A. G. Scott. Miss Saint's clothes by Rudi Gernreich. Costume co-ordinator, Hope Bryce. General Manager, Martin C. Schute. Production Manager, Eva Monley. Assistant to the Producer, Max Slater. Filmed in Israel. Technicolor and Super-Panavision 70. Running time, 212 minutes.

CAST Paul Newman, Eva Marie Saint, Ralph Richardson, Peter Lawford, Lee J. Cobb, Sal Mineo, John Derek, Hugh Griffiths, David Opatoshu, Jill Haworth, Gregory Ratoff, Felix Aylmer, Marius Goring, Alexandra Stewart, Michael Wager, Martin Benson, Paul Stevens, Betty Walker, Martin Miller, Victor Maddern, George Maharis, John Crawford, Samuel Segal, Dahn Ben Motz, Peter Madden, Ralph Truman, Joseph Furst, Paul Stassino, Marc Burns, Esther Reichstadt, Zeporrah Peled, Philo Hauser.

The hustler 1961   20th Century-Fox

CREDITS Produced and directed by Robert Rossen. Assistant Directors, Charles Maguire and Don Kranz. Screenplay by Robert Rossen and Sidney Carroll. Based on the novel by Walter Tevis. Photography, Gene Shuftan. Art Direction, Harry Horner and Albert Brenner. Set Decorations, Gene Callahan. Film Editor, Dede Allen. Sound, James Shields. Technical Advisor, Willie Mosconi. Unit Manager, John Graham. Costumes, Ruth Morley. Makeup, Bob Jiras. Hairstyles, Deneene. In CinemaScope. Filmed in New York City. Running time, 133 mins.

CAST Paul Newman, Jackie Gleason, Piper Laurie, George C. Scott, Myron McCormick, Murray Hamilton, Michael Constantine, Stefan Gierasch, Jake LaMotta, Gordon B. Clarke, Carl York, Alexander Rose, Carolyn Coates, Vincent Cardenia, Gloria Curtis, Charles Diercep, Donald Crabtree, Cliff Fellow.

Paris blues 1961 United Artists
CREDITS A Pennebaker Production. Executive Producers, George Glass and Walter Seltzer. Producer, Sam Shaw. Directed by Martin Ritt. Assistant Director, Bernard Farrel. Screenplay by Jack Sher, Irene Kamp and Walter Bernstein. Adaptation by Lulla Adler. Based on a novel by Harold Flender. Photographed by Christian Matras. Film Editor, Roger Dwyre. Music by Duke Ellington. Second unit director, Andre Smagghe. Art Direction, Alexander Trauner. Sound, Jo De Bretagne. Production Manager, Michael Rittener. Location scenes filmed in Paris. *Running time,* 98 mins.

CAST Paul Newman, Joanne Woodward, Sidney Poitier, Louis Armstrong, Diahann Carroll, Serge Reggiani, Barbara Laage, Andre Luguet, Marie Versini, Moustache, Aaron Bridgers, Guy Pederson, Maria Velasco, Roger Blin, Helene Dieudonne, Niko.

Sweet bird of youth 1962 MGM
CREDITS A Roxbury Production. Produced by Pandro S. Berman. Directed and written by Richard Brooks. Assistant Director, Hank Moonjean. Based on the play by Tennessee Williams. Photographed by Milton Krasner. Film Editor, Henry Berman. Music Supervisor, Harold Gelman. Orchestra conducted by Robert Armbruster. Art Direction, George W. Davis and Uric McCleary. Set decorations, Henry Grace and Hugh Hunt. Special Visual Effects, Lee Le Blanc. Recording Supervisor, Franklin Milton. Makeup, William Tuttle. Costumes, Orry-Kelly. Hairstyles, Sydney Guilaroff. Associate Producer, Kathryn Hereford. CinemaScope and MetroColor. Colour Consultant, Charles K. Hagedon. Running time, 120 mins.

CAST Paul Newman, Geraldine Page, Shirley Knight, Ed Begley, Rip Torn, Mildred Dunnock, Madeleine Sherwood, Philip Abbott, Corey Allen, Barry Cahill, Dug Taylor, James Douglas, Barry Atwater, Charles Arnt, Dorothy Konrad, James Chandler, Mike Steen and Kelly Thordsen.

Hemingway's adventures of a young man   1962   20th Century-Fox
CREDITS   A Company of Artists (Jerry Wald) Production for 20th Century-Fox. Produced by Jerry Wald. Directed by Martin Ritt. Assistant Director, Eli Dunn. Screenplay by A. E. Hotchner, based on stories by Ernest Hemingway. Photographed by Lee Garmes. Film Editor, Hugh S. Fowler. Music composed and conducted by Franz Waxman. Art Direction, Jack Martin Smith and Paul Groesse. Set decorations by Walter M. Scott and Robert Priestley. Special Photographic Effects by L. B. Abott and Emil Kosa Jr. Sound, E. Clayton Ward and Warren B. Delaplain. Costumes, Don Feld. Hairstyles, Helen Turpin. Makeup, Ben Nye. Associate Producer, Peter Nelson. Italian sequences filmed in Rome. CinemaScope. Colour by DeLuxe. Running time, 145 mins.

CAST   Richard Beymer, Diane Baker, Corinne Calvet, Fred Clark, Dan Dailey, James Dunn, Juano Hernandez, Arthur Kennedy, Ricardo Montalban, Susan Strasberg, Jessica Tandy, Eli Wallach, Edward Binns, Whit Bissell, Philip Bourneuf, Tullio Carminati, Marc Cavell, Charles Fredericks, Simon Oakland, Michael Pollard, Pat Hogan and Paul Newman as The Battler.

Hud   1963   Paramount
CREDITS   A Salem-Dover Production. Produced by Martin Ritt and Irving Ravetch. Directed by Martin Ritt. Assistant Director, C. C. Coleman Jr. Screenplay by Irving Ravetch and Harriet Frank, Jr. Based on the novel *Horseman, pass by*, by Larry McMurtry. Photographed by James Wong Howe. Second Unit Photography by Rex Wimpy. Art Directors, Hal Pereira and Tambi Larsen. Film Editor, Frank Bracht. Music by Elmer Bernstein. Set decorations by Sam Comer and

Robert Benton. Special Photographic Effect by Paul K. Larpae. Process Photography: Farciot Edouart. Sound, John Carter and John Wilkinson. Costumes by Edith Head. Makeup by Wally Westmore. Hairstyles by Nellie Manley. Production Managers, Lloyd Anderson and Andrew J. Durkus. Panavision. Filmed on location in Texas. Running time, 122 mins.

CAST   Paul Newman, Melvyn Douglas, Patricia Neal, Brandon de Wilde, John Ashley, Whit Bissell, Crahan Denton, Val Avery, Sheldon Allman, Pitt Herbert, Peter Brooks, Curt Conway, Yvette Vickers, George Petrie, David Kent and Frank Killmond.

A new kind of love   1963   Paramount
CREDITS   A Denroc Production. Produced, directed and written by Melville Shavelson. Assistant Director, Arthur Jacobson. Photography by Daniel Fapp. Editor, Frank Bracht. Music by Leith Stevens. Additional themes by Erroll Garner. Title song sung by Frank Sinatra. Art Direction, Hal Pereira and Arthur Lonergan. Set Decorations by Sam Comer and James Payne. Costumes by Edith Head. Paris originals by Christian Dior, Lanvin-Castille and Pierre Cardin. Sound by John Cartier. Makeup by Wally Westmore. Assistant to the Producer, Hal Kern. Production Manager, Andrew J. Durkus. Technicolor. Colour consultant, Hoyningen-Huene. Running time, 110 mins.

CAST   Paul Newman, Joanne Woodward, Thelma Ritter, Eva Gabor, George Tobias, Marvin Kaplan, Robert Clary, Jon Moriarty, Valerie Varda, Robert Simon, Jean Staley and guest star Maurice Chevalier.

The prize   1963   MGM
CREDITS   Produced by Pandro S. Berman. Directed by Mark Robson. Assistant Director, Hank Moonjean. Screenplay by Ernest Lehman. Based on the novel by Irving Wallace. Film Editor, Adrienne Fazan. Music by Jerry Goldsmith. Photographed by William Daniels. Set Decoration, Henry Grace and

Dick Pefferle. Special Visual Effects, J. McMillan Johnson, A. Arnold Gillespie, Robert R. Hoag. Hairstyles, Sydney Guilaroff. Makeup, William Tuttle. Associate Producer, Kathryn Hereford. Art Directors, George W. Davis and Urie McCleary. In Panavision and MetroColor. A Roxbury Production. Running time, 135 minutes.

CAST Paul Newman, Edward G. Robinson, Elke Sommer, Diane Baker, Micheline Presle, Gerard Oury, Sergio Fantoni, Kevin McCarthy, Leo G. Carroll, Sacha Pitoeff, Jacqueline Beer, John Wengraf, Don Dubbins, Virginia Christine, Rudolph Anders, Martine Bartlett, Karl Swenson, John Qualen and Ned Wever.

What a way to go 1964   20th Century-Fox
CREDITS   A J. Lee Thompson Production. Produced by Arthur P. Jacobs. Directed by J. Lee Thompson. Assistant Director, Fred R. Simpson. Screenplay by Betty Comden and Adolph Green. Based on a story by Gwen Davis. Film Editor, Marjorie Fowler. The songs, *I think that you and I should get acquainted* and *Musical extravaganza*, lyrics by Betty Comden and Adolph Green. Music by Jule Styne. Choreography by Gene Kelly. Music by Nelson Riddle. Photographed by Leon Shamroy. Art direction by Jack Martin Smith and Ted Hawoorth. Set Decoration by Walter M. Scott and Stuart A. Reiss. Special Photographic Effects by L. B. Abbott and Emil Kosa, Jr. Unit Production Manager, William Eckhardt. Men's Wardrobe, Moss Mabry. Assistant to Mr Kelly, Richard Humphrey. Dialogue Coach, Leon Charles. Sound, Bernard Freerich and Elmer Raguse. Makeup, Ben Nye. Orchestration, Arthur Morton. Supervising Hair Stylist, Margaret Donovan. Miss MacLaine's Hairstyles, Sydney Guilaroff. Precious Stones, Harry Winston, Inc. Gloves, Kislav. Miss MacLaine's gowns, Edith Head. CinemaScope. Colour by De Luxe. Running time 111 mins.

CAST   Shirley MacLaine, Paul Newman, Robert Mitchum, Dean Martin, Gene Kelly, Bob Cummings, Dick Van Dyke,

Reginald Gardiner, Margaret Dumont, Lou Nova, Fifi D'Orsay, Maurice Marsac, Wally Vernon, Jane Wald, Lenny Kent.

The outrage 1964 MGM
CREDITS A Martin Ritt Production. Produced by A. Ronald Lubin. Directed by Martin Ritt. Assistant Director, Daniel J. McCauley. Screenplay by Michael Kanin. Based on the Japanese film *Rashomon,* by Akira Kurosawa, from stories by Ryunosuke Akutagawa and the play *Rashomon* by Fay and Michael Kanin. Photographed by James Wong Howe. Film Editor, Frank Santillo. Music composed and conducted by Alex North. Associate Producer, Michael Kanin. Art Direction, George W. Davis and Tambi Larsen. Set Decorations, Henry Grace and Robert R. Benton. Special Visual Effects, J. McMillan Johnson and Robert R. Hoag. Costumes by Don Felt. Hairstyles by Sydney Guilaroff. Makeup by William Tuttle. Panavision. Running time 97 mins.

CAST Paul Newman, Laurence Harvey, Claire Bloom, Edward G. Robinson, William Shatner, Howard Da Silva, Albert Salmi, Thomas Chalmers, Paul Fix.

Lady L. 1965 MGM
CREDITS A Carlo Ponti Production presented and released by Metro-Goldwyn-Mayer. Directed by Peter Ustinov. Screenplay by Peter Ustinov from the novel by Romain Gary. Photographed by Henri Alekan. Film Editor, Roger Dwyre. Music by Jean Francaix. Running time, 124 mins.

CAST Sophia Loren, Paul Newman, David Niven, Claude Dauphin, Philippe Noiret, Michel Piccoli, Marcel Dalio, Cecil Parker, Jean Wiener, Daniel Emilfork, Eugene Deckers, Jacques Dufilho, Tanya Lopert, Catherine Allegret, Peter Ustinov.

Harper 1966 Warner Bros. (*The moving target* in Britain)
CREDITS Warner Bros. release of a Jerry Gershwin–Elliott Kastner Production. Directed by Jack Smight. Assistant Dir-

ector, James H. Brown. Screenplay by William Goldman based on the novel, *The moving target*, by Ross MacDonald. Film Editor, Stefan Arnsten. Music by Johnny Mandel. Song *Livin' Alone* by Dory and André Previn. Photographed by Conrad Hall. Technicolor. Running time, 121 mins.

CAST Paul Newman, Lauren Bacall, Julie Harris, Arthur Hill, Janet Leigh, Pamela Tiffin, Robert Wagner, Robert Webber, Shelley Winters, Harold Gould, Strother Martin, Roy Jensen, Martin West, Jacqueline de Wit, Eugene Iglesias, Richard Carlyle.

Torn curtain 1966 Universal
CREDITS Produced and directed by Alfred Hitchcock. Assistant Director, Donald Baer. Screenplay by Brian Moore, based on his story. Art Director, Frank Arrigo. Photographed by John F. Warren. Unit Production Manager, Jack Carrick. Sound, Waldon O. Watson and William Russell. Miss Andrew's costumes by Edith Head. Production designer, Hein Heckroth. Pictorial Designs, Albert Whitlock. Film Editor, Bud Hoffman. Music by John Addison. Set Decorations, George Milo. Makeup Supervision, Jack Barron. Costume Supervisor, Grady Hunt. Assistant to Mr Hitchcock, Peggy Robertson. Hairstyles for Miss Andrews, Hal Saunders. Hair Stylist, Lorraine Roberson. Technicolor. Running time, 126 mins.

CAST Paul Newman, Julie Andrews, Lila Kedrova, Hansjoerg Felmy, Tamara Toumanova, Wolfgang Kieling, Gunter Strack, Ludwig Donath, David Opatoshu, Gisela Fischer, Mort Mills, Carolyn Conwell, Arthur Gould-Porter and Gloria Garvin.

Hombre 1967 20th Century-Fox
CREDITS Produced by Martin Ritt and Irving Ravetch. Directed by Martin Ritt. Assistant Director, William McGarry. Screenplay by Irving Ravetch and Harriet Frank, Jr. Based on the novel by Elmore Leonard. Second Unit Director, Ray Kellogg. Photographed by James Wong Howe. Film Editor,

Frank Bracht. Music composed and conducted by David Rose. Art Direction, Jack Martin Smith and Robert E. Smith. Set Decorations, Walter M. Scott and Raphael Bretton. Sound, John R. Carter and David Deckendorf. Orchestration, Leo Shuken and Jack Hayes. Costumes, Don Feld. Hairstyles, Margaret Donovan. Makeup, Ben Nye. Production Manager, Harry A. Caplan. Filmed on location in Arizona. Panavision. Colour by DeLuxe. Running time, 111 mins.

CAST Paul Newman, Fredric March, Richard Boone, Diane Cilento, Cameron Mitchell, Barbara Rush, Peter Lazer, Margaret Blye, Martin Balsam, Skip Ward, Frank Silvera, David Canary, Val Avery, Larry Ward, Linda Cordova, Pete Hernandez, Merrill C. Isbell.

Cool hand Luke 1967 Warner Bros.
CREDITS A Jalem Production. Produced by Gordon Carroll. Directed by Stuart Rosenberg. Assistant Director, Hank Moonjean. Screenplay by Donn Pearce and Frank R. Pierson. Based on the novel by Donn Pearce. Photographed by Conrad Hall. Film Editor, Sam O'Steen. Music by Lalo Schifrin. Art Director, Cary O'Dell. Set Decorations, Fred Price. Sound, Larry Jost. Costumes, Howard Shoup. Makeup, Gordon Bau. Hairstyles, Jean Burt Reilly. Associate Producer, Carter DeHaven Jr. Production Manager, Arthur Newman. Filmed on location in the San Joaquin area near Stockton, California. Technicolor. Panavision. Running time, 129 minutes.

CAST Paul Newman, George Kennedy, J. D. Cannon, Lou Antonio, Robert Drivas, Strother Martin, Jo Van Fleet, Clifton James, Morgan Woodward, Luke Askew, Marc Cavell, Richard Davalos, Robert Donner, Warren Finnerty, Dennis Hopper, John McLiam, Wayne Rogers, Dean Stanton, Charles Tyner, Ralph Waite, Anthony Zerbe, Buck Kartalian, Joy Harmon, Jim Gammon, Joe Don Baker, Donn Pearce, Norman Goodwins, Charles Hicks, John Pearce, Eddie Rossen, Rush Williams, James Leter, Robert Luster, Rance Howard, James Bradley, Jr, Cyril 'Chips' Robinson.

The secret war of Harry Frigg 1968 Universal
CREDITS An Albion Production for Universal. Produced by
Hal E. Chester. Directed by Jack Smight. Assistant Director,
Terence Nelson. Screenplay by Peter Stone and Frank Tarloff.
Based on a story by Frank Tarloff. Photographed by Russell
Metty. Music by Carlo Rustichelli. Musical Supervision,
Joseph Gershenson. Art Direction, Alexander Golitzen and
Henry Bumstead. Set decorations, John McCarthy and John
Austin. Sound, Walden O. Watson, William Russell and
Ronald Pierce. Costumes by Edith Head. Makeup by Bud
Westmore. Hairstyles by Larry Germain. Associate Producer,
Peter Stone. Production Manager, Arthur S. Newman, Jr.
Location scenes filmed in Sierra Madre area of Southern Cali-
fornia. Technicolor. Techniscope. Running time, 110 mins.

CAST Paul Newman, Sylva Koscina, Andrew Duggan, Tom
Bosley, John Williams, Charles D. Gray, Vito Scotti, Jacques
Roux, Werner Peters, James Gregory, Fabrizio Mioni, Johnny
Haymer, Norman Fell, Buck Henry, Horst Ebersberg, Richard
X. Slattery and George Ives.

Rachel, Rachel 1968 Warner Bros.
CREDITS A Paul Newman Production for Warner Bros. Pro-
duced and directed by Paul Newman. Assistant Director, Alan
Hopkins. Screenplay by Stewart Stern. Based on the novel
A jest of God, by Margaret Laurence. Photographed by Gayne
Rescher. Film Editor, Dede Allen. Music composed and con-
ducted by Jerome Moross. Song lyrics by Stewart Stern. Per-
formed by The Phaetons. Art Direction, Robert Gundlach.
Set Decorations, Richard Merrell. Sound, Jack Jacobsen and
Dick Vorisek. Costumes by Domingo Rodriguez. Associate
Producers, Arthur Newman and Harrison Starr. Production
Consultant, Larry Sturhahn. Production Manager, Flo Ner-
linger. Filmed entirely in Connecticut, at Bethel, Georgetown
and Danbury. Technicolor. Running time, 101 mins.

CAST Joanne Woodward, James Olson, Kate Harrington,
Estelle Parsons, Geraldine Fitzgerald, Donald Moffatt, Terry

Kiser, Frank Corsaro, Bernard Barrow, Nell Potts, Shawn Campbell, Violet Dunn, Izzy Singer, Tod Engle, Bruno Engle, Beatrice Pons, Dorothea Duckworth, Connie Robinson, Sylvia Shipman, Larry Fredericks and Wendell MacNeal.

Winning 1969 Universal
CREDITS A Universal–Newman–Foreman Production. A Jennings Lang Production. Produced by John Foreman. Directed by James Goldstone. Assistant Director, Earl Bellamy, Jr. Screenplay by Howard Rodman. Photographed by Richard Moore. Film Editors, Edward A. Biery and Richard C. Mayer. Music by Dave Grusin. Art Direction, Alexander Golitzen, John J. Lloyd and Joe Alves. Set Decorations, John McCarthy and George Milo. Sound, Waldon O. Watson and James T. Porter. Makeup, Bud Westmore. Hairstyles, Larry Germain. Associate Producer, George Santore. Production Manager, Wally Worsley. Location scenes filmed at the Indianapolis Speedway and at Elkhart Lake, Wisconsin. Technicolor. Panavision. Running time, 123 mins.

CAST Paul Newman, Joanne Woodward, Richard Thomas, Robert Wagner, David Sheiner, Clu Culager, Barry Ford, Bob Quarry, Eileen Wesson, Toni Clayton, Maxine Stuart, Karen Arthur, Paulene Myers, Ray Ballard, Charles Steel, Alma Platt, Harry Basch, Allen Emerson, Marianna Coe, Carolyn McNichol, Bobby Unser, Tony Hulman, George Mason, Mimi Littlejohn, Pat Vidan, Bruce Walkup, Timothy Galbraith, Lon Palmer and Joy Teynolds.

Butch Cassidy and the Sundance kid 1969 20th Century-Fox
CREDITS A 20th Century-Fox release of a George Roy Hill–Paul Monash (Camanile) Production. Directed by George Roy Hill. Assistant Director, Steven Bernhardt. Produced by John Foreman. A Newman–Foreman Presentation. Camera (Colour by DeLuxe) Conrad Hall. Screenplay by William Goldman. Editors, John C. Howard and Richard C. Meyer. Music by Burt Bacharach. Song *Raindrops keep falling on my head* by Burt Bacharach and Hal David, sung by B. J. Thomas. Art direction,

Jack Martin Smith, Philip Jefferies. Second Unit Director, Michael Moore. Sound, William E. Edmondson, David E. Dockendorf. Running time, 112 mins.

CAST Paul Newman, Robert Redford, Katharine Ross, Strother Martin, Henry Jones, Jeff Corey, George Furth, Cloris Leachman, Ted Cassidy, Kenneth Mars, Donnelly Rhodes, Jody Gilbert, Timothy Scott, Don Keefer, Charles Dierkop, Francisco Cordova, Nelson Olmstead, Paul Bryar, Sam Elliott, Charles Akins and Eric Sinclair.

W.U.S.A. 1970 Paramount
CREDITS A Rosenberg–Newman–Foreman Production for Paramount Pictures. Produced by John Foreman. Directed by Stuart Rosenberg. Assistant Directors, Hank Moonjean, Howard Koch, Jr, Les Gorall. Associate Producer, Hank Moonjean. Screenplay by Robert Stone from his novel, *A hall of mirrors*. Photographed by Richard Moore. Art Director, Philip Jefferies. Set Decorator, William Kiernan. Unit Production Manager Arthur Newman. Film Editor, Bob Wyman. Music composed and conducted by Lalo Schifrin. Sound Recording, Jerry Jost. Costumes by Travilla. Men's Wardrobe, Nat Tolmach. Women's Wardrobe, Norma Brown. Script Supervisor, Betty Crosby. Hairstyles by Sydney Guilaroff. Makeup artists, Lynn Reynolds and Jack Wilson. Running time, 117 minutes.

CAST Paul Newman, Joanne Woodward, Anthony Perkins, Laurence Harvey, Pat Hingle, Cloris Leachman, Don Gordon, Michael Anderson, Jr, Leigh French, Moses Gunn, Bruce Cabot, Lou Gosset and Robert Quarry.

Sometimes a great notion 1971 Universal (*Never give an inch* in Britain)
CREDITS A Newman–Foreman Production in association with Universal Pictures. A Jennings Lang Presentation. Produced by John Foreman. Directed by Paul Newman. Assistant Director, Mickey McCardle. Associate Producer, Frank Caffey.

Screenplay by John Gay from the novel by Ken Kesey. Technicolor and Panavision. Photographed on location in Oregon by Richard Moore. Editor, Bob Wyman. Music by Henry Mancini. Art director, Philip Jefferies. Second Unit Director, Michael Moore. Running time, 114 minutes.

CAST Paul Newman, Henry Fonda, Lee Remick, Michael Sarrazin, Joe Maross, Richard Jaeckel, Sam Gilman, Cliff Potts, Jim Burr, Linda Lawrence and Roy Poole.

Pocket money 1972
CREDITS A First Artists/Coleytown Production for National General Pictures release. Produced by John Foreman. Directed by Stuart Rosenberg. Second Unit Director, James Kinett. Screenplay by Terry Malick based on the novel *Jim Cane* by J. P. S. Brown. Adaptation by John Gay. Photographed by Laszlo Kovacs in Technicolor. Art Director, Tambi Larsen. Editor, Robert Wyman. Music by Alex North. Title song by Carole King. Running time, 100 minutes.

CAST Paul Newman, Lee Marvin, Strother Martin, Wayne Rogers, Christine Belford, Kelly Jean Peters, Fred Graham, Hector Elizondo, R. Camargo, Gregg Sierra, Wynn Pearce, G. Escandon, D. Herrera, John Verros, E. Baca, N. Roman, R. Manning, Terry Malick.

The life and times of Judge Roy Bean 1971–2 A National General Pictures Release. U.K. From Cinerama Releasing (UK) Ltd.
CREDITS A First Artists Production. A John Huston Film. Produced by John Foreman. Directed by John Huston. Associate Producer, Frank Caffey. Screenplay by John Milius. Edited by Hugh S. Fowler, A.C.E. Music composed and conducted by Maurice Jarre. Song, *Marmalade, molasses and honey*, lyrics by Marilyn and Alan Bergman. Sung by Andy Williams. Director of Photography, Richard Moore. Art Director, Tambi Larsen. Costumes Designed by Edith Head. Unit Production Manager, Arthur S. Newman, Jnr. Sound, Larry Jost. Makeup created by William Tuttle. Makeup, Monty Westmore.

Assistant to John Huston, Gladys Hill. Assistant to the Producer, Annabelle King. Men's Wardrobe, Jim Linn. Special Photographic Effects by Butler-Glouner. Stunt Co-ordinator James Arnett. Set Decorator, Robert Benton. Animal Trainer, Ron Oxley. Men's Hair Consultant, James Markham. Assistant Editor, Richard Wahrman. Script Supervisor, John Franco. Property Master, Robert Schultz. Panavision. Colour by Technicolor. Length, 11,115 feet. Running time, 124 mins.

CAST Paul Newman, Victoria Principal, Anthony Perkins, Frank Soto, Tab Hunter, John Huston, Neil Rivers, Howard Morton, Stacy Keach, Billy Pearson, Roddy McDowall, Stan Barrett, Don Starr, Alfred G. Bosonos, Anthony Zerbe, John Hudkins, David Sharpe and Jacqueline Bisset. Also Ava Gardner as Lily Langtry and Watch Bear played by Bruno. Also Whores, Pimps, Marshalls and Marshalls' Wives, and Outlaws, as cast by Lynn Stalmaster.

The effect of gamma rays on man-in-the-moon marigolds 1972
20th Century-Fox
CREDITS Produced and directed by Paul Newman. Assistant director, John Nicolella. Executive Producer, John Foreman. Screenplay by Alvin Sargent from the play by Paul Zindel. Camera (Colour by DeLuxe), Adam Holender. Editor, Evan Lottman. Music, Maurice Jarre. Production design, Gene Callahan. Set decoration, Richard Merrell. Sound, Dennis Maitland, Robert Fine. Running time, 101 minutes.

CAST Joanne Woodward, Nell Potts, Roberta Wallach, Judith Lowry, Richard Venture, Estelle Omens, Carolyn Coates, Will Hare, Jess Osuna, David Spielberg, Lynn Rogers, Ellen Dano, Roger Serbagi, John Lehne, Michael Kearney and Dee Victor.

The mackintosh man 1973   Columbia Warner (distributors for Newman–Foreman/John Huston Productions.)
CREDITS Producer, John Foreman. Associate Producer, William Hill. Second Unit Director, James Arnett. Assistant

Director, Colin Brewer. Screenplay by Walter Hill. Based on the novel, *The freedom trap*, by Desmond Bagley. Photography, Oswald Morris. Editor, Russell Lloyd. Special effects, Cliff Richardson and Ron Ballinger. Musical Director, Maurice Jarre. Running time, 99 mins.

CAST   Paul Newman, Dominque Sanda, James Mason, Harry Andrews, Ian Bannen, Michael Hordern, Nigel Patrick, Peter Vaughan, Roland Culver, Percy Herbert, Robert Lang, Jenny Runacre, John Bindon, Hugh Manning, Leo Genn, Wolfe Morris, Noel Purcell, Donald Webster, Keith Webster, Niall MacGuinnis, Eddie Byrne, Shane Briant, Michael Poole, Eric Mason, Ronald Clarke, Anthony Viccars, Dinny Powell, Douglas Robinson, Jack Cooper, Marc Boyle, Marcelle Castillo, Nosher Powell, Terry Plummer, Joe Cahill, Gerry Alexander, John McDarby, Donal McCann, Joe Lynch, Seamus Healy, Tom Irwin, Pascal Perry, Steve Brennan, Vernon Hayden and Brendon O'Duill.

The sting   1973   Universal
CREDITS   A Bill/Phillips production of a George Roy Hill film. A Zanuck/Brown presentation. Produced by Tony Bill and Michael and Julia Phillips. Presentation by Richard D. Zanuck and David Brown. Associate Producer, Robert L. Crawford. Directed by George Roy Hill. First Assistant Director, Ray Gosnell. Second Assistant Director, Charles Dismukes. Script, David S. Ward. Director of Photography, Robert Surtees, A.S.C. Art Director, Henry Bumstead. Set Decorations, James Payne. Sound, Robert Bertrand and Ronald Pierce. Film Editor, William Reynolds, A.S.C. Costumes by Edith Head. Music adapted by Marvin Hamlisch. Piano Rags by Scott Joplin. Production Manager, Ernest B. Wehmeyer. Special Photographic Effects by Albert Whitlock. Technical Consultant, John Scarne. Script Supervisor, Charlsie Bryant. Titles and Optical Effects, Universal Title. Title and Graphic Design Kaleidoscope Films, Ltd. Cosmetics by Cinematique. Running time, 129 mins.

CAST   Paul Newman, Robert Redford, Robert Shaw, Charles Durning, Ray Walston, Eileen Brennan, Harold Gould, John Heffernan, Dana Elcar, Jack Kehoe, Dimitra Arliss, Robert Earl Jones, James J. Sloyan, Charles Dierkop, Lee Paul, Sally Kirkland, Avon Long, Arch Johnson, Ed Bakey, Brad Sullivan, John Quade, Larry D. Mann, Leonard Barr, Paulene Myers, Joe Tornatore, Jack Collins, Tom Spratley, Ken O'Brien, Ken Sancom, Ta-Tanisha, William Benedict.

The towering inferno   1974   20th Century-Fox, Warner Bros.
CREDITS   An Irwin Allen Production. Directed by John Guillermin. Action sequences directed by Irwin Allen. Assistant Directors, Wes McAfee, Newton Arnold, Malcolm Harding. Screenplay by Stirling Silliphant. Based on the novel *The tower* by Richard Martin Stern and the novel *The glass inferno* by Thomas N. Scortia and Frank M. Robinson. Director of Photography, Fred Koenekamp. Director of Photography, Action Sequences, Joseph Biroc. Film Editing, Harold F. Kress and Carl Kress. Associate Producer, Sidney Marshall. Music, John Williams. Costumes, Paul Zastupnevich. Art Director, Ward Preston. Set Decorator, Raphael Bretton. Sound, John Bonner. Makeup, Emile La Vigne and Monte Westmore. Executive Production Manager, Hal Herman. Panavision. Colour by DeLuxe.

CAST   Paul Newman, Steve McQueen, William Holden, Faye Dunaway, Fred Astaire, Susan Blakely, Richard Chamberlain, Jennifer Jones, O. J. Simpson, Robert Vaughn, Robert Wagner, Susan Flannery, Sheila Mathews, Normann Burton, Jack Collins, Don Gordon, Felton Perry, Gregory Sierra, Ernie Orsatti.

The drowning pool   1975   Warner Bros.
CREDITS   A Coleytown Inc./Turman-Foster Production. Produced by Lawrence Turman and David Foster. Director, Stuart Rosenberg. Assistant Director and Producer, Howard

W. Koch, Jr. Screenplay by Tracy Keenan Wynn, Lorenzo Semple, Jr., and Walter Hill. Based on a novel by Ross MacDonald. Photography, Gordon Willis. Film Editor, John Howard. Music, Michael Small. Art Director, Ed O'Donovan. Set Decorations, Phil Abramson. Sound, Larry Jost. Costumes, Dick Bruno. Makeup, Monty Westmore. Hairstyles, Kaye Pownall. Production Manager, Arthur Newman. Filmed on location in Louisiana and California. Technicolor. Panavision.

CAST   Paul Newman, Joanne Woodward, Tony Franciosa, Linda Haynes, Murray Hamilton, Gail Strickland, Melanie Griffith, Richard Jaeckel, Paul Koslo, Andy Robinson, Coral Browne, Richard Derr, Helena Kallianiotes, Leigh French, Cecil Elliott.

*   *   *   *

NOTE   As a director, Paul Newman is also responsible for a short feature film *On the harmfulness of tobacco*, released in the USA in 1959. It is black and white, with a running time of 28 mins. (Not released in Great Britain at time of publication.) This short was filmed at the New York Actors' Studio and adapted from the monologue by Anton Chekhov.

Paul Newman was the narrator for the NBC News television special when the network devoted $2\frac{1}{2}$ hours to the premise, *From here to the seventies*, transmitted early in October, 1969. This programme sought to do no less than sum up one decade and anticipate the next. The very choice of Newman, as narrator, lent the fillip of a concerned actor discussing the concerns of the era. And a dozen NBC correspondents—in essays on topics like race, youth, environment, hunger—suggested points of view towards their material which made it an honourable landmark in American television. With the music beating out the rock-folk sounds of the times, the programme conveyed the irony of an era full of violence and tragedy pursuing pleasure to a rock beat.

On the New York stage

Following repertory work and summer stock in provincial theatres in and around his home state of Ohio, in Williams Bay, Wisconsin, and with the Woodstock Players in Woodstock, Illinois, and having also appeared extensively in college dramatics at Kenyon, Paul Newman studied for a year at the Drama Department of Yale University in Connecticut. He was persuaded to try his luck as a professional actor in New York before he could sit for a Master's Degree in Drama. He was almost immediately given work in the then busy television drama scene and within six months was cast in the long-running stage play, *Picnic*, which not only helped him to consolidate his position as a notable television actor but to study at the Actors' Studio under the inspirational teaching of Lee Strasberg. Four years later he said, 'If I've shown any development as an actor, it's mostly to be credited to the Actors' Studio and my work there under Lee Strasberg. In fact, I still consider myself a student and whenever I am in New York, I attend classes twice a week.' The following are cast and production details of the three plays in which he appeared on 'Broadway' and also the 1964 play in which he appeared at the Little Theatre, New York, with Joanne Woodward, which the Newmans did as a special presentation for the Actors' Studio.

Picnic 1953
CREDITS Produced by the Theater Guild. A play by William Inge. Staged by Joshua Logan. Setting by Jo Mielziner. Costumes by Mildred Trebor. Presented by the Theater Guild and Mr Logan at the Music Box Theatre, New York, 19 February 1953.

CAST Ralph Meeker, Janice Rule, Kim Stanley, Eileen Heckart, Paul Newman, Arthur O'Connell, Ruth McDevitt, Maurice Miller, Peggy Conklin, Reta Shaw, Elizabeth Wilson.

The desperate hours   1955
CREDITS   A play by Joseph Hayes, based on his novel of the same name. Staged by Robert Montgomery. Setting and lighting by Howard Bay. Costumes by Robert Randolph. Presented by Howard Erskine and Mr Hayes at the Ethel Barrymore Theater, 10 February 1955.

CAST   Karl Malden, Nancy Coleman, Paul Newman, James Gregory, George Grizzard, George Mathews, Fred Eisley, Judson Pratt, Kendall Clark, Malcolm Broderick, Patricia Pearson, Wyrley Birch, Rusty Lane and Mary Orr.

Sweet bird of youth   1959
CREDITS   A play in three acts and five scenes by Tennessee Williams. Staged by Elia Kazan. Settings and lighting by Jo Mielziner. Costumes by Anna Hill Johnstone. Presented by Cheryl Crawford at the Martin Beck Theater, New York, 10 March 1959.

CAST   Geraldine Page, Paul Newman, Sidney Blackmer, Madeleine Sherwood, Rip Torn, Diana Hyland, Logan Ramsey, John Napier, Patricia Ripley, Milton J. Williams, Martine Bartlett, Earl Snyder, Bruce Dern, Charles Tyner, Monica May, Hilda Browner, Charles McDaniel, James Jeter.

Baby want a kiss   1964
CREDITS   A comedy in two acts by James Costigan. Staged by Frank Corsaro. Settings and costumes by Peter Harvey. Lighting by David Hays. Presented by the Actors' Studio, Inc. at the Little Theater, New York, 19 April 1964.

CAST   Paul Newman, Joanne Woodward, James Costigan, Patrick (a dog).